STAGS AND SERPENTS

Stags and Serpents

THE STORY OF
THE HOUSE OF CAVENDISH
AND THE DUKES OF DEVONSHIRE

by

John Pearson

MACMILLAN LONDON

ISBN 0 333 28454 2

First published 1983 by
MACMILLAN LONDON LIMITED
4 Little Essex Street London WC2R 3LF
and Basingstoke
Associated Companies in Auckland, Dallas, Delhi, Dublin,
Hong Kong, Johannesburg, Lagos, Manzini, Melbourne, Nairobi,
New York, Singapore, Tokyo, Washington and Zaria

Photoset by Rowland Phototypesetting Ltd
Bury St Edmunds, Suffolk
Printed in Hong Kong

Contents

List of Illustrations
between pages 18 and 19

Acknowledgements for illustrations

5, 9, 10, 13, 15, 16, 17, 18, 19, 20, 22, 23, 24, 25, 28 from
    paintings at Chatsworth by permission of the Chatsworth Settlement
    Trust.

29, 30, 32, 33, 34, 35, 36 from photographs by permission of the
    Chatsworth Settlement Trust.

2, 3, 7, 11 by permission of the National Trust (Hardwick Hall).

1, 4, 6, 8 by permission of the National Trust Photographic Library.

2, 3, 7, 11, 13, 15, 16, 17, 18, 19, 20, 28 photographs by
    courtesy of the Courtauld Institute.

14 Private collection, photograph *Country Life*.

21 Courtesy of the Trustees of the British Museum.

Preface

This has been an unusually pleasant book to write – not least because of the unfailing kindness and support I have received from such a range of people who have helped me over countless aspects of this fascinating story. The chance of doing one's research in a house like Chatsworth was in itself the sort of bonus few books offer to their authors; and few authors can have received such good-humoured hospitality and intelligent interest as I did from the present Duke and Duchess.

I often regretted not having had a chance to meet the two legendary Chatsworth librarians, Francis Thompson and Tom Wragg before they died – if only to thank them for their skill in cataloguing and arranging the splendid archives, and to draw on their knowledge of the house and its history. But their successors – the librarian, Peter Day, and his deputy, Michael Pearman – were both learned and indefatigable in guiding me through the intricacies of fifteen generations of Cavendishes.

Many of the present Chatsworth staff also helped me with their reminiscences – among them Bert Link, the late William Shimwell and his wife Maud Shimwell, Dennis Fisher, Hugo Read, Sally Barnes, Jesse and Gladys Grafton.

I must also thank the following for their invaluable assistance and advice: Clodagh Anson, Melissa Bakewell, Tim Burrows, Paul and Arabella Burton, Peter Browne, David Cannadine, Lady Elizabeth Cavendish, Lady Blanche Cobbold, Angela Conner, David Durant, Dr Evans, Mathew Frankland, Lady Gage, Lord Hartington, Professor Francis Haskell, Harold Macmillan, Noel Malcolm, Lady Mersey, Sir Jack Plumb, Karl Schweizer, William Spowers, Lady Anne Tree, Professor John Vincent.

My agent, Deborah Rogers, first suggested I should write this book. Alan Maclean, my publisher, sustained me while I was writing it. My son Mark made a number of surprisingly apposite suggestions to the completed manuscript, and Peter Day and Michael Pearman both corrected various mistakes with remarkable courtesy and skill.

To all I remain immensely grateful, as I am also to my wife, Lynette, who has helped in more ways than she will ever realize.

J. P.

1527–1608 Bess of Hardwick = (1) Robert Barlow –1544   = (2) Sir William Cavendish 1505–1557

Frances Cavendish   Henry Cavendish   1552–1625 William Cavendish = Anne Keighley –1625
                                    1st Earl of Devonshire (1618) | *dau of Henry Keighley*

1590–1628 William Cavendish = Hon. Christian Bruce 1595–1675
     2nd Earl of Devonshire | *dau of 1st Lord Kinloss*

1617–1684 William Cavendish = Lady Elizabeth Cecil 1619–1689   Charles Cavendish 1620–1643
     3rd Earl of Devonshire | *dau of the Earl of Salisbury*   *Royalist general*

1640–1707 William Cavendish = Lady Mary Butler 1646–1710
     4th Earl of Devonshire | *dau of the Duke of Ormonde*
1st Duke of Devonshire (1694)

1673–1729 William Cavendish = Hon. Rachel Russell 1674–1725
     2nd Duke of Devonshire | *dau of William Lord Russell*

1698–1755 William Cavendish = Katherine Hoskyns –1777   Lord Charles Cavendish = Anne Grey –1733
     3rd Duke of Devonshire | *dau of John Hoskyns* | *dau of the Duke of Ken*

                                          1731–1810 Henry Cavendish *Scientist*

1720–1764 William Cavendish = Lady Charlotte Boyle 1731–1754
     4th Duke of Devonshire | *dau of 4th Earl of Cork and 3rd Earl of Burlington,*
                          estates in Yorkshire and Ireland, Chiswick House, Burlington House

1748–1811 William Cavendish ≈ Charlotte Spencer   = (1) Lady Georgiana Spencer ≈ Charles Grey
     5th Duke of Devonshire ⋮   1757–1806   ⋮   *2nd Earl Grey*

          Charlotte Williams   Eliza Courtney

1783–1858 Lady Georgiana Cavendish = George Howard 1773–1844   Lady Harriet Cavendish 1785–1862
                            6th Earl of Carlisle   *married 1st Earl Granville*

1803–1881 Lady Caroline Howard = Hon. William Lascelles 1798–1851
                            son of the Earl of Harewood

1838–1920 Emma Lascelles = Lord Edward Cavendish 1838–1891

1868–1938 Victor Cavendish = Lady Evelyn Fitzmaurice 1870–1960
     9th Duke of Devonshire | *dau of the Marquess of Lansdowne*

1895–1950 Edward Cavendish = Lady Mary Cecil 1895–
     10th Duke of Devonshire | *dau of the Marquess of Salisbury*

1920– Andrew Cavendish = Hon. Deborah Mitford 1920–
     11th Duke of Devonshire   *dau of Lord Redesdale*

= (3) Sir William St Loe –1565   = (4) George Talbot 1528?–1590
6th Earl of Shrewsbury

Charles Cavendish = (2) Katherine Ogle   Elizabeth Cavendish = Charles Stuart   Mary Cavendish = Gilbert Talbot
1553–1617   1570–1629   1555–1582   1556–1632   *7th Earl of Shrewsbury*

illiam Cavendish 1593–1676   Charles Cavendish –1654   Arbella Stuart
Duke of Newcastle   *Mathematician*   1575–1615

Family Tree

= (2) Lady Elizabeth Foster   1754–1834 George Cavendish = Lady Elizabeth Compton 1760–1835
1759–1824   *1st Earl of Burlington (2nd creation)* *heiress to the Earls of Northampton*
Caroline St Jules   Augustus Clifford   *estates in Sussex*

William Spencer George Cavendish 1790–1858   1783–1812 William Cavendish = Hon. Louisa O'Callaghan –1863
6th Duke of Devonshire   *killed in carriage accident* *dau of Lord Lismore*

12–1840 Lady Blanche Howard = William Cavendish 1808–1891
2nd Earl of Burlington (2nd creation)
7th Duke of Devonshire

833–1908 Spencer Compton Cavendish = Louise von Alten 1832–1911   1836–1882 Lord Frederick Cavendish = Lady Lucy Lyttelton
8th Duke of Devonshire   *Duchess of Manchester*   *assassinated in Dublin*   *dau of Lord Lyttelton*

–1944 William Cavendish = Kathleen Kennedy 1920–1948
Marquess of Hartington   *sister of President Kennedy*
killed in action

1. Prologue

The Devonshires Today

As you drive up the M1 motorway to the north there comes a point, just past the turn-off to Nottingham, where the landscape changes. The coal-tips and winding-towers of the Nottinghamshire coalfields disappear, and for five or six miles the dual carriageway is flanked to the right by a ridge of thickly-wooded hillside. From its highest point, just visible among the clustered oaks, peers the fretted silhouette of that strange masterpiece of late Elizabethan architecture, Hardwick Hall. Four miles further on, just as the mines and rows of houses start again, the skyline is briefly crowned with the lonely keep of Bolsover.

Bolsover Castle is a shell, partially refurbished and administered by Her Majesty's Department of the Environment and, since 1957, Hardwick, with its gardens and miraculously-preserved interior, has been tended, devotedly if a shade impersonally, by the National Trust. In their time, both were strongholds of the family which ruled this stretch of northern Midlands – the Cavendishes. The family then had other ample outposts close at hand as well: Welbeck Abbey, six miles to the east (in the late seventeenth century it passed through a branch of the Cavendishes in the female line to the Cavendish-Bentinck Dukes of Portland); Nottingham Castle, rebuilt by the most vainglorious of all the Cavendishes, the seventeenth-century First Duke of Newcastle, and now a museum; and a great Elizabethan house at Oldcotes, long relinquished and demolished.

But although so much of this private kingdom of the Cavendishes has gone, the core remains nearby, protected by the moors and peaks of Derbyshire. These limestone uplands are themselves a spectacular survival with their tors and fells and stone-walled fields encircled by the densest industrial conurbation in the country – on clear nights from the High Peak the lights of Manchester and Stockport are reflected to the west and those of Sheffield to the east. And just past Baslow village, at the point where the Derwent widens out from a mountain stream to a gentler lowland river, stands Chatsworth, 'the Palace of the Peak', for centuries the show-place of the Cavendish dynasty of the Dukes of Devonshire and now their ultimate redoubt.

The first glimpse is unforgettable, for you see it suddenly on the far side of the valley as you take the old road through the park from Baslow, and at first sight it appears not so much a house as part of some imagined classical Italian city placed by a painter in an ideal landscape. It looks even bigger than in fact it is, set against the far woods and overhanging moors, and everything about it still proclaims the vanished power – and partly vanished wealth – of the family who proudly erected and adorned it.

It was created by the Cavendishes over many generations out of what Defoe once called 'a houling wilderness'. There is nearby Edensor village which was demolished in the late eighteenth century by the Fourth Duke and rebuilt a mile away by the Sixth, so as to leave unmarred the perfect vista of his park; the great fountain in the middle of the long canal, once the highest in the world and constructed to impress an Emperor of Russia (who never found the time to see it); the immense nineteenth-century north wing which contains the last stately-home theatre built in Britain (by the unmarried Sixth Duke who sometimes appeared in his own theatricals); and the seventeenth-century body of the house, with its gold-leafed window-frames and finely-carved façade (which reminded Horace Walpole of 'neatly wrought plate') stands like a sumptuous stone casket carefully designed to house the riches almost casually acquired by assorted Cavendishes in the intervals between their horses and mistresses and governing the country.

Like any threatened species, the Devonshires have been quietly withdrawing to this habitat from which they originally emerged, and on the surface there seems little change. The Duke still owns Pilsley and several nearby villages, as his family has done for centuries. He is still the major land-owner in this part of Derbyshire, and Chatsworth itself is paradoxically more splendid now than ever in its history. The gardens are wonderfully maintained; trees planted long ago are in their prime; and as the family has stoically sold or leased off such distant and expendable great houses as Chiswick House, Compton Place at Eastbourne, and Burlington House and Devonshire House in Piccadilly (they still own Lismore Castle in Ireland and Bolton Abbey with its Yorkshire grouse moors), the best of their furniture and pictures have come here, and Chatsworth bulges with inestimable possessions.

With death duties some have inevitably disappeared. In 1912, after the Eighth Duke's death, the Shakespeare folios and Caxtons in the library were quietly disposed of (for what seems now a ludicrously small amount), and when, at a fiscally awkward moment in 1950, the Tenth Duke joined him in the local churchyard, a Memling triptych and the Chatsworth Apollo – a unique fifth-century Greek bronze head, now in the British Museum – also fell victims to the Inland Revenue.

Their absence is barely noticed amid so much that still remains: paintings by Rembrandt and Rubens, Gainsborough and Reynolds, one of the greatest private libraries in the land, a cellarful of ducal silver, the Cavendish jewellery, cabinets containing a now legendary collection of old master drawings, and a separate gallery housing the Sixth Duke's unique collection of sculpture by Canova and his early nineteenth-century neo-classical disciples in Rome. The list is endless and the mind grows slightly weary at this grand array of worldly treasures.

But the house is not a mere museum for the Devonshire possessions: it is also a place of record for the family which, for four hundred years, has survived and prospered with more consistent splendour than any other English dynasty, producing statesmen, proconsuls, great builders and collectors, leading figures in society and fashion, patrons of the turf, several notable eccentrics and at least one scientist of genius. Chatsworth has been held through fifteen generations, and, although the house was totally rebuilt at the end of the seventeenth century in much of its present outward grandeur, it remains a curiously personal house which is also a part of English history.

In the Park, once part of Sherwood Forest, stands 'Queen Mary's Bower', where Mary Queen of Scots is supposed to have exercised during the years she was held prisoner at Chatsworth, and in the State Apartments is George II's deathbed. (The Fourth Duke was his Chamberlain and received the bed as a macabre but legitimate official perk at the monarch's death.) Johnson and Sheridan and Charles James Fox were guests here of the languid Fifth Duke and his gambling-mad Duchess, Georgiana. (Fox broke his leg running races in the garden and was finally to die in 1806 at the Duke's Thames-side house at Chiswick.) The gardens were magnificently illuminated when Victoria came to see the Sixth Duke's Great Conservatory, and the game-book still records the prodigious quantities of Chatsworth pheasants which fell to the twelve-bore of her plump successor during his rakish visits to the Eighth Duke in the 1890s.

A hundred years ago this rural palace functioned with the discipline and man-power of a full-scale man-of-war, and below stairs everything was organized with all the snobberies and careful class gradations of Victorian society in miniature: an honoured aristocracy of butler, cook and house-keeper ruling a deferential work-force of footmen, grooms, maids, odd-job men and messengers as well as a vast outside staff of gardeners, labourers and keepers, on whom the smooth running of the whole great house depended.

Most have gone. High up beneath the roof are corridors of small undeco-rated empty rooms where Chatsworth's population of living-in servants once resided out of sight and sound of family and guests below. But by a sort of sleight-of-hand, Chatsworth appears to function much as it always did. The deer still roam the park, the gardens are immaculately maintained (although the state of the nineteenth-century water-valves no longer lets the Emperor Fountain reach its former glory), the estates are run from Chatsworth by an efficient modern manager, and the home farm and hot-houses supply the kitchens with all the vegetables and meat and fruit they need.

For Chatsworth remains a very lived-in house. The present Duke and Duchess have their own extremely comfortable apartments and have paid considerable attention to ensuring that their heir, Lord Hartington, will finally succeed them here. Since he has a son and heir as well, the twelve-year-old Lord Burlington, there seems no shortage of potential Dukes of Devonshire to inhabit Chatsworth for many years to come.

And, whatever the social or political implications of this sort of continuity, there is no question of its effect on Chatsworth. The house lives, in a way that unlived-in but lovingly-preserved great houses never can, and it is largely this that still attracts the visitors. Hardwick Hall is architecturally more interesting than Chatsworth, and as a building it is unquestionably more romantic. But every year for every visitor who comes to Hardwick, five come to Chatsworth, for houses such as this are virtually unique to England.

The aristocracy of France had largely given up living in their châteaux even before they were pillaged in the turmoil of their revolution. Nowhere in

Germany or Italy does one find a great ancestral house still lived in by the original family with such a mass of inherited treasures more or less intact, as one does in England – still less in the rest of Europe. Only in a house like Chatsworth does one see this extraordinary survival of a famous family with so much that still bears witness to its history. And as one sees it, one inevitably wonders how so much wealth and splendour was achieved, how it changed across the centuries, and how, against all the odds, it has been so tenaciously preserved. Above all, one asks oneself about the characters who have inhabited the house, the lives they lived amid such grandeur – and how it all began.

2. The Third Wiffe

Bess of Hardwick (I. 1527–1565)

In the small hours of 20 August 1547, in a manor-house in Leicestershire, a wedding occurred between a middle-aged civil servant who had buried two wives already, and a childless red-haired widow in her early twenties. Little is known about the ceremony beyond the fact that the house, Bradgate Manor, was the property of Henry Grey, Marquis of Dorset and father – by his wife, Frances, grand-daughter of Henry VII – of the hapless Lady Jane.

The bride, the orphaned daughter of penurious Derbyshire gentry, brought no money to the match, but the groom had little need to worry, being a self-made man of some importance, with a house in London, land in Hertfordshire and Wales, and a recent knighthood earned by service to the Crown. A solid, heavy-featured man, he was by training an accountant and by nature a survivor who had already taken in his stride the change in his religion with the Reformation, the fall of his mighty patron, Thomas Cromwell, and the intrigues at court following the accession of the whey-faced young King Edward VI. Something of his dry accountant's mind can be seen in the record of his marriage he duly entered in his notebook:

> *Memorandum*: That I was marryed to *Elizabeth Hardwick*, my third Wiffe, in *Lecestersheere*, at *Brodgat*, my Lord Marquesse's House the 20th of *August*, in the first Yeare of King *Edward* the 6. at 2 of the Clock after Midnight, the domynical Letter *B*.*

Reading that bleak little business entry, one rather wonders if Sir William Cavendish, cautious discreet man that he was, can have guessed what he was taking on with that 'third Wiffe' of his.

Bess of Hardwick was always reticent about her age, but it is probable that she was born around 1527, the fourth child and third daughter of a Derbyshire farmer-squire who took his name from the few hundred acres he owned and farmed at Hardwick, near the ancient town of Chesterfield. Her life would have formed a chilling but appropriate subject for the Victorian gospel of self-help and the power of will to triumph over every obstacle in life – and as in all such stories it begins with hardship and almost all life's odds stacked formidably against her.

The family had little money; the farm was poor (ironically her father, John of Hardwick, had no way of knowing of the seams of top-grade coal his daughter would one day exploit beneath his fields); and Derbyshire was a cold

---

*This is an astrological reference making it clear that the unusual hour of the wedding had been worked out in accordance with a propitious conjunction of the stars.

and largely undeveloped county, five days' journey over frightful roads from London. What scant inheritance the family possessed would naturally descend to Bess's elder brother, James; and daughters without dowries were expendable in Tudor times. Had she been a raging beauty or a rich man's daughter, Bess might have dreamed of a romantic marriage, but she was neither. Her surviving portraits all suggest that even when young her features were powerful but never pretty, and John of Hardwick gave his child one final handicap when she had barely tottered from the cradle. Aged forty-one, the poor man died.

It is interesting that no personal reference to Bess's childhood has come down to us: she was never one for dwelling on the past, and even had she been, hers was hardly the sort of childhood she would have wanted to recall. When John of Hardwick died, the hard-pushed exchequer of Henry VIII was reviving and enforcing the old feudal claims of royal wardship over lands inherited by a minor and, through the Court of Wards, was claiming the right to administer them until the heir was twenty-one. Bess's brother James was eight: and although on his deathbed her father did his best to protect what inheritance there was by leaving the land to nominees, this failed to work. The royal lawyers went to work. The widow, Elizabeth Hardwick, lost the case. The Hardwick lands were leased off by the Crown to a local businessman called Bugby, and Widow Hardwick and her children – victims of these early Tudor death duties – were left penniless and virtually without support.

No one knows how they survived. Bess's biographer suggests that Bugby may have let them stay on at Hardwick for a while. But although Elizabeth finally remarried – and bore her unfortunate new husband three more female children – Bess's situation was as grim as ever. Ralph Leche, her new stepfather, was himself a penniless younger son of impecunious nearby local gentry, and the family was soon involved in further legal wrangles over small amounts of money.

It was now that Bess of Hardwick took her most important step in the sixteenth-century English school of life. Tudor England was not sentimental over childhood: Ralph Leche must have had problems supporting his own infant family, let alone all the stepchildren he had taken on, and Bess, though still a child herself was found a suitable position in the household of a noble family, the Zouches. Cut off at a stroke from her mother and her sisters, Bess of Hardwick's short and hard-pressed childhood was over.

By Derbyshire standards the Zouches must have seemed immensely grand, particularly to an intelligent, impressionable child like Bess. An old Norman family, they owned abundant lands throughout the country and a great house in London. Once they had ruled much of Wales for King Edward II, and the family produced a great Archbishop of York in the reign of his successor. Although they backed the wrong side in the Wars of the Roses, they had managed to recoup something of their old prestige and by the 1530s were maintaining a semblance of the feudal life-style of their past. Romantic, rich and ineffectual, the Zouches epitomized the feudal aristocracy the Tudors were largely to dispense with in their great social and religious revolution of the Reformation and the Dissolution of the Monasteries.

Although the Hardwicks claimed a tenuous relationship with the current Lady Zouche – which almost certainly explains Bess's presence in her household – her status must have been distinctly humble: part unpaid female retainer, and part infant poor relation, earning her keep and getting some rough and ready schooling in this extended semi-feudal family. Such service in a noble family was a traditional way for the children of kinsmen and hangers-on to gain some sort of education as well as useful connections for the future and practical experience in the running of a household.

For Bess it offered something more. At an impressionable time of life this sharp young lady from a poor home in Derbyshire was being shown a world of enviable riches, and would certainly have heard nostalgic legends of the former grandeur of the Zouches together with their lost power and feudal privileges. For the remainder of her long, ambitious life, Bess herself would prove as obsessive as any Zouche could be about such things.

Any hope she had of such a future for herself must have been dashed abruptly when at fifteen, or possibly a little younger, Bess of Hardwick's life in London ended, and she returned to Derbyshire to be a bride. Unless she was very much in love with her adolescent bridegroom, Robert Barlow – which from all one knows about her temperament and situation would seem unlikely – she must have viewed her fate with resignation. For the marriage, which was almost certainly arranged by her family, was not the sort of match for which a young, ambitious female in a noble household would have hoped, and it was a sharp step backwards from the exciting world of London. The Barlows were from her own part of Derbyshire; they were far from rich, and although her father-in-law was ailing, there was little to be hoped for from the inheritance.

Had the marriage lasted we would have heard no more of Bess, but the Barlows were evidently an unhealthy family. According to the Duchess of Newcastle, Robert Barlow was already 'lying sick of the Chronical Distemper' – probably tuberculosis – when Bess first saw him, and his health continued to decline. On Christmas Eve, 1544, he made the most effective contribution to his young wife's future greatness that was in his power: he quietly expired.

As a teenage widow, Bess was a distinctly better proposition than she had been as an undowered virgin. She had no claim on the Barlow lands, but she possessed a certain status as a widow and an annual income from her marriage settlement of £8 15s. a year. Even in early Tudor terms this was certainly not riches, but it was something, and it was her own.

There is an almost total blank over these four years or so of her first widowhood, but there was clearly no question of her remaining patiently among the Leches back in Derbyshire until another local husband could be found for her. Her fate was in her own hands now, and her future lay in London. Once back there, and with her Zouche contacts to rely on, it cannot have been too difficult for a young resourceful widow to find herself a fresh appointment with an important family. She was already rising in the social scale, and at some time she joined the Dorsets as a fully-fledged lady-in-waiting.

Henry Grey, Marquis of Dorset (and soon to become Duke of Suffolk) was a vain, ambitious, ultimately disastrous character, a fervent Protestant who on King Edward's death would tacitly encourage his daughter's suicidal bid against the Catholic Mary, disown her at the crucial moment, raise his own rebellion in the north and die on Tower Hill. But in the 1540, as Henry VIII's reign drew to its close and Edward VI succeeded him, the Dorsets were a power in the land. Immensely rich and related to the young Protestant king by marriage, they held court in London on a regal scale.

Bess was alone in a worldly society that must have held considerable temptations, but it is significant that there was never a breath of scandal round her name – nor would there be throughout the years to come, for she was not one to waste time or reputation on passing love-affairs, however tempting. She was careful and prudent, like a true provincial; for Bess it would always be the marriage-bed or nothing.

Within the circle of the Dorsets she would have met a range of eligible young men, but it says much for the caste-consciousness of this society that, with her background and her birth, not even someone as determined as the indomitable Bess was able yet to land a husband of inherited wealth and noble name. Instead she got twice-widowed William Cavendish. He was not particularly romantic – but nor was she.

He had three children living from his first marriage, and was more than twice her age, but he was just the sort of father-figure to appeal to a fatherless girl like Bess. He had other virtues too – money, his own comfortable house in London, and an increasingly important role in government. Perhaps they detected in each other kindred spirits, for William Cavendish was also prudent and ambitious, and rising fast in the free-for-all of mid-term Tudor politics.

Inevitably in centuries to come, efforts would be made to fit the Cavendishes with golden origins, most of which, they now cheerfully admit themselves, were bogus. No discernible Cavendish crossed the Channel with the Conqueror, and one tradition has it that the family name began in the thirteenth century when a man called Gernon married the daughter of a Suffolk gentleman called Potkin, and duly inherited the Potkin house at Cavendish in Suffolk near the Essex border. In honour of his wife's inheritance, he changed his name from Gernon to Cavendish; and a century later the family rose to prominence when one John de Cavendish, a lawyer, became Richard II's Lord Chief Justice, and in 1380, Chancellor of Cambridge University. A year later he was murdered by Wat Tyler's followers during the Peasants' Revolt, and the severed head of the Chancellor of Cambridge University was exhibited for several days in Bury St Edmunds market-place.

After this the fortunes of the Cavendishes not surprisingly declined, but the family remained in Suffolk as people of substance and lords of Cavendish manor through the fifteenth century. Then with the coming of the Tudors the family began to rise again.* One of them, Thomas Cavendish, married well, added lands in Buckinghamshire and Bedfordshire to those in Suffolk, and

---

*A distant branch of the family produced the great Elizabethan buccaneer and explorer Thomas Cavendish, who in 1588 became the second English captain to circumnavigate the globe.

served in the King's Exchequer as Clerk of the Pipe with a house in London. He produced three sons, and the eldest of them, George Cavendish, entered the service of the greatest self-made Englishman of his century, another Suffolk man, the Ipswich butcher's son, Thomas Cardinal Wolsey.

Through his obvious abilities, George Cavendish became Gentleman Usher to the Cardinal, a position of importance in his household: he was a loyal, courtly man and when the 'overmighty' Wolsey fell, George stayed beside him to the end. Henry VIII invited him to enter his service, but with considerable dignity George declined, collected his wages and a cart for his possessions and trudged his way back to Cavendish, 'for he had no goodwill to the dissolution of the monasteries or respect for Anne Boleyn.' At Cavendish he lived out the remainder of his days in retirement with his wife, a niece of Thomas More, and it was there that he wrote a long-unpublished minor Tudor classic, the life of his friend and patron, Thomas Wolsey.

George Cavendish must have had many of the qualities ascribed to later generations of the family – courtly manners, a retiring disposition, honesty and literary ability; but such virtues did not get one very far in Tudor England, and George's younger brother, William, was not similarly encumbered. William must have owed his start in life to George, for he first appears among the keen young men, who included Thomas Cromwell, in Wolsey's entourage. When Wolsey fell and Cromwell in due course became Secretary of State, William, unlike his brother, switched allegiance to the new master. Cromwell, already engaged in the destruction of the monasteries and the distribution of their wealth, needed able men to do his bidding. William Cavendish was more than willing.

He had qualities perfectly adapted for the task – abundant energy, precision and the sort of conscientious ruthlessness that frequently accompanies the actuarial mentality. He had also learned to treat his betters with what G. M. Young once called 'profound and profitable reverence'. It was an effective, if not particularly engaging combination, and the face one sees in the portrait of William Cavendish at Hardwick Hall is what one might possibly expect: the small sharp eyes and heavy features of the hard-faced men who did well out of the Reformation.

One sees him still more clearly in the letters he addressed to Thomas Cromwell during 1539, when at the height of his activities, touring the country as Cromwell's representative, making his inventories of confiscated monastic property, and dealing with the former owners.

Three years before, Cromwell had appointed him one of the ten official auditors of the Royal Court of Augmentation and by now he was adept at his work. March 1539 saw him at Dover assessing the lands and rents once owned by 'Saynt Radegund and Saynt Sepulcres in Canterbury', and he reported back to Cromwell that the money owed was 'Very arduous and paynfull to gather and receyve'. He was concerned about his fees and asked Cromwell for authority, signed by the King, to collect the money for himself as well.

A few months later he moved on to Little Marlow and seems to have found the work of dismembering the priory easier than his work at Dover. As he told Cromwell, he had soon persuaded the Prioress to take 'the matter very well like a wise woman', and he was wise enough himself to present his own activities to Cromwell in a conscientious light. Thanks to him the Prioress would now 'make delivery of every thing of which we made an inventory . . . and also of many other thing more which was not contained in our said inventory with such circumspection and diligence that the King's Highness (as far as we can learn and apperceyve) shall not be the loser of one penny belonging to the forsaid priory.'

He was much tougher with the monks at St Albans whom he found 'very obstynate refusing to accomplish the same that they have already granted, alleging how many ways it would be prejudicial unto them and to their house', and in December it was the Prior of Ely's turn to face the royal auditor. He tried to challenge William's right to confiscate monastic property, and when this failed, 'Beganne to wax melancholie saying he had friends that counselled him rather to die than to suffere me to meddle by virtue of my commission.'

William refused to listen, the confiscations went ahead, and he was able to add a postscript to his letter which he knew would please his master: 'I have sent you xi pieces of plate waying xlviii ounces.' He signed himself, to Cromwell, 'Your servant and bedesman during my lyff, William Cavendish.'

But throughout this busy period, William was not exclusively concerned with the King's and Thomas Cromwell's business. He did some on his own account as well and, considering the comparatively slender nature of his resources, did not do badly. The Cavendishes were not among the favoured beneficiaries of what Belloc emotionally refered to as 'the great orgy of loot' that accompanied the Reformation. As Cromwell's paid official he was not in the same league as important courtiers and capitalists like the Russells and the Talbots and the Dorsets who were able to carve great estates from the monastic lands.

But William had a sharp eye for a bargain. Fees like those he received at Dover Priory gave him a source of ready money, and with Cromwell behind him he was strategically placed to benefit from the slush fund of the Tudor Reformation and pick up the occasional small property at knock-down valuation. From the 'very obstynate' monks he dealt with at St Albans he acquired the manor-house and lands at Northaw in Hertfordshire, and a few months later he also obtained Cardigan Priory in Wales, and a favourable lease on a small former abbey at Lilleshall in Shropshire. As the busy year, 1539, drew to its close, he still found time to write again to Cromwell, as 'a poor and honest man', begging for the lucrative auditorship of the old Priory of St John in Clerkenwell.

William could always write effusively for what he wanted: 'You are the only fountayne and procession of my aide and succor, and the patronne of my poor living.' But this was not strictly true, for by now he was also working as auditor to the Queen's brother, Lord Beauchamp, and must have known that Cromwell's star was waning. When Cromwell overreached himself, was accused of treason, and lost his head in July 1540, his 'lifelong servant and bedesman' swiftly found service with the King who had ordered his execution. William was now a royal Commissioner in Southern Ireland, charged with reasserting King Henry's claims in that turbulent country after the Fitzgerald risings. He stayed two years in Ireland, was knighted for his work and, in 1546, just a few months before he married Bess, was appointed Treasurer of the Royal Chamber back in London, the post he held when Henry died and Edward VI succeeded him.

So when William took his young wife home from Bradgate Manor to his London house in Newgate Street behind St Paul's, he must have been expecting to enjoy the hard-earned fruits of an already long and profitable official life. He was forty-six, with country properties, children by his first marriage and an honoured place at court. Now he possessed a young, attractive wife as well. Life must have seemed sweet for both of them, with their ambitions satisfied at last.

For Bess had fallen on her feet, and the one-time retainer of the Zouches and the Greys now had a well-appointed household of her own and a husband old and rich enough to dote on her. Children were no problem for Bess's sturdy constitution: she conceived at once, and within the year the old accountant had his notebook out for another of his inimitable entries:

Frances, my 9 Childe, and the first by the said Woman, was borne on *Munday*, betweene the Howers of 3 and 4 at Afternone, *viz.* the 18 of *June*, *Anno* 2 R. *E*. 6 the domynical Letter then *G*.

Bess's half-sister, Jane Leche, came down from Derbyshire to be with her and act as her gentlewoman, and further offspring now appeared at yearly intervals – a short-lived second daughter, Temperance, in 1549, followed by a long-awaited son and heir for William in 1550. He was christened Henry, and his three god-parents show the rising fortunes of the family: all were Protestant and all extremely grand. The first was William's patron, Henry Grey, now Duke of Suffolk; the second, the powerful Earl of Warwick, and the third, the youngest child of Henry VIII and future Queen of England, Elizabeth Tudor.

The young Princess was a close friend of her kinswoman Suffolk's wife, Frances Grey, and was of an age with Bess; their temperaments were not dissimilar, and they began a friendship which, despite its setbacks, would continue for the remainder of their lives, with important benefits for all the Cavendishes.

But her friendship with Princess Elizabeth was only one of several signs that Mistress Cavendish had set her sights on something more than the submissive wifely role of her dutiful but drab predecessors in Sir William's bed. Household expenditure at Newgate Street and Northaw Manor rapidly increased; so did the servants and the visitors, with regular guests including the Derbyshire Fitzherberts and the Earl of Huntingdon. The Cavendishes offered food and wine to match. A priest joined the household, and 'a harpist and two minstrels were part of the permanent establishment; the Cavendishes had silver and the finest linens and napkins, while their servants wore a blue livery.'

From his detailed survey of the Cavendish accounts, David Durant has calculated that Sir William paid out £352, not including household wages, during eleven weeks in 1551. This was a life-style on the scale of the Zouches and the Suffolks, and although Sir William's income (including his land rents and his more or less accepted bribes of office) was considerable, the family was clearly living far beyond its means.

This was not in character for dry old William, and one can picture Bess behaving like most exigent young wives with elderly indulgent husbands, as she insisted on keeping up with the Suffolks and the Warwicks. But the expenditure did not end there. Important families had to have important country houses, and scattered lands in far-off Cardigan and Shropshire did little for the Cavendish prestige; nor did what William himself had called, 'my pore house at Northawe' in uninspiring Hertfordshire.

It may have been good enough for him and the previous Mistress Cavendishes, but Bess thought on a grander scale, and when she married it is more than likely she already had her eye on the place she wanted. For many years the Agard family, relations of the Leches, had been living on the site of a former Saxon settlement with some water-logged meadowland near Edensor village, fifteen miles from Hardwick. The Agards were far from rich and their manor-house, Chatsworth – derived from the Anglo-Saxon Chetelsuorde, Chetel's manor – was certainly not up to current Cavendish standards.

But as Bess would prove on several subsequent occasions, she had an eye for country and the perfect spot to build a house, and Chatsworth appealed to her. The site was spectacular, set between the river and the moors, and was well placed in the middle of rich undeveloped country. Bess as a local girl would have known of the profits to be gained from the nearby sheep-runs on the moors and the ancient lead-mines in the Peak; from her connections with the Leches she would have also known that Chatsworth was on the market for anyone with ready money. This was something Sir William had and, on 31 December 1549, just two years after he had married Bess, he bought it in their joint names for £600. From now on Bess possessed a geographic focus for her extraordinary ambitions.

The initiative for buying it was clearly hers; William had no knowledge of the country, and as a court official based in London, no earthly need for such a place. Indeed, he had frequently complained to Cromwell that even Northaw was, if anything, too far from London. But by now the tough old Treasurer was being twisted fairly deftly round his young wife's little finger; the fatherless girl from Hardwick was going home to Derbyshire in style, and Chatsworth would show the world the scale of her success.

But the estate would have to be enlarged, for the existing Chatsworth holding by the river was only a beginning. Whatever her husband's feelings for his 'pore house at Northawe', it would have to go – together with the lands in Cardigan and Shropshire. They served no useful purpose now and William, sharp as ever, managed, through the Crown Commissioners, an adroit exchange of all his scattered lands for a considerable tract beside the Derbyshire River Dove and the valuable Meadow Place manor almost adjoining Chatsworth. Even this was not enough for Bess. In this same period she and her husband also purchased an enormous nearby holding, nearly

8,000 acres of good sheep-rearing country, from the Earl of Westmorland and, within the first four years of marriage the Cavendishes were established as important Derbyshire land-owners and a power in the county. With such a grand position, the house at Chatsworth had to be improved as well, and one gets a glimpse of Bess's character – including her eye for detail and economy – from a letter she wrote on the subject to her Chatsworth agent, Francis Whitfield, in 1552. She was barely in her middle twenties when she planned this visit to her house, and one can almost hear her strong commanding voice as she begins:

> Lete the weivar make bere for me fourthew, for my owne drynkyng and your mayster; and se that I have good store of ytt, for yf I lack ether good bere or charcole or wode, I wyll blame nobody so meche as I wyll do you. Cause the flore yn my bede chamber to be made even, ether wt plaster, claye or lyme: and al the wyndoues were the glasse ys broken to be mended: and al the chambers to be made as close and warme as you cane. . . .
> Lyke as I wolde not have any superfleuete or waste of any thynge, so lyke wyse wolde I have to have that whyche ys nedefoulle and nesesary.

Bess knew how to deal with servants, having been one herself; she also knew her mind and how to get exactly what she wanted, and would do so for the remainder of her life. As it was, she was intent on furnishing Chatsworth as splendidly as possible, and this letter and her visit heralded the influx of a mass of rich possessions to the house. A year later the first Chatsworth inventory shows it already furnished in considerable luxury – 2,124 ounces of gold and silver plate, scarlet silk bed-covers embroidered in gold and silver, furniture and tapestries for thirteen separate bedrooms, and as a great symbolic centre-piece, the spectacular marital bed of the Cavendishes. It was carved, gilded, hung with scarlet silk and bore the proud arms of Cavendish and Hardwick.

Its grandeur was appropriate, for Bess was using it to make still more young Cavendishes to inherit and continue the great work on which her heart was set. She had boys now – and male heirs, unlike daughters, were the true capital of an ambitious family. At the end of 1551, the eighteen-month-old Henry Cavendish was joined by a brother William. A third son, Charles, was born in November 1553. The future of the family was now secure, and shortly after William was born, sometime in 1552, work began on a brand-new house at Chatsworth.

Though William paid for it, Bess planned and saw to its creation – and, as always, she expressed herself with overwhelming confidence and ostentation. The new Chatsworth was no ordinary house. She intended it to be the most impressive place in Derbyshire, a huge, stone Tudor fortress of a house, with square turrets at each corner, an imposing gateway, a fine inner courtyard, and a hall where future generations of Cavendishes could feast and gather and receive in state.

The Cavendishes were spending more than ever, but if William feared his wife would ruin him, as it seemed she must, he stayed silent on the subject.

During her trips to Derbyshire he was tied to London with his official duties. Hardly surprisingly he was drinking heavily and having trouble with his legs, but in 1553 financial ruin must have appeared the least of William's worries. That summer the young King died, to be succeeded by his Catholic sister, Mary, and William's two great Protestant protectors, Suffolk and the Earl of Warwick – now Duke of Northumberland – became fatally involved in plots to supplant her with the Protestant Lady Jane Grey.

Suffolk and Northumberland both ended up on Tower Hill, and William must have needed all his skill to survive, but he switched his faith, declared his undying loyalty to Mary, and somehow kept his Treasurership. It was a deft performance by the old acrobat, but his days were numbered. Rumours began about the state of his accounts for the Royal Chamber; Lord Treasurer Paulet had them checked, and a deficit of more than £5,000 was revealed.

Modern equivalents of Tudor money are misleading, but at a time when a skilled carpenter or mason was lucky to earn 30 p. for a full week's work – and William's own official salary was under £30 a year – this was clearly an enormous sum. Paulet's investigation was probably set off by royal disfavour after Suffolk's execution, but the deficit was not to be disputed; and as summer ended, Bess came down from Chatsworth to be present in London with her husband when he made a shamefaced appearance before the Queen's judges in the Court of Star Chamber.

He was, he told them, 'ryghte willing and ready to confess the debt determined upon me', abjectly agreed to Paulet's figures and ended in the only way he could – by appealing for royal mercy. His actual words, recorded in the proceedings of the court, could serve as the description for an elaborate Tudor tomb:

Now therefore falling upon my knees in a most humble obedient and lamentable spirit, ready to take my leave of this poor life: do in the name of my poor wife and miserable and innocent children, and family now kneeling and standing before me, presenting over myself, appeal unto Her Majesty.

He signed himself, 'Your very humble meake and pore sick man, William Cavendish.'

The game was up, his career in ruins, and an answer offered to the mystery of at least some of those great amounts of money which had furnished the plate and land and paid the builders' bills at Chatsworth. William was not the first man nor the last to have been ruined by a young demanding wife; knowing his careful nature it is hardly likely he would have spent so much money on his own account, and knowing Bess, one can understand exactly how it happened. But this was no excuse, and Mary was no more likely to be moved by his pathetic pleas than he himself had once been by the anguish of the Prior of Ely. The stage was set for the Crown to punish the disgraced Treasurer and start recovering the debt. Chatsworth would have to go, and with it the Cavendish establishment in London. William faced imprisonment or worse, and if his 'poor wife and children end their lives in misery', so be it.

But for once he was not exaggerating when he made his plea, and a few weeks after making his confession the 'humble meake and pore sick man' collapsed and died. One thing Bess had learned from her tidy-minded husband was how to keep methodical accounts and it was her turn now to make the concluding entry in his notebook:

Memorandum. That Sir William Cavendyshe Knight my most deare and well beloved Husband departed this present Life of Mundaie being the 25th daie of October betwixt the Howers of 8 and 9 of the same daie at Night in the yeare of our Lord God 1557. the domunicall Letter then C. On whose Soule I most humbly beseeche the Lord to have Mercy and Ridd mee and his poore Children out of our greate Misserie.

This was the second time that Bess's great career was saved by the timely death of a husband whose usefulness was over. By dying, William gave his family a breathing-space; a reckoning would have to come over his debts, but it would now take time for the Crown to recover what was owed. A lesser woman might have panicked, sold up everything, and thrown herself on Queen Mary's mercy; but Bess, a gambler all her life, was not surrendering her stake because the odds were rising. For, as she knew quite well, under the terms of its purchase, Chatsworth was hers, in trust for her eldest son, young Henry Cavendish. She was still not without resources and provided she could keep her nerve, time was on her side; the Catholic Queen was ailing now and if she died the situation of the Cavendishes would be instantly transformed, with Bess's friend, the young Princess Elizabeth, taking her sister's place upon the throne.

Somehow Bess managed to delay the reckoning. A royal bill for the recovery of her husband's debt began its slow way through Parliament, but Bess had long experience of using lawyers, and there was still no settlement by the autumn of 1558. That autumn Mary died and Bess was present at the new Queen's coronation. She was thirty-two. Chatsworth and its lands remained intact and, although in theory she still owed the Crown £5,000, that could be dealt with later. Bess had everything to play for in the brave new world of Gloriana's court.

Though not of noble birth, by temperament and training Bess was entirely at home amid the splendour and intrigue of life at court. But she had her family to care for and, as an eligible wealthy widow, required a husband. She took her time, and once again she made a careful choice.

Sir William St Loe was an altogether softer and more polished gentleman than William Cavendish, more socially acceptable and one of the chief ornaments at court. 'Of ancient knightly family in the county of Somerset', he seems to have been something of a favourite of Elizabeth's, for she had made him her Captain of the Guard, and later appointed him Chief Butler of England, with an annual salary of fifty marks, and responsibility for court ceremonial. A good-looking, not over-bright, but extremely loyal ex-soldier, he was perpetually fussing over his responsibilities at court. Bess had not the slightest difficulty in captivating him; they were married in August 1559 and thereafter he stayed utterly beneath her thumb.

He seems to have been slightly stunned by her, and one wonders why they had no children. Bess was barely in her early thirties and had proved herself highly fertile; St Loe from the letters that survive appears to have been an ardent lover.

'My owne, more dearar to me than I am to myseylff,' he begins one letter in which he goes on to complain of his 'contynuall nyghtlye dreams besyde my absens', when she was away at Chatsworth, and signs himself, 'Yowre loveng husband wyth akeng hartt untyll we mete.'

His heart ached often, for Chatsworth occupied the first place in his wife's affections, and she was often there while he was tied by his duties to the court. Further children would have been an inconvenience to Bess – not least by diverting the St Loe inheritance away from her existing children – and even in Tudor times there were ways for a woman of experience to avoid conception.

Besides, her dog-like husband was one of nature's ideal stepfathers to the demanding brood of infant Cavendishes, uncomplainingly paying young Master Henry and Master William's fees at Eton, arranging their journeys up to Chatsworth in their holidays, and even offering a substantial dowry for Bess's stepdaughter, Elizabeth Cavendish.

He had other uses too, enhancing his wife's somewhat parvenu social status and cementing her influence at court. Through his help, Bess finally compounded for Sir William's debts by paying the Queen £1,000, which St Loe provided, and Her Majesty appears to have waived the remainder of the debt. Above all, St Loe never interfered with what was clearly Bess's overriding aim in life – establishing a great dynasty of Cavendishes in Derbyshire. He even added to her burgeoning resources by obediently ensuring that the St Loe inheritance, including the great ruined monastery and the monastic lands of Glastonbury, should ultimately pass to her instead of to his brother, Edward. With that his usefulness was over, and in 1564 the good man, like his predecessors, died.

Throughout her life, Bess climbed the Tudor ladder of ascending widowhoods, and this, her third, was certainly her best to date. But she had not the temperament or time for an excessive show of grief. She was busy. The construction of her great new house at Chatsworth had been delayed by Sir William's troubles. Now it was under way again.

3. Mistress of Hardwick

Bess of Hardwick (II. 1565–1608)

AT the time of her third widowhood in 1565 Bess was in her late thirties and entering her prime. She was at home at court and among the aristocracy; she had the ambition and the legal and financial skill of the rising bourgeoisie, combined with the greed and grasp of the peasant who had known poverty. She was also a rich, attractive, very clever woman, and the combination was formidable.

Thanks to the death of the amiable St Loe, she was now strategically positioned for her final coup which would set herself and her descendants among the very greatest in the land. Part of her new Chatsworth was complete and already furnished with the lavishness one would expect. Her broad Derbyshire acres and new 'Western' lands in Somerset – now firmly in her grasp despite the attempt of the dispossessed St Loes to fight the legacy – were bringing in some £1,600 a year. All this was irrevocably her own, and made her one of the richest women in her own right in the kingdom, but she still required the lustre of a noble name. There was one way for her to get it, and within a few months of the obsequies for husband number three at Great St Helen's Bishopsgate, Bess had returned to court to look for number four.

The names of various potential victims went the rounds – Lord Darcy, Sir John Thynne of Longleat, and one of the Queen's own current favourites, Lord Cobham. All three escaped, scared off perhaps by what had happened to her other husbands, but there was one great noble rich and rash enough to meet the challenge.

George Talbot, Sixth Earl of Shrewsbury, was something of a rarity in Tudor England – the head of an ancient house who was also one of the most successful and enterprising industrialists in the country. His possessions were legendary and included, besides two large London houses, great tracts of land throughout the north and eight impressive country houses, in two of which, Sheffield Manor and Sheffield Castle, the splendour of the Shrewsbury establishment was said to rival the extent and splendour of the monarch's. Indeed he was all but a monarch in the 'Forests and Chases North of the Trent', which he ruled as the Queen's specially appointed Chief Justice in Eyre. A tall, slow, somewhat humourless aristocrat, Shrewsbury was very much aware of his lineage and dignity, but he was emphatically no fool to have become the great businessman he was – still less was he a gentle cypher like St Loe. The Queen enjoyed his company and recognized his worth by appointing him Earl Marshal of England after the execution of the Duke of Norfolk.

But George Talbot was susceptible. In 1566 his wife Gertrude, sister of the Earl of Rutland, was dying. Bess was never sentimental over death and saw her opportunity. She must still have possessed great sexual magnetism, which she knew how to use to captivate the man she wanted, for the sombre earl was soon totally besotted. Sex apart, Bess had financial and territorial attractions to appeal to him as well. Her lands in Derbyshire were conveniently close to his and they could be jointly managed; her capital was considerable and, upon marriage, the Earl would expect to assume control of his wife's resources. Because of this, the marriage of Bess of Hardwick and the Earl of Shrewsbury, which took place in 1567, after the unlamented Gertrude had been decently interred, has been compared with 'the merging of two companies', which in a way it was; but it was also something more.

For Bess it marked her arrival in the ranks of the upper aristocracy at last; henceforth she was Elizabeth, Countess of Shrewsbury and, for the remainder of her life, no one was going to forget it. George on the other hand was undoubtedly in love, but while he had clearly lost his heart, Bess just as clearly kept her head. She had had husbands doting on her all her adult life and always made them do exactly what she wanted. Right from the start she tried to do the same with Shrewsbury – and at first succeeded.

For her there was one great hazard to the marriage – that all she had striven to achieve, lands, fortune, even Chatsworth, might simply end up enriching the already extraordinarily rich empire of the Talbots; and to avoid this, the hard-headed bride took considerable trouble, and the finest available legal counsel, over the all-important contract for her marriage. By now Shrewsbury was evidently in a mood to agree to almost anything and Bess persuaded him into a most curious arrangement. As well as marrying Bess, Shrewsbury also agreed to marry off his daughter, Grace, to Bess's eldest son, Henry, and his second son, Gilbert Talbot, to Bess's second daughter, Mary. Grace was barely eight and Henry just eighteen; Gilbert was fourteen and Mary Cavendish was twelve.

Nobody seemed disturbed by these infant nuptials which were duly celebrated at Sheffield parish church in February 1568, a few weeks after those of the childrens' parents.

The linking of stepchildren to a marriage was not unknown in Tudor times; according to Professor Stone such eminent families as the Bourchiers, the Egertons, the Sackvilles, the Stourtons, the Sydneys and the Touchets all tried it too, but none with quite the thoroughness of Bess and Shrewsbury. For Bess was making doubly sure of the future of the all-important Cavendish inheritance and doing her best to guarantee that the benefits accruing from the marriage would not be lost completely to the Talbots if she should predecease the Earl.

She also struck a hard bargain with him in return for the lands and wealth she was bringing to the marriage. Her marriage settlement – to provide for her widowhood if the Earl died first – was to include much of the richest Talbot lands round Sheffield, and he agreed to pay off several of her large outstanding debts and to give William and Charles Cavendish considerable lump-sums on their majorities. None of this seemed to worry him, and it was understood that Bess would still take care of Chatsworth and her business interests, while he had his eight great houses, his industries and his duties with the Queen to keep him more than busy.

1. Bess of Hardwick:
   The founder

2. Sir William Cavendish
   Her second husband

3. Sir William St Loe
   Her third husband

4. The Earl of Shrewsbury
   Her fourth husband

5. Elizabethan Chatsworth
   by Richard Wilson after Siberechts

6. Hardwick Hall
Bess's triumphant building, crowned with her overweening monogram, 'E.S.'

7. The First Earl
A good head for business

8. The Second Earl
A cosmopolitan courtier

9. The Third Earl
The survivor

10. Colonel Charles Cavendish
The gallant cavalier

11. Thomas Hobbes
The famous tutor

12. Apotheosis of William Cavendish, First Duke of Newcastle

22. The children of the Fourth Duke by Johann Zoffany
William (afterwards Fifth Duke), Dorothy (afterwards Duchess of Portland), Richard, and George (afterwards
Earl of Burlington)

24. Lady Elizabeth Foster
Second wife of the Fifth Duke
by Sir Joshua Reynolds
A sort of human catalyst

23. Lady Georgiana Spencer
First wife of the Fifth Duke

25. The Fifth Duke
by Pompeo Batoni

26. The Sixth Duke's Chatsworth

27. His new sculpture gallery

28. The Sixth Duke
by Sir George Hayter
An extremely likeable man

29. The Seventh Duke
A worthy and depressing life

30. The Eighth Duke
'Dressed like a seedy, shady sailor'

31. The Eighth Duke
as Marquis of Hartington – Ape cartoon
'His ability and industry would deserve
respect even in a man; in a Marquis they
command admiration.'

32. Evelyn Fitzmaurice, wife of the Ninth Duke
Mending tapestries at Hardwick in old age

33. The Ninth Duke
in a shooting-butt

34. The Ninth Duke
speaking to cattle-men in Canada

35. The Tenth Duke
speaking to a Conservative rally at Chatsworth

36. The present Duke and Duchess, soon after they took over Chatsworth

Perhaps because of this, George's infatuation managed to survive the first year or so of marriage, and Bess did her best, within her limits, to be a conscientious wife. Within a few months, duty called George to attend the Queen at Hampton Court, and he wrote back to Bess at Chatsworth thanking her for the 'podengs and venyson' she had sent. After a long evening playing cards with Elizabeth he could wearily declare;

offe all erthely joyes that hath happenyd unto me, I thanke God chefest for you: for wth you I have all joye & contentasyon of mynde, & wthoute you dethe is mor plesante to me than lyfe, if I thought I shulde long be from you.

Bess was his 'Dere Nonne' and he her ever faithful 'Blak Man' who was contentedly basking in such 'faithfull affection which I have never tasted so deeply of before'.

It might have been a touching honeymoon between a middle-aged rich couple, but it could not last, for they were both strong characters, each with private interests and ambitions which were bound to clash. Trouble came more swiftly than it might have done, thanks to unforeseen affairs of state. During the first summer of their marriage, Mary Queen of Scots, escaping from her rebellious kingdom, arrived in England and appealed to Elizabeth for help. The arrival of the Catholic Queen created problems for her cousin who, while wishing her treated with the dignity proper to a queen, could not allow her the freedom of her court. As her potential successor and a Catholic, the Scots Queen was dangerous, and had to be kept out of the way until the difficulties surrounding her could be resolved. Elizabeth needed somebody whose rank and loyalty were above reproach – and the man she picked for this most burdensome of honours was her Hampton Court partner at cards, her 'old man' as she called him now, the Earl of Shrewsbury.

At first the Shrewsburys were delighted, innocently seeing the task as signal proof of royal favour. Mary arrived as a resentful guest at one of the Shrewsbury castles, Tutbury – together with some thirty members of her court – where the Earl and his Countess did their best to treat her with the honour due to someone who might one day be their queen. Mary however was soon complaining hard about the lack of comfort and freedom, and rapidly became involved in the first of countless plots and counterplots that were to follow her until her death. The northern Catholics rose in a doomed attempt to free her. Shrewsbury was criticized by Elizabeth and found himself compelled to act as Mary's full-time gaoler.

It was as the Scots Queen's keeper that in 1570 he was to bring her from Tutbury – where among other things the sanitary arrangements were proving woefully inadequate for the Scottish courtiers – to be the first royal guest at Bess's rebuilt Chatsworth. Bess was there to entertain her. The two ladies got on well at first, even doing needlework and embroidery together, and Mary gave her hosts a magnificent French table carved with dolphins, which is still at Hardwick. But behind the scenes there was soon another plot to free her – this time by a disaffected former servant of the Shrewsburys'. News again reached Elizabeth; the omniscient William Cecil soon arrived to interrogate the plotters, and in the presence of that hard, cold royal servant, Bess and her husband must have had their first real inkling of their uncomfortable responsibility.

Not the least part of it, for the Earl at least, was the drain on his resources. Captive she may have been, but Mary was keeping queenly state at Chatsworth with more than sixty courtiers and servants now and, although in theory Elizabeth was paying their expenses, much of the cost of this unwilling court fell to Shrewsbury. The poor man also found his gaoler's duties were increasingly diverting his time and energies from more important matters. For apart from his estates, his sources of real income – his mines and iron-works, his complicated deals in wool and overseas adventures, – all depended on his personal direction; lacking this, they soon began to suffer.

Then, as a final blow, he found himself having to provide considerable sums of money for marriage settlements on his children – Francis, his eldest son and heir who had married a daughter of the Earl of Pembroke, and his two younger children whose agreed settlements on marrying Bess's children were still not paid. Nor had he paid all Bess's debts as promised, and the twenty-first birthdays of William and Charles Cavendish were looming. By the spring of 1572, George Earl of Shrewsbury, rich man though he was, began to feel the pinch.

Not unnaturally he asked his wife to help – and help she did, but on terms which she and her lawyers carefully devised, and which must have come as something of a shock to the embattled Earl. She agreed to absolve her husband from all current payments owing to her and to her children, but only if he would legally return Chatsworth and the lands she originally brought to the marriage, to William and Charles Cavendish, with a discretionary life interest in them for herself. It was a rugged bargain – particularly for a wife to force upon the man she loved – but the hard-pressed Shrewsbury was grateful, and put his name to the agreement.

Financially for Bess the benefits were clear. As always she had been extremely sharp at pressing her advantage for, with the lands now under her control bringing in more than £1,000 a year in rents alone, she had established financial independence from her husband at a stroke, and guaranteed the Cavendish patrimony for the future. The matrimonial advantages were less obvious – especially with a husband as powerful and proud as Shrewsbury – and although Bess had her document setting out her rights, the battle for her independence was far from over.

It would prove bitter, undignified and painful – to George at any rate if not to her; for Bess invariably kept her temper and her options open while he, poor goaded man, did not. But to start with he was evidently grateful to be saved from his most pressing debts, and two years later when Bess was beginning to have trouble with her increasingly rebellious eldest son, Henry, she could still address her husband as 'My Juwel' when she wrote to him on the subject, and sign herself, 'Your faithfoul wyffe. E. Shrouesbury.'

But shortly after this, in 1574, the Earl was jolted by a new and ominous reminder of the dangerous independence of that 'faythfoul wyffe' of his, and of her limitless ambition for the house of Cavendish. As a great exponent of the fine art of profitable marrying, Bess was inevitably turning her attention to the way her remaining unmarried children could assist the sacred interests of her family. An obvious candidate was her nineteen-year-old daughter, Elizabeth Cavendish, and for some time she had been pestering her husband to help find a suitably rich and well-connected husband for the girl. 'There is few noblemen's sons in England that she hath not prayed me to deal for at one time or the other,' he was later to complain to Burghley.

None was forthcoming soon enough for Bess, and she abruptly settled matters by herself – and in such a way as to fill her already troubled husband with alarm. The bridegroom she selected for her daughter was no ordinary presentable rich man's son and heir, but eighteen-year-old Charles Stuart, the son of her friend, the Countess of Lennox. As such he was also the brother of Mary Queen of Scots' dead husband, the Earl of Darnley, great-grandson of King Henry VII, Queen Elizabeth's first cousin once removed, and uncomfortably close to the succession to the throne of England.

Having made her choice, Bess acted swiftly, and without bothering to tell her unsuspecting husband. She must have known the risk she ran of alienating the Queen, who was more than touchy over anything concerning the succession, but she went impetuously ahead, inviting the not overbright Countess and her son to stay at Rufford, a Talbot house in Nottinghamshire, making sure the young couple met, giving them her blessing, secretly arranging the marriage – and damning the consequences.

As a gambler, Bess had shown herself prepared to take almost any risk to advance her family, and the marriage must have been an irresistible temptation, for at a stroke it connected the Cavendishes with the royal family, and a child of the marriage might one day even reach the throne. She must have been counting on her friendship with the Queen to see her through the inevitable rumpus that ensued. Shrewsbury was shocked and spluttered excuses to Burghley and the Queen; Margaret Lennox was sent promptly to the Tower, but as usual Bess survived and although she fell from royal favour for a while, the risk was worth it. Once again, through marriage, the Cavendishes had advanced a further great step upwards.

Within a year the gamble was already paying off. In November 1575, Elizabeth Lennox had a daughter; she was christened Arbella. Her father died a few months later, and the baby instantly became yet one more cause for Bess to fight for; the lawyers were summoned up to Chatsworth and Bess soon staked her claim for the Lennox lands in Scotland as part of her grandchild's inheritance.

For once, her claim did not succeed, but there was still the future. With Arbella, Bess possessed the chance to make the Cavendishes not just the greatest family in Derbyshire, but a dynasty of all but royal status. Shrewsbury must finally have realized his wife's intentions, but there was little he could do to stop her. Guarding the Scots Queen was practically a full-time occupation; Bess had financial independence, and was completely free to run her life and her affairs exactly as she wanted.

She totally ignored him, and backed by the agreement he had signed restoring her control of Chatsworth and her former lands, calmly proceeded with the construction of her now enormous house, enclosed fresh pasturage for sheep, and gathered her revenues from lead and coal. Most of her income was being carefully ploughed back to increase the Cavendish possessions for the future, as she purchased still more tracts of land in Derbyshire in the names of Charles and William Cavendish. (Henry by now was totally out of favour, having quarrelled with his dominating mother, failed to produce a legitimate heir, and as a final insult, sided with his father-in-law, Shrewsbury, against his mother.)

During this period Bess even bought back her original family land at Hardwick. Her brother James had finally inherited the small estate, but lacking his sister's business skill had failed to make it pay. Rich as she was she had allowed him to be imprisoned for debt and, after his death, bought the land cheaply from his creditors. Soon afterwards her mining engineers discovered coal.

By the early 1580s, Bess was richer and more powerful than she had ever been before: her estimated annual income was approaching £2,500, and since her marriage to the Earl, she had spent ten times that sum on buying land. It was a vast investment and not the least unusual thing about it – particularly for Tudor times – was that it had been made by a married woman in virtual defiance of her husband.

A successful wife is a dreadful burden for a hard-pressed husband to endure, and by now the Earl was suffering from gout as well as from the Queen of Scots. In 1584, his patience, what was left of it, gave out, and he exploded in a burst of truly feudal wrath and frenzy. Claiming that Bess had exceeded the terms of their agreement, and hinting that Talbot money had been taken to enrich the grasping Cavendishes, he demanded rents from Bess' tenants in Derbyshire and Somerset. The tenants had already paid the rents to Bess's agents and resisted. This was an insult Shrewsbury could deal with, and his retainers were despatched to collect the rents by force. Scuffles ensued and the disorder spread. Chatsworth was raided, workers cowed, trees uprooted, windows broken. William Cavendish barred the great doors, and his mother fled to Hardwick. Shrewsbury himself arrived from Sheffield Castle with a relieving force of forty men-at-arms, determined to reoccupy the house he claimed was his.

It was like the beginning of some fine old-fashioned feudal skirmish as William, armed with his halberd and his pistol, and surrounded by a group of loyal servants, faced his imperious father-in-law, prepared to fight for his family's inheritance. Finally, this was not necessary. The gates held and, after an exchange of insults and a lot of warlike posturing, both sides obeyed the Queen's command to call their battle off. William was brought to London by royal officials, locked up briefly in the Fleet prison, and then, on instructions from the Queen herself, a full inquiry began.

With an inquiry like this, Bess was in her element. Shrewsbury's resort to force, by endangering the Queen's Peace, had placed him fairly firmly in the wrong from the beginning, and Bess knew exactly how to exploit her considerable advantages to the full. It was probably not by chance that her friend, the Earl of Leicester, was put in charge of the commission of inquiry, and she carefully played up to him by presenting herself as the sadly injured but forgiving wife who wanted nothing but her erring husband safely back beside her.

She was quite safe maintaining this, for she knew the Earl well enough by now to realize that nothing would induce him to return to her – particularly when that irritable nobleman heard there were rumours of an affair between him and Mary Queen of Scots, rumours which wrongly, or probably rightly, were imputed to the Cavendishes. He was incensed, but Bess, all public gentleness, said she was prepared to forgive him even this.

> My Lord, how I have tended your happiness. My life would have been adventured for you. . . . I trust you will quieten my heart, receiving me into your favour, for only you can do it.

Shrewsbury knew what she was up to, and the knowledge made him angrier still. 'My wife has come to court and finds great friends. I try all [I] can to be rid of this burdensome charge,' he groaned. For by now he loathed her – especially when he heard the Royal Commissioners find entirely in her favour. Chatsworth and her pre-marital lands were hers to enjoy, in accordance with the legal deed that he had signed; the Cavendish rents that he had seized by force were to be repaid; he and his servants were henceforth to keep the peace; and he was to take back his faithful, ever-loving, ill-used wife.

The noble Earl was so enraged by this that it required Elizabeth's personal intervention before he reluctantly accepted the Commission's findings, and a token reconciliation with his wife took place on royal orders. It could not last. 'Trewly, Madame, I would wish myself a plowman than here continue,' said the Earl, and he and Bess were soon apart again and bickering like any miserable modern couple over disputed household items from the marriage. But the unseemly farce was drawing to a close, with Bess the undisputed victor, as she had been with all her husbands. She was approaching sixty, robust, rich and ready to enjoy the abundant harvest of her marriages; Shrewsbury was gouty, dying and embittered.

His last great public act occurred in 1587 when, as Earl Marshal of England, he had the grim privilege of presiding at the execution of the only woman who had rivalled Bess in the troubles she had caused him – Mary Queen of Scots. After the beheading he retired to one of his manor-houses outside Sheffield, worn out by service to his queen and battles with his wife, and found brief consolation in the arms of a lady of his household, Mistress Britton.

In the autumn of 1590 he received a letter from the Bishop of Lichfield, urging him yet again to take back Bess. The prospect may well have killed him, for within a few weeks of the letter he was dead. His funeral at Sheffield Parish Church harked back to the great obsequies for a feudal noble, 'and was more sumptuously performed than was ever to any afore in these countrys, and the assembly to see the same was marvellous, both of nobility, gentry and country folks and poor folks without number.' Three spectators tumbled from a tree and died; Bess did not attend, nor was she mentioned on his monument.

Bess had more important matters on her mind at the time of her husband's funeral. She must have known his end was near, for a few weeks before he died, her workmen had started digging foundation ditches on a site not far from the Old Hall which she had already built at Hardwick, and where she had been living with her trusty and obedient second son, William, and his wife. Chatsworth was legally entailed to faithless Henry Cavendish, and had reverted to him with Shrewsbury's death. Although as her eldest son he was technically her heir, they were still not on speaking terms, and there could be no question of her moving back to Chatsworth now. But, as Shrewsbury's widow, she required a suitably impressive residence for herself and her family – and a headquarters for her business empire. The old Hardwick Hall was hardly up to the new role Bess was planning for herself, and her new hall at Hardwick was designed by the most ingenious architect in England, the virtuoso master-builder, Robert Smythson. With Shrewsbury dead, work on the house could now proceed in earnest.

The new Hardwick Hall was a triumphant building, built on the land from which her family was once evicted, and started in that year of Bess's final widowhood and most conclusive victory. Against immense odds she had emerged from four marriages, unbelievably enriched if not entirely unscathed. Now she was free at last, after the Queen the richest woman in the realm, and undisputed mistress of her fate. Hardwick reflects this sense of freedom and the immense self-confidence of the invincible woman who built it. Even today it appears a celebratory house, full of light from the expanse of high glass windows which provide unrivalled views towards the Derbyshire possessions she had conquered, and crowned with her overweening monogram – E.S., Elizabeth Shrewsbury – six feet high in solid stone on each of its six towers.

Whatever motives possessed this tough old lady when she built it – snobbery, vainglory, ostentation – and however unscrupulously she had battled in her time for the wealth to pay for it, this was transmuted here at Hardwick into something that was new in England – a vision of courtly elegance, physical delight and earthly happiness. These are not qualities one associates with Bess, and much of the credit must redound to the mysterious genius of Robert Smythson; but much must have come from her as well. She cannot have been a passive client for an architect and, after four hundred years, the house still seems impregnated with her presence. It also stands as something of a witness to the romantic dream which drove her on with its aspirations towards feudal ceremony, noble splendour, and the ideal of beauty carefully created for the future in the family she founded.

Not that this stopped her from exploiting every material advantage to the hilt during the months that followed Shrewsbury's death. As his widow she was entitled to her massive marriage settlement of a lifetime's income from a third of his disposable lands; this came to around £3,500 a year, and she intended to have it. The Earl's heir felt as strongly to the contrary.

The new Earl of Shrewsbury was Bess's son-in-law and stepson, Gilbert Talbot, his elder brother Francis having died. Gilbert and his wife, Bess's daughter Mary, had both sided with the Cavendishes during Bess's battles with her husband, but all this changed once Bess was on the warpath for her widow's rights, for these included some of the Talbots' richest possessions – Wingfield Manor with its iron and glass works, Bolsover with its coal, the forestry of Alveton in Staffordshire, and rich pasturing in Derbyshire and Yorkshire. When he realized how much he stood to lose, Gilbert decided to contest the settlement.

He was a brave man. Hearing of his decision, Bess came down from Derbyshire to London like a triumphant general bent on a final mopping-up to finish off a long campaign. As Dowager Countess of Shrewsbury, she established herself and her entourage in style at the great Shrewsbury House in Chelsea. Soon she was bribing the Master of the Rolls and feeing the best London lawyers for her cause. She had all the influence she needed, and Gilbert had lost before he even started. The courts confirmed her tenure of the Shrewsbury possessions, and she returned to Derbyshire to make the most of them. Having risen on the coat-tails of the Talbots, she had walked off with a sizeable portion of the coat.

It was now, in this final, richest chapter of her life, that Bess revealed her true powers as an organizer and a businesswoman of quite extraordinary skill. Up till then she had prospered through a lot of luck as well as foresight, and by taking many calculated risks; for years she had overreached herself and at times been massively in debt. All this was now behind her as she began to put her house – or rather her houses – and her commercial and territorial empire in order. She had her wealth, her great prestige, and an unchallengeable title to everything she owned; the time had come to maximize her capital to create the great raft of undisputed income that would keep the house of Cavendish afloat for centuries to come.

Again she was lucky – in her timing; for these last decades of the sixteenth century were a period of economic and social turbulence, with prices and population rising, and many old land-owning families going to the wall amid the social and financial pressures of the age. It was a time of steady and at times alarming cost inflation. According to Professor Christopher Hill, the cost of wheat rose six times in the century and general costs four times; such inflation 'favoured those producing in order to sell, whether in industry or agriculture'. There was widespread hardship at all levels of society, but there were also countless opportunities for anyone with the capital and skill to take advantage of his neighbour's troubles. Many great Tudor families declined from too much indulgence in the noble attitudes of years gone by – from genteel idleness, from a feudal sense of strict responsibility for tenants and retainers, from crippling extravagance and ostentation, and above all from the feeling that the details of commerce and profit were beneath the attention of a gentleman.

But Bess was not a gentleman. As a woman she was free from the extravagant male chauvinism and the elaborate code of honour and display that could prove such crippling luxuries for the Elizabethan aristocrat. Indeed, no mere Elizabethan male could have risen from such humble origins as swiftly and securely as she. For in this society, dominated by men, where women were not supposed to indulge in the male prerogatives of independence, money-making, knowledge of the law and cool ambition, Bess had a great advantage as a woman. She was a sort of outlaw who had learned to play the system on her own carefully selected terms. As Countess of Shrewsbury she could act the part of the great lady – no true-born aristocrat except the Queen herself could do it better – while never for an instant losing the bourgeois-puritan qualities of thrift, of love of profit, and the ever-open eye for a shrewd financial deal.

From the surviving mass of her accounts preserved at Chatsworth, one can see how much she must have learned from her accountant husband, William Cavendish. Most of the items are in her own firm hand, and every penny rigidly accounted for.

To Goode the Ropper for the great Rope uppon a Reckoninge for the great Rope	£1 6s. 8d
To him that Browghte the Rope	1 0
To Steven Bell and Clayton for foure dayes worck att macking the Bridge	2 0
For five hundredth six peny nayll for the gutters.	2 6

These items picked at random from the Hardwick Hall building accounts also reveal how she was able to indulge in what today appears her one great extravagance. 'Put not your finger in the mortar,' counselled one shrewd adviser some years later, having seen how many noble families foundered through ambitious building. But 'Building Bess' was never in danger of hare-brained over-spending, with every gutter-nail obsessively accounted for. She built magnificently but economically. Labour was cheap; timber, lead, mortar, bricks were all produced from her own estates, and the finest craftsmen could be hired for a pittance. Smythson himself was paid a pound for his original plan for Hardwick, and the building costs were never more than £300 a year. David Durant calculates the total cost of Hardwick Hall as something under £3,000.

Bess's great expenditure was not on building, and still less on ostentatious living, but on land and lawyers; for land, as she knew, was the one infallible elixir that could guarantee the life of all great families. It was the source of power and dignity and profit, and it could last when all else faded; but it needed to be properly administered, and here again old Bess revealed her genius in the way she ran her great possessions.

She knew exactly how to delegate to men she trained and trusted. Up at Hardwick she had her 'Northern Receiver' carefully accounting to her for the rents and demesne profits rendered by the lesser agents on each of her highly profitable estates. From this income all the local costs were met, and the substantial surplus then despatched to her 'Southern Receiver' based in London. It was at Hardwick that Bess kept her book-keepers and lawyers, and from here that she supervised a very modern business operation, managing her mines and foundries, marketing her wool, checking (and often increasing and shortening) her tenants' rents and leases, and lending her surplus capital at considerable profit.

A crucial element in this empire Bess was creating for the future was its size. She has inevitably been criticized for what appears like chronic greed in the way she went on amassing more and yet more lands and profits almost until the day she died. But here again there was method in her meanness. In the survival stakes of the English aristocracy, big is beautiful; winner has invariably taken all, and Bess was shrewd enough to know that only through massive wealth and the greatest possible inheritance of land would the house of Cavendish be able to maintain itself against the hazards of the years to come.

This policy of hers was strictly realistic, and proved itself during the crisis caused by the succession of wet summers and ruined harvests of the 1590s. Agricultural income plummeted but, where this spelled disaster for the lesser land-owner, the Cavendish resources were so wide and so diversified that Bess was able to ride out the slump with ease: indeed she benefited by being able to absorb still more lands from her less resistant neighbours, a process that one often sees being repeated by the Cavendishes during the centuries ahead.

Elizabethan England was a period of prodigies, and Bess of Hardwick has her place among them, for her achievement was unique. Until late middle-age, the odds against her own survival were enormous, but this never seems to have deterred her. Her courage was as remarkable as her ruthlessness and, although she inhabited a world where women's rights were minimal, she paradoxically achieved what no man could possibly have done, raising her family in a single generation to the ranks of the upper aristocracy and endowing them with such assured possessions and prestige that it was as if the family had been great for generations.

No other great Elizabethan family rose more swiftly than the Cavendishes or was left better placed to face the future. Yet, apart from the embittered Shrewsbury, who in one final outburst did refer to Bess's 'base breeding', no one objected to the Cavendishes as parvenus. This was partly due to the rapid social changes in the period, but mainly to Bess herself. Unlike a man she could rise socially through marriage, and she also took advantage of the fact that under the Tudors the English aristocracy had ceased to be based exclusively on birth. Upper-class acceptability could also come through royal favour, great territorial possessions, and the ability and willingness to play the part of a great aristocrat with suitable panache. By her final widowhood, Bess possessed each of these attributes in abundance – particularly the third – and she used them to coat the Cavendishes with a sort of instant gloss of aristocracy.

But the future was what mattered to her most, for she lived in a world still powerfully concerned with immortality. During the Middle Ages, this obsession found expression in the chantries and cathedrals built by the powerful and rich for priests to pray for ever for their souls' repose. Bess had much the same obsession, but as a sound materialist, she expressed it in a more earthly way: her great houses were her chantries for the future and her generously endowed descendants were a surer way of continuing her name than through the prayers of priests.

With hindsight one can see this beady-eyed old lady as the great mother of these future gilded generations with their palaces and parks and privileges, for their honours and achievements all derived from the great Cavendish collective she had so solidly created. She also left them sound family traditions which would ensure their continuing success for many years to come – frugality and shrewdness, skill with money and knowledge of accounts, a passionate concern for land, an eye for business and the careful use of marriage, as the surest way of acquiring ever more possessions. Possessions were what mattered: all else, happiness included, was distinctly secondary.

In old age Bess lived on at Hardwick until her death there in her early eighties in February 1608. By then she had lived long enough to see the outlines of her great plans for the Cavendishes coming true. She remained unreconciled with Henry to the end, but must have known that her son William could be relied on to carry on her work and dutifully ensure the future of the dynasty. He had been already knighted in 1581 and, three years before she died, Bess had the satisfaction of seeing him promoted Baron Cavendish; she had made sure that he inherited the bulk of her possessions. Her third son, Charles Cavendish, was also well provided for and, before she died, Bess even brought herself to be reconciled with Gilbert Shrewsbury and his wife and her daughter Mary, Countess of Shrewsbury.

Apart from Henry Cavendish, Bess's only real failure was in her great ambition for her granddaughter, Arbella Stuart. Despite the girl's royal blood, and despite elaborate attempts to find her an appropriate husband – including the Farnese Prince, the Duke of Parma – she never did achieve the resounding marriage Bess had planned for her. While Elizabeth was still on the throne, Arbella proved a dangerous responsibility for Bess who, with poetic justice, had the task of acting as her keeper up at Hardwick, rather as Shrewsbury had had the burden of guarding Mary Queen of Scots. They had not got on together. With the succession of her kinsman, James I, Arbella was suddenly in favour at court; she, too, was reconciled with Bess in the end and did her best to further the fortunes of the Cavendishes, but her own life was doomed and, after a hopeless marriage to the dissolute Earl of Hertford in 1610, she herself died miserably at forty, five years later, childless, out of royal favour, and one of the human casualties of Bess's relentless ambitions for the House of Cavendish.

During her final years at Hardwick, Bess herself would pass the time embroidering, as she had done many years before at Chatsworth with the Queen of Scots, and creating meticulously-worked hangings to decorate the walls and provide yet more heirlooms for the Cavendish inheritance – a consoling occupation to absorb the energies of a precise, powerful old woman, with time heavy on her hands, waiting for her end. One of the symbols she inevitably incorporated in her work was the Cavendish stag, but as she stitched she also worked another animal into her designs. This was a coiled serpent, which she originally copied from a book of prints with Mary Queen of Scots, and it became adopted as the second of the Cavendish heraldic beasts.

In years to come it would seem apt that the Cavendishes, who possess more of most things than most other people, should have two animals to represent them. It was also appropriate that Bess herself should be remembered by these two animals which embody the complementary sides of her own distinctly larger than life-sized nature. The aim of her life had been to achieve for her family the grandeur of the stag, the kingly beast of the North Midland forest-lands she owned. But the methods she had used had often been those of the serpent, a cautious creature symbolizing continuity and cunning, who survives when others overreach themselves.

The serpent and the stag both played their part in the founding of the House of Cavendish. They would recur throughout its history.

4. The Foundations of the House

The First Earl, William (1552–1625)

The Second Earl, William (1590–1628)

The Third Earl, William (1617–1684)

Temporall possessions are the life of a man, and by riches is worshipp and honour preserved in familyes, whereas by poverty they grow contemptible.

John Smyth of Nibley

BESS had lived too long for comfort; as uncrowned queen of Derbyshire she had had ample time to school her pliant son, William, as her obedient Prince of Wales, and there were hardly likely to be any great surprises when he finally succeeded her. Unlike his elder brother, Henry, he possessed little of his mother's drive or daring, which was just as well. After the storms and upheavals of its creation, the House of Cavendish required a period of calm. William provided it.

He was very like his father, a precise, domesticated man with a good head for figures and a prickly awareness of his wealth and dignity, but none of that absolute obsession to acquire and build which had ruled his mother. During her lifetime he was generally seen as Bess's shadow, for she had dominated him, just as she had his father. Even as a married man in middle-age he was still living on at Hardwick (his younger brother Charles at least had the independence to establish himself at Stoke Manor, four miles north of Chatsworth) but he knew exactly where his interests lay. Now the old matriarch was dead, he set about tidying up her work with considerable circumspection.

His qualities were largely negative ones, but none the less valuable for that: a marked talent for avoiding trouble and excess, a careful business brain to keep the Cavendish estates and enterprises steadily on their course, and a conscientious sense of duty. He was a sound managing director of Cavendish Incorporated, and his real work lay in Derbyshire. He had little taste for London or for life at Court, but in Derbyshire as Lord Lieutenant, a post he had held since 1595, he was a figure of importance in his own considerable right, great land-owner, official representative of the Crown and head of the militia and judiciary.

This was enough for him, and he is the first of the long line of succeeding Cavendishes who enjoyed unquestioned semi-feudal power as rulers of this virtual principality in the north Midlands. A true Cavendish, he had made sure that both his marriages enriched the family with useful jointures but, with Bess's death, he began a policy of peace with his neighbours. The Talbot lands, which Bess had so long exploited as part of her marriage settlement, were returned to his brother-in-law Gilbert, and there was no more trouble from that dangerous quarter.

In 1605, three years before his mother died, William had already got a foot on the first rung of the profitable ladder of the aristocracy by purchasing a barony from James I, through the useful intervention of his niece, Arbella Stuart. He was also shrewd enough to purchase Chatsworth from his elder brother, Henry. (Since the house and estate had originally been entailed to her eldest son, Bess had been unable to disinherit Henry entirely when he fell from favour, but he was now seriously in debt.) And for the most part it was here beside the Derwent, in the high, turreted, stone fortress-palace, which in its time had been the scene of so many of his mother's dramas, that this middle-aged magnate lived in somewhat frugal state and played the unexciting part society allotted him.

It is only now that one begins to see the full extent of all that Bess of Hardwick had accomplished for the House of Cavendish. With her unsated genius for acquisition, she had created something radically new with this enormous holding of land and wealth she left for her descendants. Previously, all great families had depended on feudal title or political service to the Crown for their position. Not so the Cavendishes; from Bess they had inherited an unencumbered territorial and commercial empire, along with the personnel and skills and family traditions to run it profitably. This was the true source of their power and their position in society; it would be where their final loyalties would always lie; it would see them safely through the centuries ahead. And, because of this, the Cavendishes already seem to be foreshadowing the great Whig landed families of the eighteenth century, at the head of whom they would effortlessly take their place.

According to Sir Lewis Namier, Whiggism possessed 'one immutable, unchanging element, the overriding absolute belief in property.' Bess had this absolute belief as well. On land and property she built her power and independence – and that of her descendants – and Bess, like all true Cavendishes was something of a Whig before the term had been invented.

Not all her family would serve the dynasty as faithfully as William, but they would fail at their cost. Henry Cavendish, who should have been her heir, had proved to be a maverick, and was ruthlessly discarded. He had no ingrained sense of property and dynasty. A spendthrift, adventurous, restless man, his life was a rejection of everything his mother stood for. He sought his fortune, not in his rent-rolls, but by fighting in the Netherlands and travelling to Turkey. He had sided with Shrewsbury, he produced no lawful issue, but his extra-marital amours earned him the title of 'the common bull of Derbyshire and Staffordshire'. Rejected by Bess, he foundered and, after selling Chatsworth to his brother, retired to his nearby small estate of Doveridge, which until recently was still owned by his descendants in the illegitimate line, the Lords Waterpark.

Bess's third son, Charles, though not so malleable as brother William, was considerably more adroit than Henry. He managed to avoid his mother's total domination, but he had something of her flair for profitable marrying. After the speedy death of his first wife Margaret (herself the heiress of the wealthy

Kitson family) he made a still more profitable, but surprisingly happy marriage with an Ogle heiress whose father was last of a line of Northumbrian border barons. He also maintained a loyal friendship with his Talbot stepbrother, Gilbert, which persisted through the latter's succession to his father's titles and his disputes with Bess.

His loyalty to Gilbert did not exactly endear him to his mother, but Charles did not lose by it. Gilbert lent him Handsworth Manor in Sheffield, where his first son, yet another William Cavendish, was born in 1593, and later leased him Welbeck Abbey and its surrounding lands, which had come to the Shrewsburys at the Dissolution. Later still he leased – and ultimately – sold him the ruins of the Norman castle at Bolsover, three miles from Hardwick. Charles had the sense to make his peace with Bess before she died. Thanks to his wife he was already rich, but he had inherited his share of Bess's fortune. He had also inherited her passion for building, and after her death would have Bolsover Castle ambitiously restored to plans by Robert Smythson. Welbeck was soon purchased outright from the Shrewsburys, and before long Charles was rebuilding it as his principal residence.

This meant that, by the second generation, there were in fact two separate, thriving lines of Cavendishes; each possessed two stately houses and immense estates, and before long each would be enhanced with the rank and title that followed great wealth almost automatically in Stuart England.

Stolid old William Cavendish's turn came first, just as his mother would have wished. Queen Elizabeth had been rigorously opposed to watering down her upper aristocracy with lavish new creations; James, always short of money and an unromantic Scot, had no such inhibitions. 'Lords we have right cheap in England,' wrote one realistic commentator, and Baron Cavendish's next step up the peerage, though not exactly cheap, was a sound commercial proposition for the Crown. (It was one further good investment for the future of the House of Cavendish.) In 1618, thanks to a payment of around ten thousand pounds, William Lord Cavendish was granted the strawberry-leaves and ermine mantle of an Earl – the same rank that his brother-in-law, Gilbert, enjoyed as the seventh generation of the ancient House of Shrewsbury.

It was one more tribute to old Bess's wealth – and also an indication of the declining status of the upper aristocracy under the Stuarts. (Between 1615 and 1628 the numbers of the peerage rose dramatically – from 81 to 126 – as the venal court became increasingly caught up in the outright sale of titles.) The only mystery in this somewhat inelegant transaction is the title the new earl assumed; at the time no one appears to have commented on the curious fact that he was given the title of the Earl of Devonshire when he possessed no property or interests or connections in that county. Presumably, it did not matter. When rank could be bought for money, the ancient feudal practice of relating honour to the land from which it sprang had little meaning, and William's earldom in no way changed him from the essentially bourgeois businessman he really was.

What did matter were his wealth and the Cavendish inheritance, and these, rather than any elevated duties at King James' Court, were what occupied the Earl's attention to the last, and under his shrewd direction the wealth went on accumulating. He was the foremost magnate of his day to invest heavily in trading companies abroad. According to Lawrence Stone, 'he was probably unique in putting about £1,000 a year into the East India Company for nearly fifteen years', and speculated profitably in the Russian trade, in the Bermudas Company, and in the settlement of Virginia.

But Bess's lands remained the golden plank of the Devonshire fortunes with the steady rise in rents and population preceding the Civil War. Economic forces were as usual on the side of the big battalions – the determined land-owners who 'could benefit from booming farm prices and were content to save and reinvest their gains instead of consuming them in gracious living.'

Gracious living was not one of William's weaknesses, and his account-books, all carefully checked and minutely entered up, show just how profitably the Devonshire inheritance was being run. For the year 1620–1, for instance, the total collected by his Chatsworth agent came to £8,390 17s. 2½d, and his London collection – which included profits from the Devonshire estates at Leicester Abbey, Latimers, Chesham, Redbourne and Glastonbury – brought in a further £15,660 5s. 11d. Of this sum, nearly £5,000 came from the sale of wool, £843 from cattle sold on the London market, and £1,000 from the East Indies trade. With such an income the Devonshires were doing nicely, and were among the very richest families in the land.

But what was the point of all this money, and where exactly were the Cavendishes going in the kaleidoscopic world of Stuart England? Would they continue as ennobled but commercially-minded Derbyshire magnates like old William, with the love of profit and the self-denying attitudes of sound bourgeois businessmen? Or would they become caught up in the decorative but profligate and rootless aristocracy that clustered round the Stuart court? Great families are fragile things. Excessive wealth could prove a hazardous inheritance and, having risen so rapidly in times of social instability, there was a danger that the Devonshires could soon fall victim to fresh instability themselves when William died.

The weak point in every dynasty lies in the succession, and the House of Cavendish was no exception. The example of disgraceful Henry Cavendish was still too close for comfort. Luckily for the safety of the line, Bess had been smart enough to spot the danger early on. Chatsworth and all its lands were now safely entailed to William and his heirs and, when the reprobate Henry died in 1616, all his remaining lands, apart from Doveridge, returned to William.

But even so, old William must have had his moments of uneasiness about the future for, despite his wealth and lands and title, there was no earthly guarantee that the Devonshire inheritance could survive another heir like Henry. And, although the Earl had called his eldest son William Cavendish, the bestowing of the talismanic family name showed little sign of bringing with it all important Cavendish virtues.

As early as 1608, when the boy was barely eighteen, his father had had trouble with him over the crucial question of his marriage. Here, if anywhere, young William should have known where his duty lay, and that with any family as rich but still as vulnerable as the Cavendishes, the marriage of the heir was too important to be left to the inclinations of the mere participants.

True, it was another of those carefully manoeuvred infant dynastic marriages the Cavendishes were so good at, and the intended bride, young Christian Bruce, the daughter of the Scottish Lord Kinloss, was only twelve; but King James himself had given it his benediction. More than this, he was rumoured to be offering Kinloss 'this alliance with a rich and rising English house as a reward for his share in setting him on the English throne', and had graciously increased the schoolgirl's dowry to an enticing £10,000 out of the royal pocket. His Majesty had also made his wishes known to the bridegroom's father in the bluntest Scottish manner – and as a loyal and ambitious subject, old William saw the point at once. Young William did not.

Although the girl was earthily described as 'a pretty, red-headed wench', the cause of the youth's reluctance was not far to seek. One of the problems that had plagued Bess on her death-bed was her discovery that her eldest grandson had seduced – or been seduced by – one of the ladies of her household, Margaret Chatterton. Parental authority, hard cash, and royal favour were all suddenly at stake, and old William put his foot down. Didn't the young fool realize that if he still refused, he would antagonize the king, and moreover 'it would make him the worse by £100,000'? He was thinking of the profits to be made at court and probably exaggerating, as fathers do with sons, but it was on this sour note of paternal insistence and sharp financial gain that the marriage finally took place.

'Alas, poor Wylkyn!' sighed his uncle Charles Cavendish. 'He desired and deserved a woman already grown, and may evil stay twelve weeks, much less twelve months. They were bedded together, to his great punishment, some two hours.'

Punishment or not, it is unlikely that the marriage was physically consummated during those uncomfortable two hours, for part of the deal appears to have been that the bridegroom was allowed to keep his freedom – and probably Mistress Chatterton – and generally amuse himself at least until his wife could bear him children. But, although old William's will was done, it hardly augured well for the future of the Cavendishes.

One historian has claimed that the First Earl 'shattered the boy's happiness and blighted his life' by his 'determination to use his son's marriage to improve his political prospects.' This is another slight exaggeration, for young Wylkyn seems to have enjoyed himself, if anything too much, in his first years as a married man. The trouble went much deeper: by nature and by inclination, young Sir William Cavendish (the King had already knighted him in 1606) could hardly have been more different from his father had he tried; and try he did, for the remainder of his life, in what psychologists might term a total rejection of the father image.

Possessed of such great prospects, and resentful of his enforced but unsatisfying marriage, he had no problem finding compensating pleasures. Thanks to his marriage, he had earned King James's favour, and backed by the approbation of that most unpleasant monarch, was soon thoroughly at home in a Court that was probably the most corrupt and dissolute in Europe.

How could he possibly be bothered with the cares of far-off Derbyshire and all that boring, money-grubbing business of rents and mineral sales and leases which formed the life-blood of the Cavendishes? (His signature is notably lacking from the Chatsworth balance-sheets throughout his life.) Instead, by his early twenties he was already a polished courtier and a good-looking man of fashion; he was also a spendthrift, a brawler and a rake.

But there was considerably more to him than this. In him the house of Cavendish had finally produced its first approximation to the contemporary ideal of a presentable young aristocrat, with courtly manners, easy generosity with money, and cosmopolitan knowledge of the world. Since he had money and could play the part expected of him, the parvenu status of the Cavendishes could hardly be held against him in a court that was full of freshly-purchased titles, Scots adventurers and royal catamites.

Apart from his great-uncle, old George Cavendish, with his Life of Thomas Wolsey, none of the family had been people of much culture; Bess's library at Hardwick numbered six books at her death, and there is no evidence that her son William was any better read. But young William had an open and inquiring mind, which was soon strongly influenced by close contact with one of the most powerful and original thinkers of his age, that curious genius, the philosopher Thomas Hobbes of Malmesbury.

The long relationship between the Cavendishes and the author of *Leviathan* is the first and one of the most important acts of patronage the family can claim in the four centuries of its existence, yet strangely enough it happened entirely by chance. For the teenage marriage of young William Cavendish had created one unexpected difficulty: as a married man he was now barred from completing his education at the university. To solve the problem, his father asked the Master of Magdalen College, Oxford, to suggest a tutor. He proposed Thomas Hobbes, who at twenty was a tall, dark-haired, penurious classics scholar who had just graduated from the college; and an unlikely friendship started.

It seems to have been a formative friendship for them both. They were of an age and, while Hobbes did his best to introduce the young master to the classics, his pupil was more successful at showing the sheltered philosopher something of the wicked world. They were soon hawking and riding together, so much so that Hobbes admitted later that he began to lose his Latin. And the courtier had other work for his easy-going tutor.

That omniscient old gossip, John Aubrey, picked up a tale about the pair of them around this time that has the ring of truth:

His lord (this only *inter nos*), who was a waster sent him up and down to borrow money, and to get gentlemen to be bound for him, being ashamed to speak for himself: he took colde, being wet in his feet (there were no hackney carriages standing in the streets) and trod both his shoes the same way. Notwithstanding he was well-loved: they loved his company for his pleasant facetiousness and good-nature.

Old William must have been tightening the purse-strings for his son already, but in 1610 did pay for him and his facetious tutor to visit Europe on what later young aristocrats would call the 'Grand Tour' of France, Germany and Italy. He should have known better. For Hobbes, who henceforth was styled Cavendish's 'secretary', it was the beginning of that broadening of interests and speculation which would ultimately lead him to a foremost place in European thought; but it must also have added to old William's anxieties about his son and heir.

In Elizabethan times, Italy had been the alluring source of all that was new in literature and art and architecture; the allure remained, but 'the Englishman Italianate' was starting to reveal himself 'the Devil incarnate', and young Lord Cavendish (as he had now become with his father's earldom) was no exception. Italy had certainly improved his mind. Between 1615 and 1628 he corresponded regularly with the Italian humanist, Fulgenzio Micanzio, and at Court he had a useful reputation as an accomplished linguist. But he had also picked up something of the Italianate ideal of the accomplished courtier as a man of heedless magnificence and display, as ready to spend a fortune on a doublet as to settle a point of honour with his rapier. He had all the pride and ostentation of the Cavendish stag, and none of the self-preserving caution of the Cavendish serpent.

One has a brief glimpse of the sort of man he was in 1623, when he emerged as a notorious protagonist in the troubled affairs of the Virginia Company. By now he was in his early thirties, and had brought himself to father three children – William, Charles and Ann – on his young wife Christian. He was M.P. for Derbyshire, still living magnificently and well beyond his means, and enjoying a considerable income from his position as a Governor of the Bermudas Company. (As a courtier he was well placed to take maximum advantage of the Cavendish investments in this highly promising exploitation of the resources of the New World; and he and his secretary, Thomas Hobbes, were both conscientious participants at the meetings of the Company.)

But, by 1623, disputes had broken out within the company and, somewhat surprisingly, Cavendish emerged as one of the most vehement opponents of the royal supporters in the company led by the Earl of Warwick. In May, the Privy Council placed him under virtual house arrest for several days for the violence of his language to the Earl; and a few weeks later the two men were only just prevented from settling matters with a duel.

This sort of profligate, romantic living was all very well. The devoted Thomas Hobbes, comfortably established in his house and hard at work on his first major work, his translation of Thucydides, said later that 'no one needed a university in the household of such a splendid lord'. His wife's biographer described his house as 'appearing rather like a prince's court than a subject's'. And, despite his behaviour over the Virginia affair, he remained one of the grandest and most decorative figures at the Court of the young King Charles. But courtly splendour and a knowledge of Italian did little for the long-term prospects of the House of Cavendish. Chronic overspending did even less. Old William Cavendish survived to check the balance-sheets and guarantee the steady flow of rents from the Cavendish possessions until his death in 1626. Then came the reckoning.

It was obvious that the new Earl of Devonshire had been borrowing steadily for years at compound interest on the strength of his inheritance. As a discreet eighteenth-century historian of the family put it, 'by his excessive gallantry and glorious way of living, he had contracted a vast debt and greatly impaired his fortune'. Even the rent-rolls and mineral rights from Derbyshire were not enough to meet the debts, and maintain the Earl in the style to which he had so long become accustomed. The time had come to do what, for a Cavendish, was virtually unthinkable; and in 1627 a bill was introduced in the House of Lords to break the entail which preserved the Cavendish inheritance, so that land could now be sold to pay the debts.

Perhaps the Earl was tempting fate. In Bess's time, death had intervened so often and propitiously to keep the Cavendish lands intact that a superstitious man might well have wondered what would happen. The answer came within a year. In June 1628, at his splendid house near Bishopsgate on the site of the present Devonshire Square, the cultured, wild and spendthrift Second Earl of Devonshire expired. His death was charitably ascribed to 'excessive indulgence in good living', and the future of the House of Cavendish was once again effectively in the hands of a woman, the thirty-two-year old Countess Christian, 'a vast and increasing debt and upwards of thirty lawsuits, constituting her inheritance.'

The Earl's death brought into relief the problem that would always dog the Devonshires – and every great landed dynasty trying to survive and prosper at the apex of the aristocracy. This was the conflict there would always be between the serpent and the stag, between the cautious, bourgeois business instincts which were crucial for survival and the demands of liberality and reckless show, which were part of the essential way of life of the true-born aristocrat. Bess had been able to reconcile these two opposed demands as far as had been necessary – partly because she was a business genius but also because she was a woman. The Widow Christian was not a genius, but she possessed a Scottish shrewdness, and must have been a woman of considerably more natural charm than Bess. Lucky again, the House of Cavendish had found a saviour whose character ideally matched the task that faced her.

If she felt any grief for her departed spouse she kept it to herself. Her loyalties lay with her children and their inheritance and, having obtained full legal guardianship of her eldest son and heir, the Third Earl of Devonshire, she set about clearing up the mess in a straightforward Scottish manner that would have earned her the approval of Bess herself.

She was a serpent, not a stag, and economy and strict retrenchment were the order of the day – no more glittering entertainments at the London house, no more literary patronage, (poor Hobbes was soon sent on his way, despite a glowing dedication to her dear departed in his translation of Thucydides) and a regiment of all-consuming servants was summarily dismissed.

Outlying lands were sold to meet the most pressing debts, but none of the really profitable Cavendish patrimony was sacrificed. She still had her own marriage jointure of £5,000 a year, a useful income, and with this she started whittling away at those thirty lawsuits hanging over the Devonshire estates. Again like Bess, she knew exactly how to work the law to her advantage, and before long every case was settled satisfactorily. 'Madam,' exclaimed the King in genuine surprise, 'you have all my judges at your disposal!' And the judges themselves responded with rare legal gallantry. The Countess was, they said, 'A mirror of a woman.'

Under her eagle eye the Cavendish estates and enterprises started to thrive again. Hobbes returned to the household as tutor to the young Third Earl (in which capacity the great man did a repeat performance of the European tour which he had done with the young man's father, twenty years before, meeting the aged Galileo in Florence and Descartes in Paris), and although she left Chatsworth for her house at Leicester Abbey when the Earl was twenty-one, one gets a strong impression that young William remained as firmly under his mother's thumb as his grandfather, old William, had been under Bess's.

In fact it was the other thriving branch of the Cavendishes, sired by Bess's third son, Charles, that now produced the grandest, and in many ways the most disastrous, Cavendish stag of all. As with the Devonshires under the Second Earl, the disaster stemmed from the lunatic extravagance of a *nouveau riche* heir desperate to act the great aristocrat and splendid courtier in a vulgar age, but in his case he lived longer, and enjoyed a far wider stage for his acts of folly and magnificence. There was also no Christian Devonshire to restrain him or to deal with his debts.

On his second wife, the rich, nobly born Elizabeth Ogle, Charles Cavendish had sired two sons. The younger, duly christened Charles after his father, had been born deformed; but, despite his stunted body he possessed high intelligence, which was to earn him a circle of learned friends and a reputation as one of the most accomplished mathematicians of his age. According to Clarendon he was 'a man of the noblest and largest mind, though the least and most inconvenient body that ever lived', and history remembers him as the man who all but persuaded his friend Descartes to come to live in England at the invitation of Charles I.

But the elder brother, yet another William Cavendish, and heir to the great possessions and the titles of his parents, was a vain, rich, and quixotic nobleman. A good-looking, dapper man of some learning, considerable courage, and immense ambition, he set out to play the part of a very *grand seigneur*. It was not entirely his fault that the times he lived in made him suffer so much for his grandiose ambitions.

He started life promisingly enough. According to his second wife, 'his education was according to his birth; for as he was born a gentleman, so he was bred a gentleman'. At Cambridge the fellows of St John's 'could not persuade him to read or study much', but he spoke good courtly French, was created Knight of the Bath by King James in 1610 and, two years later, aged eighteen, went off on the inevitable trip to the Continent – in an honoured position in the embassy of Sir Henry Wotton to the court of the Duke of Savoy.

As with his cousin, Devonshire, it was probably this contact with a polished, extravagant European court that sealed his fate, for he made a great impression on the Duke of Savoy and never seems to have got over it. The remainder of his life was dedicated to the dangerous role of playing the splendid European nobleman.

He did make one thoroughly Cavendish gesture by marrying an heiress – Elizabeth, the daughter of wealthy William Basset of Blore in Staffordshire – and, on his father's death in 1617, continued rebuilding Welbeck and Bolsover on a still grander scale. At the same time his mother was granted by royal patent the right to continue the ancient Ogle title, so that on her death in 1629, William picked up the historic rank of Baron Ogle in addition to the titles he already held as Viscount Mansfield of Nottinghamshire, Baron Cavendish of Bolsover and Earl of Newcastle-on-Tyne.

It was a truly resounding collection of honours, which he owed partly to his Shrewsbury connections and partly to the favour of the King, whom he had entertained in extraordinary magnificence and pomp at Welbeck in 1619. But titles, however pleasing, were an expensive luxury, and William was not the man to skimp on the princely state expected of him now. Bolsover,with its great range of new apartments and its keep rebuilt as a miniature Renaissance palace, was his pleasure dome, and it was here he planned his Italianate gardens, bred his splendid horses and patronized his poets.

He had his own pretensions as a poet and a playwright, but he is remembered for his patronage of Davenant and Shirley and above all for his generosity to Ben Jonson when the great man was sick and past his prime. In the early 1630s, William employed him on two masques – *Love's Welcome at Welbeck*, and *Love's Welcome at Bolsover*, which were staged at vast expense as part of his princely entertainment for King Charles and his Court during the royal progress through the north Midlands.

But splendour and titles on their own were not enough for the Earl of Newcastle-on-Tyne. Hobbes, who knew him well, has described that 'perpetual and restless desire of power after power that ceaseth only in death' – and William was certainly obsessed by it. He was also seriously in debt with all that royal entertaining and had set his heart on gaining some suitable and lucrative position at King Charles's court in recompense for all the trouble he had taken as a courtier.

The poor man had to work for it, enduring the venom and intrigue of the Stuart court, but he had much in common with the King and finally, in 1638, weary but triumphant, he received the post on which he had set his heart – the Governorship of the eight-year-old Prince Charles. It was the ideal role for him (although snob that he was, he drew the line at dining with the Prince's tutor, learned Bishop Duppa), for the King and Queen were distant and undemonstrative parents, and the courtly Governor seemed to take their place in the affections of the royal heir.

William was the perfect pedagogue, teaching the young Prince riding, swordsmanship and laying down suitable attainments for a future king of England. The Prince, he said, should not be over-studious or too devout and, while he should be gracious to his subjects, he should not be so familiar that he forgot his great position; to ladies, particularly great ones, he could never be too civil or obliging. Charles II's career suggests that he took his Governor's advice to heart.

But sadly this influential and distinguished post at court soon ended, for the Civil War was looming. Glory beckoned and, when hostilities began in 1641, the bustling Governor took the field in splendour for the royal cause.

With his castles, his hereditary following in the north and his pride in all those great but somewhat pointless titles – to say nothing of his accomplishments on horseback and his prowess and his sword – it should have been his finest hour; and just for a while it was. From pedagogue he suddenly assumed the trappings of a feudal war-lord, raising a highly decorative troop of over a hundred knights and well-born gentleman at his own expense, and by 1642 was given command of the royal forces in the north. It was a key position, stretching from Northumberland to parts of Essex – and no king, who could appoint a man like Newcastle to such a post, could possibly deserve to win.

William was personally extremely brave and, thanks to his mother's Northumberland connections, he could arouse considerable local loyalty, but he was quite bereft of even the most rudimentary warlike skills of his Ogle ancestors. Indeed he rather typified what was happening to much of the English aristocracy – he was a rich, extravagant country gentleman with Court connections, playing at soldiers and totally obsessed with precedence and honour and his noble reputation.

When his fellow general, Lord Holland, marched his troops ahead of his, he challenged him to a duel. When he failed in his siege of Hull and had his troops in Lincolnshire destroyed by Cromwell, the King consoled him with a marquisate. At Marston Moor, where Prince Rupert, who was in command, disastrously misread Cromwell's intentions, he was in his carriage sheltering from the rain and lighting his pipe when the Parliamentary army charged. Newcastle fought bravely, but nothing could prevent Cromwell routing the Royalist army and decisively winning the day.

The King had lost the north to Parliament, and Newcastle fled to Holland, not from cowardice, but once again from vanity. As he replied to Prince Rupert, who begged him to rally the remnants of his forces, 'No, I will not endure the laughter of the Court,' and he asked the Prince to tell the King that, throughout the battle, 'he had behaved himself like an honest man, a gentleman and a loyal subject.'

This was what mattered, and in exile – first in Hamburg and Paris, then in style in Rubens's former house in Antwerp – the Marquis of Newcastle still preserved his honour and his noble state. True he was all but bankrupt, his English lands confiscated and his total losses were later computed by his wife at the enormous sum of £941,303, but he did not repine. He received money through his faithful mathematician brother Charles, he was in close contact with the exiled English court at St Germains and, his first wife having died, he now remarried – Margaret Lucas, a young blue-stocking lady-in-waiting to the Queen.

Here in Antwerp, with his adoring young wife, honoured but out of touch with all reality, the Marquis was probably as happy as he would ever be. He now had the Order of the Garter for services to the royal cause; he published his appalling plays; and at last he was able to devote his time to what had become the all-consuming passion of his life, the training of his horses.

There is something at once ridiculous and touching in the spectacle of this would-be warrior who had failed so lamentably at warfare, showing such total dedication to the knightly art of horsemanship. Here he was in his element at last, the greatest horseman of his time and, as a scholar on the subject, he decided to condense a lifetime's equine wisdom into a book. The result, his fantastic *Méthode et Invention Nouvelle de Dresser les Chevaux* is his own most faithful monument. A stately folio – the printing alone cost £1,300 – it is adorned with forty-three copperplate engravings showing not just the horses, but the bold Marquis as he presumably liked to see himself, an upright and commanding nobleman, gleaming with honours and self-confidence against a background of his loved but far-off properties at Bolsover, Welbeck and Ogle in Northumberland. In the most memorable print of all, an audience of adoring horses kneels around the Marquis as he spurs his charger ever upwards to a chivalrous apotheosis in a horseman's heaven.

Meanwhile, the serpentine qualities of the Devonshire Cavendishes had carried them safely through the crisis of the Civil War. *Cavendo tutus*, the family motto, was an appropriate play on words which meant 'Safe by being cautious', and the Third Earl, guided as usual by his mother, took it thoroughly to heart.

Both were staunch Royalists of course – Christian Devonshire was a friend of Queen Henrietta Maria – and when the war began in 1641, the Earl and his younger brother, Charles, hurried off to York to offer their services, and fortunes, to the Crown. Charles was the perfect cavalier, adventurous (he had already made a celebrated journey on his own as far as Cairo), physically brave and keen for glory. Within a few weeks he was on horseback with the *jeunesse dorée* of the royal army and he followed Prince Rupert in the cavalry charge which nearly lost the day at the battle of Edgehill.

Dissatisfied, he persuaded King Charles to let him raise a regiment of his own, financed with Cavendish money, and by 1643, young Colonel Cavendish had had several victories to his credit and was in command of the royal forces in Lincolnshire and Nottinghamshire. He was also something of a favourite of the Queen's.

But what of his elder brother, Devonshire? He too had been following the path of duty, but, as heir to the house of Cavendish, it had taken a somewhat different course. One hero in the family was enough and, guided as always by his mother, he understood his obligations to the line. In 1639 he had married Elizabeth, the daughter of the Earl of Salisbury (the first but not the last marital linking up between Cavendish and Cecil) and early in 1641 a son and heir had duly made his appearance and been given the by now all but statutory Cavendish name of William.

As a Cavendish, a husband and a father, the Earl had a duty to survive; and doubtless with heavy heart, he slipped away to France leaving his tough old mother to protect his interests in his absence. Courage and wisdom do not always coincide; the Cavendish estates were more important now than profitless loyalty to the King, and the wisdom of this exercise of Cavendish caution was shown in the spring of 1643, when the gallant Colonel Charles came face to face with Cromwell on the field of Gainsborough. Daring was no match for military genius. The Colonel was outflanked, attacked swiftly from the rear, trapped in a quagmire, unhorsed, beaten to the ground, and summarily despatched with 'a thrust under the short ribs' from the famous Roundhead leader, James Berry.

The Countess was distraught but typically controlled her grief. What mattered for the future was her eldest son, and he was safe; so for the moment were the Cavendish possessions and, in 1645, with no end to Cromwell's power in sight, she persuaded him to make his private peace with the King's enemies and return to his rightful place at the head of the Devonshire domains.

There are some survivors one feels sorry for – and although the Third Earl saved his skin and his estates, the wind had gone out of him. Ruled by his mother, overshadowed by the memory of his heroic brother, he spent the remainder of his life (he died in 1684) as an amiable and unassuming titled caretaker of the Devonshire possessions. During the Commonwealth he lived in powerless but comfortable obscurity, wisely not moving back to ostentatious Chatsworth – which had been occupied by both sides in the fighting – but residing first at his smaller house, Latimers in Buckinghamshire, then at Hardwick. He seems to have been rather bored, but consoled himself with horses and, as a conscientious Cavendish, kept businesslike accounts which show that even now the great inheritance was flourishing.

His mother, on the other hand, was inextinguishable. Tired of her cut-off life at Ampthill, in 1650 she moved close to London, buying a house and small estate at Roehampton, and continued to keep in lively, often dangerous touch with the Stuarts and their sympathizers until the Restoration. In 1660 when the King returned, the Cavendishes should all have been among the greatest beneficiaries of the restored regime, but after nearly twenty years there were clearly limits to what the King could do for his old friends, and Charles II was never the most grateful of English monarchs.

Other royalists were slightly luckier: the Newcastles returned exultantly by boat from Rotterdam. Seeing the distant smoke of London as he sailed up the Thames the Marquis told one of the sailors 'to jog and awake him out of his dream, for surely, said he, I have been sixteen years asleep, and am not thoroughly awake yet'. But, although Bolsover and Welbeck had already been restored to his son and heir, Lord Mansfield, and most of his confiscated estates were finally returned by act of Parliament, the great post of state he naturally expected never came. Nor had he the faintest hope of recovering the £941,303 (including interest) he claimed to have expended in the royal cause.

But he was still immensely rich, and there remained one consolation which Charles II knew would satisfy his old Governor at no cost to the Crown: the Earl was made a Duke, the highest and most decorative rank in the English aristocracy and, until he died in his early eighties in 1676, his titles and his horses were the unfailing interest of this sad and slightly fatuous old gentleman. For although he befriended Dryden, published another massive tome on horses, and occupied his old age seducing his chambermaids and constructing an Italianate and quite unnecessary palace on the site of Nottingham Castle, he was a figure belonging to the past. Pepys laughed at him and ridiculed his plays, and it is ironic that, for all his honours and his sacrifices to the royal cause, he is remembered chiefly through his extraordinary Duchess, Lamb's 'Thrice-Noble Margaret Duchess of Newcastle', poet, eccentric and self-proclaimed philosopher. She was, wrote Virginia Woolf, 'garish in her dress, eccentric in her habits, chaste in her conduct, coarse in her speech [and] she succeeded during her lifetime in drawing upon herself the ridicule of the great and the applause of the learned'. Her most readable book remains the devoted biography of her husband (included in the thirteen massive volumes of her collected works), which presents him as the greatest gentleman and general of his age.

Clarendon's verdict was sourer, but more realistic: 'A very lamentable man' he wrote, 'and as fit to be a general as a bishop.'

The Civil War and its aftermath had been a period of crisis for the English aristocracy, but although both branches of the House of Cavendish had experienced their setbacks and disasters, the family itself, unlike so many other noble houses, had actually prospered and enhanced itself throughout this time of troubles. Those massive foundations laid by Bess were still as sure as ever. The lands, the rent-rolls, the great houses were intact, and with an earldom and a dukedom to their credit, as the century drew towards its close, the Cavendishes 'were collectively, without exception, the richest landed proprietors in Great Britain.'

While Newcastle and his literary Duchess were busily enjoying the last years of their princely lives at Welbeck, the Third Earl of Devonshire had now returned to Chatsworth, although he still visited London regularly. The gardens were restored, the farms were flourishing and, while the great old house must have seemed out of date and horribly uncomfortable, it suited his undemanding and reclusive character. He had little of his uncle Newcastle's passion for rebuilding – nor his ambitions for great offices of state – but he loved Derbyshire, and he loved books. By the 1670s he had laid the foundations of the great Cavendish library of the future – but more important still was his librarian.

This was old Thomas Hobbes who, by now, as author of the *Leviathan*, was as famous throughout Europe as he was notorious in Restoration England. Although during the Protectorate he had briefly taught the exiled King philosophy in Paris, Hobbes was generally reviled as a dangerous atheist, and it is to Devonshire's undying credit that he thought it 'inconsistent with his grandeur or humanity to discard a man in his old age, who had, by his long services, so well deserved of his family.'

Hobbes died at Hardwick Hall in 1679, and the amiable Third Earl, having done his unheroic duty by his family, followed him five years later. By making a life-work of his own survival, he had ensured the survival of the Devonshire inheritance as well, and this was what mattered. He had started as a devoted Royalist, compromised with Cromwell under the Protectorate, regained honours and prestige at the Restoration, and lived out his last years as an egregious political ostrich, head firmly buried in the rent-rich soil of Derbyshire.

But times were changing far too rapidly for such a passive role to last indefinitely. A would-be absolutist monarchy was once more on the war-path and threatening the power of the aristocracy; London's merchants were rivalling the Dutch as the richest in the world and staking their own claims for the future; the fight between Crown and Parliament was unresolved, and with a Catholic Duke of York now Charles II's acknowledged heir, the Protestant succession seemed in danger.

The Devonshires could not remain immune to such great issues. At the Third Earl's death in 1684, his son, thinking his father ungratefully treated by the King, insisted on burying him with all the honours of a duke. It was a proud but somewhat pointless gesture, for it was the future, not the past, that mattered now, and the fortunes of the entire House of Cavendish were soon crucially involved with the fate of England and the future of the Crown itself.

5. The Patron of Our Liberty

The First Duke, William (1640–1707)

Dukedoms were originally introduced into Britain for the sons of kings, and were only given later to other noblemen to honour them with equivalent status.

Sir Iain Moncreiffe of that Ilk

THE new William Cavendish, who inherited the title of Fourth Earl of Devonshire in 1684, must have appeared a distinctly bad bet as the defender and repository of the fortunes of his family. He was forty-three. Bishop Burnet described him as 'one of the finest and handsomest gentlemen of his time . . . and of a nice honour in everything but the paying of his tradesmen'; as Lord Cavendish he had already made his name as one of the most notorious and controversial figures of the reign of Charles II, so notorious in fact that the King, no paragon himself, is supposed to have forbidden Nell Gwyn to have anything to do with him.

A famous womanizer almost to the day he died, Cavendish was arrogant, aggressive and extravagant. An irritable man, he fought – or tried to fight – innumerable duels, and might have been a throwback to his disastrous grandfather, the Second Earl. Yet strangely, it is this handsome, uncomfortable and 'withal exasperating man', who would be revered as one of the architects of English liberty, defender of the Protestant religion, and the greatest enhancer of the House of Cavendish after Bess of Hardwick.

Although his childhood was spent under Cromwell's Protectorate, and in the shadow of his slain, heroic Uncle Charles, he had certainly not suffered in the Stuart cause. Rich, acquiescent families like the Devonshires had been left to enjoy their wealth and their estates – provided they kept clear of politics – and as the treasured heir, young William seems to have passed an idyllic boyhood between his father's establishment at Latimers and his grandmother Christian's house at Roehampton. In 1658, aged seventeen, he even made the obligatory grand tour of France and Italy, bear-led by the playwright-parson Henry Killigrew, who seems to have implanted literary ambitions in his charge. Throughout his life, Devonshire remained a would-be poet and a man of European taste and culture. His taste was better than his poetry, and with the Restoration he inevitably became a notable courtier of fashion – one of the four young noblemen who bore Charles II's train at the Coronation – and just as inevitably something of a rake.

His life in the following few years was fairly predictable: first, in 1662, a sound Cavendish-style marriage to a barely pubescent heiress, the fifteen-year-old Mary Butler, daughter of the Duke of Ormonde, in Kilkenny Castle; a fairly swift return from Ireland to the delights of Charles II's court; a spot of fashionable campaigning with the Duke of York against de Ruyter in the Battle of Lowestoft; then off to France once more, to escape his creditors, while his young Countess stayed dutifully at home.

Disaster dogged him. In Paris he was almost killed in a brawl with three drunken Frenchmen at the opera. Back in England there were more mistresses, more debts and a messy duel with an Irish captain who was supposed to have insulted one of his favourite ladies, the celebrated actress, Mrs Heneage (by whom he had several children). The Captain and Cavendish survived intact, but his lordship's second, the unfortunate Lord Mohun, took an incidental sabre cut from which he eventually expired.

None of this enhanced the young Lord's reputation – and it did nothing for his temper. For shortly afterwards there was a still more serious row with an intemperate gentleman called Howard, whose brother, Colonel John Howard, had been killed in battle fighting for the French. Lord Cavendish – as an Earl's son he enjoyed a courtesy title – was Member of Parliament for Derbyshire, by now an all but hereditary Cavendish seat. As an M.P. he had strongly criticized Englishmen who fought for France, and he said in public that the Colonel had merely got his just deserts. Howard responded angrily, also in public and, to stop the trouble going any further, Parliament passed a motion forbidding the cantankerous Member for Derbyshire from issuing or accepting a challenge on the subject.

Naturally it made no difference, and next day His Lordship personally fixed a paper to the gate of the Palace of Whitehall proclaiming Howard 'a rogue, a rascal and a coward', which was most unwise. Parliament reacted angrily and within a few hours the Member for Derbyshire was cooling his lordly heels in the Tower of London. Howard was also imprisoned, but it took the personal intervention of the Speaker of the House and of the King himself before Cavendish would reluctantly let the matter drop.

The introduction of the rapier from Italy had made the cult of duelling a serious problem. It had been rife in France throughout the sixteenth century and began to afflict England in the seventeenth. And when the upper-class exiles returned from France at the Restoration, at times 'it looked as if the English nobility, like fighting-cocks in the ring, were about to indulge in wholesale mutual slaughter.' But in Cavendish's case, aggressiveness and patent relish for a fight were not so self-destructive as they might have been. For by the 1670s the ever-ready brawler had become a dedicated politician, and his arrogance and his undoubted courage were becoming channelled into the running battle being waged in Parliament against the King.

It was a fairly gradual process that converted a Cavendish of all people into a convinced opponent of a Stuart king. His cousin Henry Cavendish, Viscount Mansfield (the future Second Duke of Newcastle), gave unquestioning loyalty to the Stuarts to the last. So did his father to the day he died. But, as Member for Derbyshire, young Lord Cavendish could hardly fail to be aware of certain ominous tendencies in the way the King was starting to conduct his government.

Great issues were at stake in the conflicts between Court and Parliament during the 1670s – the power and prerogative of Parliament itself, the threat of the revived Catholicism of the Counter-Reformation to the Protestant establishment, and Charles' attempts to free himself from Parliament by secret money from the King of France, in return for help in Louis' wars against the Netherlands. As Protestant, parliamentarian and self-proclaimed patriot, Cavendish's instincts were inevitably against such measures. But instinct alone would not have driven him to take the important role he now assumed in opposition to the King.

Brought up as heir to the Devonshire inheritance, he had a keen sense of where his interests lay and, as an intelligent and realistic man with personal experience of what was happening in France, he was convinced of the dangerous road he saw his monarch following. At Versailles he had witnessed for himself the way the aristocracy, after their failed outburst in the Fronde, had lost their real power to the Sun King and his centralizing ministers, and passively exchanged the independence of their great estates for honourable but impotent attendance on an absolutist king.

In England – so far – things were different. Great families like the Cavendishes had made their sacrifices for the Royalist cause during the Civil War, and in return had kept their power in the counties and their rights in Parliament. Now they were being undermined; the old order was at risk from absolutist theories, creeping Catholicism and the French connection. For a man like Cavendish, who had so much to lose, no sentimental loyalty to the House of Stuart could obscure the revolutionary trends behind King Charles's government.

Lord Cavendish was not a sentimental man. He was tough, forthright and self-confident. At Newmarket races he was quite ready to offend the King by refusing to acknowledge his brother and the royal heir, the Catholic James, Duke of York, and in Parliament he inevitably took his place, along with great noblemen like Shaftesbury and Russell, as one of the most embattled leaders of the so-called Country Party of the Whig opposition, pledged to excluding York from the succession.

But unlike Shaftesbury and Russell he had inherited a hidden share of the old Cavendish caution – at least where politics were concerned – and was loyal enough, or shrewd enough, to steer clear of the treasonable plotting, to assassinate the Duke of York and even Charles II, in which some of his fellow Whigs were certainly involved in the early 1680s. But when the conspiracy was revealed (in the so-called Rye House Plot of 1683), and Shaftesbury fled, leaving the brave but slow-witted William Russell to face the royal wrath, Cavendish proved himself the most loyal of friends, doing everything he could to save him, and speaking out bravely at his trial.

It is hard to separate what happened then from the legends that grew up around the episode in years to come when Cavendish had been received into the realms of Whig mythology. According to one account he visited his friend in the condemned cell at Newgate and in an heroic if unlikely scene (the two men were not at all alike) suggested they changed clothes and places; Russell naturally refused. Another legend has it that Cavendish was boldly set to organize a rescue party ready to snatch the peer *en route* to his actual execution. This failed too, but what is certain is that Cavendish stood with the 'Patriot' to the last, and Russell's all but final words were a sincere if fruitless exhortation to his friend to embrace the purity of Christ. Either from remorse or pity – or moved by the sheer impossibility of such a course – Cavendish was copiously moved to tears.

Possibly Russell's words, or his example, did have some effect, for he kept out of trouble during the crammed and crucial months that followed – for a while. In November 1684 his gentle father went to meet his Maker, and he succeeded to the Earldom. Two months later the old Earl was followed by King Charles II, which was in turn the signal for the bloodthirsty fiasco of the rebellion of his indecisive natural son, the Duke of Monmouth. However much the new Protestant Fourth Earl of Devonshire might personally dislike the new Catholic King James of England, he stayed nominally loyal to the succession, playing no part in the rebellion.

But it was unlikely that a man as controversial and as touchy as the Earl could stay out of trouble at a time like this; and, sure enough, he was soon at the centre of another fracas. At first it seemed like one more of those violent scrapes he was so prone to in his youth, but this time the brawl would have important consequences for the Earl himself, for the Devonshire inheritance, and for the fate of Bess's ancient house at Chatsworth.

It all began quite accidentally. For some time the Devonshires had been having trouble with a bumptious military gentleman called Colonel Culpeper, who was attempting to recover lands in Derbyshire which he claimed as part of his wife's dowry. The facts were complicated and not particularly important, except that they left the Colonel with a grudge against the Devonshires. He was a keen supporter of King James and, meeting the new Earl in the Palace of Whitehall, a few days after Monmouth's defeat at the Battle of Sedgemoor, he insulted him and questioned his loyalty to the Crown. Devonshire ignored him. The insult was repeated. The Earl called the Colonel a liar.

> On which Culpeper struck him a box on the ear, which my Lord returned, and felled him. They were soon parted, Culpeper was seized, and his Majesty, who was all the while in his bedchamber, ordered him to be carried to the Green-Cloth officer, who sent him to the Marshalsea, as he deserved. My Lord Devon had nothing said to him.

The wretched Culpeper was to languish in the Marshalsea for the next eight months, and the Earl, remembering the King's frigid silence after this bout of fisticuffs outside the royal bedroom, spent most of his time in Derbyshire. He kept firmly out of London politics and, whatever he felt about the way the King was busily undermining the old aristocratic order in the counties, with his own private, often Catholic nominees, he kept his opinions to himself. He and King James disliked each other heartily, and Devonshire was pinning his hopes for the future on the ultimate succession of the Duke of York's daughter, Mary, and her sound Dutch Protestant husband, William of Orange.

But during this trying time the Culpeper incident evidently rankled and, early in 1687, the unfortunate Colonel, now freed from gaol, was once again frequenting the Palace of Whitehall. It was there that, fresh from Derbyshire, the Earl encountered him. This time the Earl took the initiative, and challenged him to a fight. The Colonel, evidently chastened by imprisonment, refused; at which the Earl, 'took him by the Nose, led him out of the Room, and gave him some despising Blow with the Head of his Cane.'

This time the Earl was clearly in the wrong, and as the whole incident took place in the royal drawing-room it was also something of an insult to the King. Uproar ensued, and the Earl was hustled off to the ignominy and considerable discomfort of the King's Bench Prison. His plea of parliamentary privilege was overruled and, almost certainly on instructions from the King himself, the King's Bench Judge summarily fined him the enormous sum of £30,000, and ordered him into custody until the fine was paid.

The Devonshires had no intention of being treated in this way by any King – least of all by James II. The Earl disdainfully refused to acknowledge the competence of a mere royal magistrate to fine him; and his mother, the old Dowager, flounced into Whitehall to present the unrelenting King with bonds signed by Charles I for £60,000 which the Cavendishes had spent on the Stuart cause but had never been repaid, in return for 'her son Billy's' immediate release. The King dismissed her.

But if the King could be high-handed, so could the Earl and, with a splendid show of Cavendish pride and noble rectitude, he informed the Marshal of the King's Bench Prison that he had stayed there long enough and was leaving for the north. His bags were packed, nobody dared contradict him, and a few days later he was back at Chatsworth, still simmering with anger at the ungrateful and unlawful way this upstart member of the House of Stuart had treated a member of the House of Cavendish.

A warrant followed from the Lord Chancellor to the High Sheriff of Derbyshire, Sir Paul Jenkinson, promptly ordering the Earl's arrest; but accounts differ over what exactly happened then. According to one highly-coloured version of events, Sir Paul and his posse rode to Chatsworth, were themselves arrested at the gates and swiftly sent about their business. A more credible account has it that the Sheriff ignored the warrant and was himself berated by the King for failing to perform his duty. Whatever the actual details, the affair provides extraordinary evidence of the authority and independence of the Earl of Devonshire, and shows that in Derbyshire by 1687 the Cavendishes enjoyed more effective power than James II.

When he had finally calmed down, the Earl brought himself to compose a letter for the King, not so much justifying his behaviour (he was too proud an Earl for that) as to read His Majesty a lesson in good manners, the privileges of the English peerage, and simple human gratitude. He addressed it to the King's confidant, Lord Middleton, and it shows so much of the Earl's self-confidence and character, that it is well worth quoting here in full.

My Lord,

About three weeks since, I was obliged to make a journey into the country, as well for my health as to look after my private affaires, still retaining and paying for a lodging in the prison, which I hope may free me from the imputation of an escape. Since that the Lord Chancellor, (who I conceive has nothing to do in this matter, it being forraign to his Jurisdiction) has not only revil'd ye Marshall of ye King's Bench with ye most opprobrious language and threaten'd to hang him, but likewise process'd a warrant to be sent after me signed by a privy judge, which your lordship well knows is not of force all over England. But had it been signed by my Lord Justice himself, I cannot but insist upon that which I insist to be ye right of all ye Peers of England, not to be imprison'd for debt.

I think I have pretty well shew'd my readiness to submit to His Majesty's pleasure in all things that concern myself alone, but hope His Majesty in his justice will allow ye great sumes which my father lent and was bound in for ye Earl his father (not to mention the loss of his estate for many years) to be at least as just a debt as any that may arise from the late scandalous judgement given against me in the Court of King's Bench.

I am yet to learn in what I have given His Majesty any just cause of offence. . . .

My Lord, I beg of the favour of your Lordship to acquaint His Majesty with the contents of this letter, and to excuse this trouble from,

William Cavendish, Earl of Devonshire.

And there, for a while at least, the matter rested. The King could not arrest the Earl in Derbyshire. The Earl sent the King an I.O.U. for £30,000 – which was no more use than those celebrated bonds from Charles I. And for a year his Lordship would remain safe and sound at Chatsworth, 'thinking the farthest retreat from the court to be at that time the fittest place for a good subject.' Here in Derbyshire he had much to occupy his mind and many-sided talents.

According to that good Whig Bishop Kennet, it was now,

under this load of difficulties, that he first projected the new glorious pile at Chatsworth, as if his mind rose on the depression of his fortunes; for he now contracted with workmen to pull down the South side of that good old seat, and to rebuild it in a plan he gave them, for a front to his gardens, so fair and august, that it looked like a model only of what might be done in after ages.

In fact Bess's 'good old seat' must have been growing increasingly decrepit and inconvenient with the years, and despite some renovations by the Third Earl, his overseer James Whildon reported to the Fourth Earl on his succession that the whole edifice was still 'decaying and weak'; the new Earl's immediate reaction was that he 'did determine to pull down the same or a great part thereof'.

This was entirely in character. Devonshire was a man who liked his comfort, and he seems to have been devoid of any great feeling for the past. So Kennet's suggestion that the tweaking of the Colonel's nose led directly to the Chatsworth that we see today is not quite accurate – although like most such legends it contains an element of truth.

The fact was that from his succession, and throughout the reign of James II, the Earl was ceasing to be the confirmed Londoner he had been before. After the London house he was renting from Lord Montagu was dramatically burned down in 1686, he spent almost all his time in Derbyshire, and could devote his energies to remedying this ramshackle great house he had inherited.

But he had other more serious matters on his mind which his anger over Culpeper kept firmly on the boil. According to one of his earliest biographers, 'while reflecting in his mind on the deplorable state of his country' he was reading Tacitus; and it was from Tacitus, with his dangerously republican denunciations of the Emperor Domitian, that 'he drew many useful reflections in respect to power and liberty'. James II's tyranny in suppressing Monmouth's rebels through the notorious Judge Jeffreys's Bloody Assizes, and the Trial of the Seven Bishops must have given him further food for thought, and he finally decided that although 'a Prince governing by law deserved his allegiance, yet he could never digest the notion of passive obedience to tyrants', be they the Emperor Domitian or James II.

But while the Earl was coming to these rebellious conclusions in his library, he was also working out his plans for Chatsworth in much the same idiosyncratic manner. Indeed, the whole transformation of Elizabethan Chatsworth into the great Whig palace that he left to his descendants was a very odd, tentative and piecemeal process coinciding quite uncannily with the transformation he was also pondering for the government of his country. Even the source of his ideals was the same for his house as for his country – ancient Rome; in one case through Tacitus, and in the other from the classical Roman models he was studying in the architectural plan books of Vitruvius and Palladio. Rebellion and rebuilding were proceeding hand in hand, and he conducted both cautiously, pragmatically, and in accordance with what he believed were ancient principles. It is this that makes his Chatsworth an extraordinary political document, as well the symbol it would finally become of the power of the great Whig aristocracy against the unlawful 'tyranny' of kings.

Early in 1687, and before he had tweaked the Colonel's nose, the Earl had already paid his labourers for 'carrying away an oulde sealeing' from the Elizabethan south front. When he sent the King his bond for £30,000, the demolition of the south front was under way. And that summer, when the Earl was in secret correspondence with King William in his palace in the Hague, he was also busy with his architect.

For this task he chose William Talman, a relatively unknown man who has been credited with the classical design of Thoresby Hall for the Earl of Kingston. But Talman's obscurity was no great disadvantage, for it suited the Earl to have an architect prepared to do as he was told. Because of this it will always be debatable how much of the present south front of Chatsworth is Talman's, and how much the Earl's. The overall concept of this long, imposing, rather heavy classical façade of local stone was undoubtedly Devonshire's idea; so was the motto, *Cavendo Tutus*, like a slogan for the times, carved in great Roman capitals beneath the balustrade. And to start with this was apparently as much as Devonshire intended in his work of restoration. His first idea was simply to tack this classical façade onto his Tudor house and have done with it. But for him rebuilding and rebellion were to become all or nothing occupations which could not be halted halfway through.

As far as the country was concerned, the point of no return for the opponents of the King arrived early in 1688 when, to considerable disbelief and general consternation, James II's Queen produced a son and heir to the throne of England. It was no longer possible to hope that Protestant William and Mary would now legitimately ascend the throne when James expired. The Stuarts, their government and the Catholic succession to the Crown were now secure – unless their enemies were prepared to act. By the summer of 1688 they were, and few more decisively than James's old enemy, the Earl of Devonshire, who was one of the leading Whig conspirators against the Crown. The great man's finest – and most profitable – hour had come.

Too late the King realized how dangerous a foe he had in Devonshire, and he sent William's cousin (now the Second Duke of Newcastle and almost as loyal to the Stuarts as his father) in an attempt to woo him back to court. Devonshire declined the invitation, for by now he was totally committed to the revolutionaries.

Although the King was generally unpopular, the lead to dethrone him was taken by the disaffected aristocracy who had so much to lose from James's government, and wielded effective power in many of the counties. Devonshire was all-important in the north Midlands, and in the spring of 1688 he and Lord Delamere and Charles II's former minister, the Earl of Danby, rode out secretly to meet on Wittington Moor, 'to discuss about the Revolution then in agitation'. Local legend had it that a heavy shower of rain drove them to shelter in Wittington village, and it was there in the so-called 'Plotting Chamber' of an inn called the 'Cock and Pynot' that these three very grand conspirators completed their plans to secure the north for Dutch William before marching south against the King. Devonshire himself was set to lead Derbyshire and capture Nottingham, and shortly after the meeting in the so-called 'Revolution House' (as the 'Cock and Pynot' was inevitably renamed), he signed the historic letter from the revolutionary lords, sent in cypher to the Hague, inviting William of Orange to assume the Crown of England.

Devonshire never did enjoy the great military role in the Revolution he must have hoped for. Thanks to the November North Sea gales, William's fleet was blown from the Yorkshire coast where he had planned to disembark, and finally made landfall at Torbay. The Earl is supposed to have received the news in an almost illegible letter which a courier from London concealed in his boot; but if he was disappointed he was too proud to show it. He read a stirring 'Declaration in Defence of the Protestant Religion' to the gentry of Derby, and proceeded gallantly to Nottingham, where he raised a regiment of horse, received James II's younger Protestant daughter, Princess Anne, with all due honour in his cousin Newcastle's now vacated castle, then heard the glad but unheroic tidings that James had ignominiously fled to France. The bloodless 'Glorious Revolution' of 1688 was over, and the time had come for great Whig aristocrats like Devonshire to collect their winnings. These were not inconsiderable.

But in London Devonshire still had one important part to play, over the crucial question of Dutch William's status. The Tories in the House of Lords, keen to preserve the principles of hereditary monarchy, were anxious to declare him the mere consort of the legitimate sovereign, his Stuart wife,

Queen Mary. William himself indignantly refused the role of Regent, or as he put it, of 'my wife's gentleman usher'; and it was Devonshire who led the Whig lords in the debates that finally established William and Mary as co-equal King and Queen in accordance with the will of Parliament.

And so it was that Devonshire, having started as a conspirator against King James II, ended as something of a kingmaker for his successor. William would not forget it – nor would Devonshire. The Revolution was hailed by the Whigs as a vindication of the resounding principles laid down in Parliament's Declaration of Rights and soon enshrined in popular mythology – liberty under the law, the inalienable rights of property, the supreme authority of Parliament and the Protestant religion. It was for all this that one of Devonshire's most fervent sycophants would solemnly beg his readers to

> Adore the wondrous hand of Providence, which put it in the heart of such patriots as the Duke of Devonshire to fix the tottering throne upon its antient foundations, and to restore those laws to their due course, under which the meanest subject in the kingdom may sit as securely as the greatest, under his own vine and fig-tree.

More to the point, the Earl had led a totally successful aristocratic coup to replace an unpopular king with their own carefully circumscribed nominee.

It was another triumph for the big battalions. Not for the first time a Cavendish had acted to protect his great inheritance, and the 'Glorious Revolution' was an attempt to guarantee that the vast estates, the political power and the ensuing profits of the aristocracy would be safe for many generations. It had also placed Devonshire in sacrosanct position at the apex of society. Old Bess would have been proud of him.

The King was not ungrateful either, and honours flowed – membership of the Privy Council, the Most Noble Order of the Garter, the Lord Lieutenancy of Derbyshire, and the Lord Stewardship of the Royal Household; at the Coronation he enjoyed the role of Lord High Steward of England by carrying the Crown; while his daughter Elizabeth bore the Queen's train. Money flowed in as well. Along with the rewards of office, the Devonshires in 1690 were granted in perpetuity the Crown rights to the High Peak Hundred in Derbyshire, together with the valuable lead deposits around Castleton. A year later, when he accompanied the King to a royal congress at the Hague, the Earl is said to have 'outshin'd most of the Princes there: his plate and furniture were so magnificent, that the sight of them drew a greater concourse of people to his house than to any other palace.'

In somewhat poignant contrast his cousin, Henry, the Second Duke of Newcastle, was not merely out of favour, but desperately unlucky. His attempts to make a great marriage for his son Henry to the daughter of the Earl of Northumberland were defeated after the settlement had been arranged by the young lord's unexpected death; and at his own death in 1691 the Newcastle title would die out, and the bulk of his great estates pass to his son-in-law, John Holles, son of the Third Earl of Clare. As a favourite of William III, Holles was able to persuade the King to grant him the Dukedom of Newcastle-on-Tyne in a new creation. The history of the dukedom was a timely warning on the vulnerability of even the greatest houses.

But Devonshire had no need to worry on that score. His Countess had dutifully presented him with two sons and two daughters, and in 1689 his heir, Lord William Cavendish, was married to fourteen-year-old Rachel Russell, the daughter of his old friend and fellow parliamentarian, the 'slain patriot', William Russell. Then came the final honour that the Earl could gather for his dynasty. On 12 May 1694, as Macaulay puts it,

> the two great houses of Russell and Cavendish, which had long been closely connected by friendship and by marriage, by common opinions, common sufferings, and common triumphs, received on the same day the highest honour which it is in the power of the Crown to confer.

Devonshire and William Russell's father, the sad old Earl of Bedford,* were both created dukes.

The preamble to the royal patent creating him Marquis of Hartington and Duke of Devonshire praised him as

> one who in a corrupted age, and sinking into the basest flattery, had constantly retained the manners of the ancients, and would never suffer himself to be moved either by the threats or the insinuations of a deceitful court.

It might have been praise from his beloved Tacitus, and it described the role that he had set himself and would entrust to his successors, now he was great enough and powerful enough to play the independent part of some ancient Roman tribune, honoured, inflexible, the revered trustee of the 'ancient' constitution and its laws.

His new title certainly reflected this. In the Continental nobility it would have carried with it the appellation 'Prince' and he was unquestionably more powerful than those petty German princelings he 'outshin'd' at the Hague. On Queen Mary's death he was appointed one of the three Lords Justice administering the kingdom during King William's frequent absences abroad; he was the last great English courtier to be admitted among the despairing Dutch favourites at the King's own death-bed; and he inevitably continued as High Steward to the Queen Anne he had once welcomed to his cousin's castle during the Revolution.

But he still had one self-appointed task to occupy his years of greatness – transforming Chatsworth into a fit setting for his ducal dynasty, as 'a Testimony of Ease and Joy' to the successful outcome of the Revolution. The simplest and most painless way of doing this would have been to raze the 'good

---

*According to Macaulay, Bedford had been reluctant to accept the honour on the practical grounds that 'An Earl who had a numerous family might send one son to the Temple and another to a counting house in the city. But the sons of a Duke were all lords; and a lord could not make his bread either at the bar or on Change. The old man's objections, however, were overcome.'

old seat' entirely, and construct a brand new ducal Chatsworth on the old foundations – but this was not his way, nor his intention. Instead, by fits and starts, for the remainder of his life, he wrestled with the obstinate old building, never sure quite what he wanted or how much he would do, and creating endless problems for himself, his architects, and his frequently rebellious work-force. As a builder he was an egregious old muddler and the only wonder is that out of all the chaos the new Chatsworth actually emerged as such a symbol of the power and new magnificence of the Dukes of Devonshire.

In effect he proceeded with the building, a side at a time, and the work went on for nearly twenty years. Talman's classical south front was more or less complete by the time King William landed at Torbay, but some months earlier Devonshire had already set his workmen to dismantle the Tudor stonework of the inner East court, and

> by the early 1690s a mighty confusion reigned at Chatsworth. Because the Earl would embark upon new schemes before finishing the old, a nightmare overlapping was in process. Simultaneously the south wing rooms were being decorated, the great staircase was being built, the old hall being pulled down and put up again, the garden side of the east wing being exposed to the elements, and the north-east tower of the old house being releaded and recased as though for preservation, then as suddenly demolished.

According to the historian of Chatsworth, Francis Thompson, most of the trouble stemmed from the Duke himself, who was very much in charge, but who suffered from 'a curious disability. His imagination would not work *in vacuo*: always he required the sight of something solid and embodied in the concrete to start the flow of his ideas'; and once flowing, his ideas led swiftly onto others, often contradicting what had gone before.

But one thing and one alone was clear – Devonshire's determination to make Chatsworth worthy of his freshly acquired importance in the state, and he was able to employ several of the leading decorative artists of the late baroque who had 'overflowed' from the France of Louis XIV to seek their fortunes at the Court of Charles II or among the fashionably rich who, like Devonshire himself, were eager to update their houses in the latest French and Italian manner. None of these artists was comparable with their great stay-at-home contemporaries like Lebrun or Pietro da Cortona from whom they often learned their craft, but they brought something new to these murky shores in the great houses where they painted – an illusion of extraordinary luxury and splendour, theatrical grandeur and superhuman character which, though often ponderous, was always on the most heroic scale. It was the princely style *par excellence*, which had reached its apogee in the palaces of Rome and the great apartments of Versailles – and it suited Devonshire's requirements admirably.

He was fortunate in being able to attract the two most adept of these immigrant scene-painters up to Chatsworth: the former 'first and chief painter to His Majesty Charles II', Antonio Verrio, and his rival and occasional collaborator, Louis Laguerre. Verrio was born at Lecce, that Mecca of the baroque in the heel of Italy, and was something of an adventurer and womanizer, an immensely facile painter who had worked in Rome and Toulouse before woman trouble sent him scurrying to England where he found fame and fortune frescoing a vast acreage of walls and ceilings for the King at Windsor. A loyal admirer of James II, he refused at first to work for his successor, but by 1689 his conscience had permitted him to come to Chatsworth where he painted on, with intermissions, until 1698, his work including

> the spirited and well-composed 'Triumph of Cybele' over the great stairs, and some of the figures in the vast ceiling of the State Dining-room, in particular the witch-like Atropos, eagerly bending forward to cut the thread of life, her sharp features – it is said – being those of the Chatsworth housekeeper and Verrio's enemy of the day, Mrs Hacket.

He also contributed a decorative if not wildly inspired altarpiece on 'The Incredulity of St Thomas' to the fine new chapel which the Duke was busy building.

But it is the younger painter, Louis Laguerre, who provides the closest connection between the First Duke's Chatsworth and the authoritative style of the court of Louis XIV. Born at Versailles in 1663, he was actually a godson of the King, trained with the French court painter, Le Brun, and, after working for a while as Verrio's assistant at Windsor, found his first major commission at Chatsworth. Here he worked away until 1697, aided by anonymous assistants, to turn the great interior of restructured Chatsworth into a sort of Derbyshire outpost of the Palace of Versailles. The chapel, the great painted hall – with the inevitable scenes from the life and death of Caesar – and the walls and ceilings of the grandiose state apartments all testify to Laguerre's amazing industry. Critics may find much of his work 'decidedly dull' compared with the work of his more inspired contemporaries in France, but nobody seemed to notice at the time, and he was giving the Duke exactly what the great man wanted in his enormous scenes from classical mythology.

Chatsworth was being rapidly transformed into an immense theatre, skilfully tricked out with all the splendour and illusion of the late baroque, where the Duke and his successors could now perform the stately role their rank demanded. Other artists made their contribution to this ducal *mise en scène* – the great French iron-master, Tijou and the local smith, John Gardom who together wrought the elaborate stair-rails and internal balustrades; James Thornhill, most famous of English late baroque decorative painters, whose Chatsworth Sabine Room has been hailed by James Lees-Milne as 'one of the great baroque interiors of an English country house'; and an extraordinary home-grown genius encouraged by the Duke, the carver Samuel Watson whose work in wood and stone, once mistakenly attributed to Grinling Gibbons, is one of the glories of the house.

Copying Versailles again, the Duke transformed the ancient gardens round the house, commissioned the Frenchman, Grillet, to design him a long, elaborate cascade, and constructed avenues, parterres, fountains and a brand new bowling-green. With a fine ducal gesture, he commanded a hill obscuring the southward view from the house to be removed, and replaced with the present long canal in which the south front of Chatsworth is so splendidly reflected.

The Duke was undoubtedly a vain man with an instinctive love of luxury, but vanity and self-indulgence were not what really lay behind so much extravagant display. It had a purpose that was strictly practical. As Sir John Plumb has said,

> in Chatsworth, in the great rooms of state, the power and the riches of the Devonshires was there for all men of Derbyshire to see. Knights of the Shire, Justices of the Peace, Deputy Lieutenants, Mayors and Aldermen, came for the Duke's favour which alone could ensure their success. And this territorial greatness gave the Devonshires a voice in the affairs of the nation as of right.

And there was more to it than this. In France, as the Duke knew all too well, that dangerous enslaver of the aristocracy, Louis XIV, had made the great palace of Versailles the symbol and the centre of their servitude to the elaborate, all-embracing cult of the Divine Right of Kings. Chatsworth, like some miniature Versailles, was to be a symbol of the Divine Right of Dukes, and in particular of the Duke of Devonshire, who, having helped to make an English king, was not letting him or anyone forget the fact.

It was not chance that made the Duke choose artists with such close connections with Versailles and the former Stuart court. At Chatsworth with its regal State Apartments, he could now entertain the King in equal splendour, and the princely nature of the house grew with the years. Verrio, Laguerre and Thornhill all went on to decorate the extended Royal palace at Hampton Court in much the same style as at Chatsworth – thus underlining Chatsworth's near-equality with the palace of a king. The new and splendid west front which the Duke began in 1700 was, again to quote Lees-Milne, 'an obvious yet extremely clever adaptation of the two-storeyed pavilion at Marly, built by J. H. Mansart for Louis Quatorze in 1683'. And in terms of solid comfort and amenities, Chatsworth was actually ahead of many palaces. Even at Versailles, members of the royal family were having to make do with portable commodes on wheels until well into the eighteenth century, but the First Duke was a demon for efficient sanitation. He and the Duchess had a marble bath with hot and cold running water, and by the early 1690s he had installed at least ten fully flushing water-closets in the house; 'their woodwork was mostly of cedar, their fittings of brass, and their bowls of local alabaster, except those for the Duke and Duchess which were of marble.'

But, despite the splendour and the luxury the Duke had brought to Chatsworth, his work there ended on a note of sadness rather than the triumph the house itself suggests. The beginning of the eighteenth century saw the Duke havering as usual over its completion, and constantly putting off the decision over what was to be done – if anything – with the one remaining front, the north, which was still as Bess had left it. Not until the summer of 1702 did he gird himself to finish it.

By then he was in his sixties, and the abounding confidence of his great years following the Revolution had faded. He was no longer universally revered by the younger, brasher, often Tory, politicians who were rising now, and he was losing favour with Queen Anne. There were malicious rumours – almost certainly untrue – that he was in treasonable contact with the exiled Stuart Court in France. And the excesses of his youth had finally caught up with him, making him old beyond his years with gout and dropsy. He was even short of money: a great gambler all his days, he had been losing heavily and steadily at Newmarket, and what with the costs of Chatsworth and of the new London house he had built in Piccadilly, he had finally overstrained even the Cavendish resources.

Despite this, he now pushed on with the work at Chatsworth with a certain dithering desperation that was typical of him. Even before he started on the west wing, he had quarrelled irretrievably with Talman. He too was now successfully at work at Hampton Court, along with so many of the former Chatsworth artists, and the Duke had found a young, unknown draughtsman called Thomas Archer to help him with his ever-changing plans and to supervise the builders. What with the duns and the delays the work went slowly.

But the decaying Duke still found an ever-ready consolation in his extra-marital amours. His amiable Duchess had long grown used to sharing his affections with a string of mistresses and openly acknowledged bastard offspring. A dignified and pious lady, she had the friendship of Queen Anne, and the devotion of her children. According to her chaplain, Mr Williamson, 'All the offices of love and friendship passed between them, and she appeared never better pleased than in their company.' Her staple reading lay in Bishop Taylor's *Holy Living* and *Holy Dying*, and he praised her for her 'exemplary patience and resignation to the will of God.'

Patience and resignation must have been needed in abundance when coping with her husband, for despite his physical afflictions he was insatiable as ever. At sixty-five he exercised his *droit de seigneur* over Mary Anne Campion, the seventeen-year-old actress daughter of his valet, and promptly made her pregnant. Early in 1706 she bore a daughter, who was given the same name as her mother. But this was to be the old rake's last and most melancholy conquest. It must have been a complicated birth, for the young actress never properly recovered. The Duke had given her a house in Bolton Street, conveniently close to Devonshire House, and according to a note now in the British Museum, it was there on 19 May 1706, that 'she died in the bloom of youth of a hectic fever which she had had four months.'

The Duke was shocked, and there is something rather splendid in the way he made no secret of his grief. Most old seducers would have hushed the matter up, but not the Duke. The baby was 'put to nurse' at Devonshire House, and he added a codicil to his will, leaving the child 'the sum of £10,000 to be paid to her at her age of one and twenty, or on the day of her marriage.' Mary Campion herself was buried at the church next to his house at Latimers.

According to a scandalmonger writing about the funeral some years later, 'there was nothing set on the coffin, as I can hear of, and her burial was a sort of secret, for it was a private funeral and but one coach with the hearse.' But the Duke made no secret of his feelings for his dead mistress and set up a tablet in her memory for all to see.

Here lie the mortal remains of Mrs. A.C——n
She died in the 19th year of her age. . . .
The virtues of her mind excelled the beauties of her
body, that was admired with so many charms. . . .
At the playhouse where she acted she was modest and
untainted and is a person to be lamented by all that
are imbued with humanity.

The epitaph ended with a reference to her 'beloved remains' and was signed, 'W——D. of D.'

By the time the tablet was erected, the north front of Chatsworth was complete, more or less matching the remainder of the house. Apart from Queen Mary's Bower and the Stand Tower, Bess of Hardwick's hunting tower above it on the hill, no sign was left of her work, for the Duke had totally transformed the 'good old seat' into the great Whig palace that, together with his dukedom, was the legacy he left to his descendants. It was also his own monument, for as Christopher Hobhouse put it, 'there is no house in England which illustrates more vividly the magnificence to which an English subject can attain.'

But, now that the house was finished, so was he. 'When the house is complete, death enters,' runs an Arab proverb, and on 18 August 1707 the great prince of the Whigs resigned his dropsical old body to his Protestant maker, and departed, to the sort of lamentations that he would have loved:

Is Cavendish dead, and yet the Heavens not bear
In such a publick loss an equal share?
Can such a patron of our liberty,
Without some grand eclipse or comet die?
Tho' not at death, yet Devonshire will have
The sun itself a mourner at his grave.
Great Devonshire! Oh speak not of his title's Fame!
But tell his virtues, give his soul a name:
If you will have all excellence appear,
All that is good and great, say Devonshire.
In short, his native qualities were such,
No pen, nor tongue could ever say too much.

6. The Great Collector

The Second Duke, William (1673–1729)

Government has no other end but the preservation of property.

John Locke

'A MAN of very poor understanding,' growled that old Tory misanthrope, Dean Swift, about the balding, somewhat startled-looking Whig politician who became the Second Duke of Devonshire in 1707. Few sons could have seemed more different from that flamboyant, intemperate, very stylish old rake, his father; but, not for the first time, Swift had made a profound misjudgment on human nature, and the new Duke was not exactly what he seemed. He may have appeared a distinctly dull dog to the Dean, but there was little wrong with his understanding – particularly when it came to the interests of the House of Cavendish. Indeed, he proved to be the near perfect complement and successor to his wild old father: unsung and practically unnoticed, he immeasurably enriched his house, and played a crucial part behind the scenes in making eighteenth-century England such an agreeable, well-padded place to be a duke in.

In contrast to his father, he lived a blameless and largely uneventful life, making him an admirable example of the cautious, serpentine sort of Cavendish – just as his father had been one of the most successful of the family stags. In youth he campaigned briefly in King William's wars against the French in Flanders, but soldiering and foreign parts were not for him. He never ventured far from London or Derbyshire again, for other all-important matters occupied his time.

The truth was that the First Duke's work was incomplete, and the 'Glorious Revolution' which had carried his family to fresh fame and political pre-eminence under the new monarchy, offered no lasting guarantee that the supremacy of the great Whig revolutionary families would endure for long. The Tories, essentially the party of the lesser country gentry, had potentially more power in Parliament and throughout the country than the Whigs, and were soon to make their own determined comeback with Queen Anne through ambitious leaders like Harley and Godolphin. The rising middle classes, though for the most part powerless politically, were another clear threat lying in the future. If the great Whig 'Revolutionary' families were to retain their power, they still had to fight for it – in Parliament, at Court, and in the country – and no one understood this better than the Second Duke who, long before his father died, was already an engaged and skilful politician in the interests of his family and class.

It may seem strange that someone as rich and favoured as the young Lord

Hartington should have concerned himself with the undignified, time-consuming, often squalid ins-and-outs of early eighteenth-century politics. In France the absurd and highly decorative aristocracy had long since given up such tedious activities in favour of an absolutist monarchy and the pleasures of Versailles. But the English aristocracy was not absurd. It was highly functional. It was very much concerned with the pursuit and exercise of power – which is rarely boring – and it was this that made of politics such a personal and all-absorbing interest to generation upon generation of future Cavendishes.

This was particularly so for Hartington, for the turn of the century was a crucial time when political success had rarely meant so much for those who sought it. Behind the bitter parliamentary squabbling lay something more than who was 'in' or 'out'. The governmental gravy-train was up for grabs, and with it went wealth and influence throughout the country – jobs, spoils, sinecures; that golden network which controlled elections, offered or refused preferment, guaranteed a great man's standing in his county and ultimately ruled the nation. This was what mattered. In the last resort the social structure of the country was at stake, and in particular the fate of the great Whig landed families who had so much to gain – and lose – from what happened at Westminster.

But although threatened, families like the Devonshires had distinct advantages over their clamorous opponents. There was the influence and grandeur of their houses and their great estates. As founding families of the Revolution, they had a certain claim at court. They had resounding 'principles' – like liberty, the sacred rights of property and the Protestant succession. Above all they were powerfully united, with all the arrogant self-confidence of the very rich; already they were starting to exhibit the close family connections of a ruling caste, and sharing an exclusive social life which continued through the year, in their great country houses, on the racecourse, and in the lavish entertaining and the club life of the London season.

All they needed was effective parliamentary leadership, and for a while it seemed as if the young Lord Hartington was going to provide it. Soon after his majority he represented Derbyshire and, according to Bishop Burnet (who saw things somewhat differently from Swift), rapidly proved himself 'A gentleman of very good sense, a bold orator, and zealous asserter of the liberties of the people: one of the best beloved gentlemen by the Country Party in England.'

As his father's son he was duly honoured by Queen Anne, who made him her Captain of the Yeomen of the Guard; and after succeeding to the Dukedom, he was one of the very few leading Whigs to keep his place at Court. The Tory Queen somewhat warily remarked that 'she had lost a loyal subject and a good friend in his father, but did not doubt to find them again in him' – and to demonstrate continuing royal goodwill, awarded him his father's influential post as Steward of the Household and appointed him Privy Councillor.

But despite his honours and his early parliamentary success, the Duke was not the man to lead the Whigs. They needed someone with more ruthlessness and skill at the minutiae of politics, and the role was ultimately taken by that portly parliamentary genius, the Norfolk squire, Sir Robert Walpole. If you cannot be the greatest politician of your time, there is something to be said for being his best friend – and the understanding between Devonshire and Walpole proved of immense importance to them both.

Although a convivial man, Walpole was understandably mistrustful of close friendships in the political jungle he inhabited, but the Duke was somebody he trusted to the end. In their youth, after Hartington had actually lost his seat in Derbyshire, they had served in Parliament together as joint members for the safe Whig pocket borough of Castle Rising, and it was through Hartington that the unaristocratic but ambitious Walpole gained the entrée to the all-important social life he aimed at – the racy, hard-drinking world of young Whig noblemen who centred round 'the most fashionable of all Whig clubs, the Kit-Cat Club'. Hartington was inevitably a member, and Walpole joined in 1703.

Here, he could mix – and drink – on terms of near-equality with the best and brightest of the young Whig aristocrats, whose parliamentary leader he would finally become; men like Stanhope, Spencer Compton, Henry Boyle and Charles, Earl of Sunderland. They readily accepted him: 'His lively spirits stimulated their own and in a curious way he possessed great charm.' Without such acceptance, Walpole's career would have been doomed from the beginning but, with Hartington as something of a patron, Walpole's star was rising.

As it was, the final years of Queen Anne's reign were a fraught period for all the Whigs – especially for Devonshire. He had played his part in the increasingly unpopular Whig ministry which supported Marlborough's wars against the French, and when the Queen dismissed them in 1710 – after their attempt to impeach the rabble-rousing Tory cleric, Dr Sacheverell – the Duke, along with all his friends, was in the wilderness. He was completely out of favour with the Queen by now; according to Harley, that emotional lady found his behaviour 'so very peevish and so very distasteful' that she irritably refused to see him, and promptly dismissed him from his stewardship.

This was no way to treat the head of a family to whom she owed so much, and the Duke in turn was seriously put out. Soon the Tories were gleefully relating how he had 'flown into a passion which did little credit to his dignity' when Lord Dartmouth came to ask him for his staff of office. But, apart from the denting of his dignity, the Duke had really little need to worry; for, as he knew, the Queen was ailing. James I's great-grandson, George of Hanover, was ready, if not over-willing, to take up the Crown of England at her death. And the Hanoverian Succession, already set and sealed by Act of Parliament, was the great insurance policy for the future of the Whigs. It was something more than this for Devonshire, for while in office he had already introduced a bill to grant precedence to the King of Hanover's son, the Duke of Cambridge. It was a shrewd move to have done so notable a favour to the man who would one day follow his father as the King of England; not for the first time, nor the last, a Cavendish had shown exactly how to pick a winning horse.

So the Duke retired to Derbyshire – and waited. So did Walpole. And in 1714, their patience was rewarded: Queen Anne died. The ill-planned efforts of the Jacobites and Tory extremists like Lord Bolingbroke to make a comeback utterly misfired. The new King in far-off Hanover appointed the loyal Duke of Devonshire one of the Lords Justice to govern England in his name until he reluctantly arrived. And when he did – to be proclaimed King George the First of England – the Whigs had entered into their own unshakable inheritance at last.

With effortless assurance, the great men of property and their dependants – that unshakable aristocracy likened later by Disraeli to a 'Venetian Oligarchy' – had calmly taken over the eighteenth century. The squirearchy would grumble on but never rule; the middle classes prosper but stay out of power politically for more than a hundred years; and under the Hanoverians a few great families like the Devonshires would be practically co-equals with the Royal Family, running their counties like small principalities, taking their place in government by all but hereditary right, and forming an élite at the apex of polite society. In the whole of human history it would be hard to find a group more utterly and effortlessly blessed.

The political theorist of Whiggery, John Locke, had dutifully defined the aim and basis of the state as 'men's enjoyment of their Properties in Peace and Safety' – and none enjoyed so much so peaceably and safely as the House of Cavendish at the top of a peerage which was rapidly becoming something it had never been before, a tight landed caste of all but unassailable influence and power, self-perpetuating, revered and, in the absence of a strong native royal family, almost sublimely independent.

The Duke himself was now adroitly placed to make the most of the advantages history was offering this very happy few. Loyal to Walpole, he resigned his Presidency of the Council early in 1717 when the Whig Government split, and his friend resigned the Chancellorship of the Exchequer. But he did not lose out by his loyalty. He undoubtedly gained financially from Walpole's shrewd advice during the highly profitable early stages of financial speculation when the notorious South Sea Company offered to fund the National Debt. (He was also a keen investor in such lucrative new schemes as the York Building Waterworks, along with other well-placed noblemen like the Earl of Nottingham and the Duke of Chandos.) And when the South Sea Company collapsed in the scandal of the so-called 'South Sea Bubble', giving Walpole the chance he needed to return to power, the Duke automatically resumed his interrupted place in government.

The next quarter of a century is often called 'the Age of Robert Walpole' as his domination of the scene of British politics gave him the effective power of the first 'Prime Minister'. It was also a great age for the Dukes of Devonshire, for it was under Walpole's government that the great 'system' of the power of the English aristocracy, with it 'adamantine strength and profound inertia', finally took shape.

For, more than anyone, Walpole knew exactly how to use government and aristocratic patronage to build a permanent majority in Parliament and govern in the interests of the great Whig country magnates, just as another close friend of Devonshire's, Thomas Pelham-Holles (soon to be rewarded with the reconstituted title of Duke of Newcastle, inherited from his uncle), became the indefatigable organizer of Whig electoral influence throughout the country. Walpole and Devonshire saw eye to eye on policy, which was really very simple – peace abroad, low taxes and stability at home, and the calm continuation of the *status quo*. The great had inherited the earth, and were making sure that their inheritance would prosper everlastingly in the best of all possible worlds for the English landed aristocracy.

A tactful, conciliatory man, the Second Duke continued to perform his own not unimportant part in the great Whig cause of property and primogeniture. With his vast wealth he could afford to be incorruptible: with his immense prestige he was likewise immune to the lure of any greater place in government. Instead he performed the role that suited his cautious Cavendish nature to perfection – that of an influential power broker working quietly but effectively behind the scenes, and always guaranteed his place in Walpole's inner 'Cabinet'.

His most important public act was very much in character. As an extra safeguard for the Whig supremacy in Parliament – and to save on unnecessary effort and expenditure at elections – he was responsible for the comfortable law that extended the life of parliaments from five to seven years. (This curious measure from a party claiming to defend the English constitution was not repealed until Asquith brought back five-year parliaments in 1910.)

But apart from this, the Duke's true work was as Walpole's ally and most trusted friend at Court. An intimate of the Prince and Princess of Wales, he did his best to patch up the notoriously bad relations between George I and his successor. A diplomatic man, he also did all he could to foster an understanding between Walpole and the intelligent and influential Princess of Wales – the future George II's wife, Queen Caroline. And it was largely thanks to her that, when the old king died in 1727, Walpole calmly but unexpectedly remained in office.

The Second Duke himself had only two more years to live, but Walpole would stay on in power till 1744, his very presence guaranteeing the consolidation of that increasingly rigid eighteenth-century world of deference and dukes which the House of Cavendish had done so much to foster in the cause of English liberty.

Throughout this period the family would tighten its electoral hold on Derbyshire. The Second Duke's younger brother, Lord James Cavendish, was loyally returned for Derby for over forty years, and the seat began to be regarded as something of an 'heirloom' of the Cavendishes which they would keep continuously in the family until 1835. Derbyshire itself stayed all but solid for the Whigs, and it was now that Chatsworth itself really came into its own as the archetypal great Whig house, the centre and the symbol of the unquestioned power of the Dukes of Devonshire.

The eighteenth century was the great age of the English country house, the period when building mania gripped the aristocracy and immense fortunes were heedlessly expended in the creation of great new country palaces flaunting the wealth of their possessors. It was an expensive pastime, often bringing ruin and a crippling load of debt to its practitioners, but here again the Dukes of Devonshire had a head start over all their possible competitors. Indeed, they had no need to bother to compete. Thanks yet again to Bess of Hardwick – and to the First Duke's massive reconstructions – they had their great house built already in the height of fashion which lesser noblemen could copy if they dared. (They also had Hardwick, but since there was little kudos now in inconvenient Elizabethan buildings, the old house was left to slumber on in peace and rarely occupied.)

Freed from the building frenzy of his peers, the Second Duke was left to devote his surplus wealth and energies to something else – the civilized enrichment of his father's house. And here again this quiet cautious man displayed the shrewdness and discretion that had produced such rich rewards in politics.

Lord David Cecil once remarked on a certain philistinism prevalent in the artistic taste of the great Whig families of the eighteenth century. This was inevitable, since they generally bought their pictures as they built their enormous houses, for prestige and for display. The First Duke had done this when he hired Verrio and Laguerre to decorate his walls and ceilings, but his son acted very differently in artistic matters.

Here, more than anywhere, one sees how singular a man he was. He was a passionate collector – one of the very greatest in a century of great collections – yet he was quite unlike the fashionable *virtuosi* who came a few years later. He never saw Italy, never based his education on the Grand Tour, and was never even tempted to revisit Holland, home of several of his favourite painters, where he had soldiered in his youth. He was a plain man with an uncomplicated passion for the best; this, combined with a genuine collector's flair, led him quite early on in life to an area where, with unerring skill, he was able to amass superb examples of the work of almost all the European masters from the Italian Quattrocento to the Flemish, French and German masters of his own day.

In his early twenties he seems to have spotted one important source of great art which, on the whole, the rich still ignored – old master drawings. Unlike paintings, these had little use as objects of display, and were relatively cheap. Apart from examples in the great royal collections – in particular that of the Kings of France – old master drawings had tended to be bought by artists themselves; and it was at the sale of one of these – that of Sir Peter Lely – that the twenty-one-year old future Second Duke made his debut as a true collector.

In his diary, Lely's executor, Roger North, describes the young Marquis's enthusiasm when the bidding started for a drawing thought to have been by Raphael. He already knew exactly what he wanted. 'Damn me!' the young aristocrat exclaimed. 'What care I whether the owner bids or not, so long as I can tell whether I wish to bid and for what?'

According to North, he went on to bid up to £70 for the drawing – which in fact was not by Raphael at all, but by his pupil, Penni – only to cry off when the bidding went still higher. He was to get the drawing later through another sale, and purchased a number of Lely's other drawings. North's remark makes it clear that, even as a young man, the future duke was already a determined and serious collector, who would go on buying, eagerly and shrewdly, for the remainder of his life.

As a collector his earliest competitors in England were scholarly connoisseurs like the son of his father's former architect, John Talman, and John Guise, whose own fine collection of old master drawings is at Christ Church, Oxford; and it was the sort of esoteric, rather private interest, that obviously suited someone of his temperament. His most prized possession was probably Claude Lorrain's *Liber Veritatis* – the sketchbook in which the painter methodically recorded the outlines of most of the major paintings he created. And his major *coup* as a collector was his purchase two years before his death of the extraordinarily rich collection made by the son of Rembrandt's former pupil, Flinck. With this collection, the Second Duke's legacy to Chatsworth achieved the legendary status that it has today, as the greatest collection of old master drawings in Britain outside the royal collection at Windsor.

According to one recent expert,

no great period or phase of art, hardly a great name, except Michelangelo's . . . is not represented. The Italian quattrocento, the high renaissance, with its magnificent Raphaels, and its extraordinarily rich representation of Raphael's school, Dürer and Holbein in Germany, Rubens, and above all Van Dyck and Rembrandt in the Netherlands . . . the mannerist and baroque painters of Italy, all are there.

7. A Man of His Word

The Third Duke, William (1698–1755)

WITH the death of the Second Duke, it must have seemed as if the House of Cavendish, after almost two centuries of spectacular advance, had finally slipped past its zenith, and that from now on it would quietly decline, safely enjoying its possessions and assured prestige at a time when a Whig grandee had everything in life a man could wish for. Certainly the new Duke showed little inclination to advance the fortunes of his family any further – nor did his presence or his character give the faintest hint of the extraordinary fresh turn of fate which would come to the Cavendishes in his lifetime.

He was a simple man, more like some homespun Tory squire than a Whig magnifico, 'plain in manners, negligent of dress', a solid, heavy-drinking, hunting man whose placid features gaze from his portrait like the epitome of the well-fed century in which he lived. He was not particularly bright, but this was no great disadvantage in a duke, and it says much for him that he was one of the few 'Whig dogs' ever to have been praised by Dr Johnson:

He was not a man of superior abilities, but he was a man strictly faithful to his word. If, for instance, he had promised you an acorn, and none had grown that year in his woods, he would not have contented himself with that excuse; he would have sent to Denmark for it. So unconditional was he in keeping his word; so high as to the point of honour.

A somewhat lazy man, and a nearly inaudible public speaker, he seems to have assumed his allotted place in eighteenth-century politics more as a duty than an honour. Within a few months of leaving Oxford he was duly found an uncontested seat in parliament – for the pocket borough of Lostwithiel – and was soon sharing his father's friendship with Sir Robert Walpole. The friendship prospered with his father's death, and according to Walpole's son – the feline letter-writer, Horace – old Walpole deferentially set him up 'as the standard of Whiggism', just as he had his father.

Horace Walpole disliked the Third Duke,* and was fairly cynical about the way he and his son, the future Fourth Duke, tended to be cited as 'the fashionable models of goodness, though their chief merit was a habit of caution'. The Third Duke, he suggested, was not quite the paragon of bluff simplicity that he appeared:

---

* The origins of the feud between Horace Walpole and the Third Duke lie in the way the Duke sided with the diarist's namesake and cousin, later Lord Orford, after his marriage to the Duke's daughter Rachel Cavendish. Horace always called his cousin 'Prince Pigwiggin', and henceforth presented the Third Duke as rather the same sort of humbug and buffoon.

The Duke's outside was unpolished, his inside unpolishable . . . but the dexterity of raising his son to . . . the Master of the Horse during his own life, and obtaining a Peerage for his own son-in-law [Lord Duncannon], by retiring from power himself, extremely lessened the value of the rough diamond that he had hitherto contrived to be thought.

Certainly the Third Duke, like his father, did very nicely out of his friendship with Robert Walpole, who made him his Lord Privy Seal and then in 1737 gave him the most lucrative appointment that was in his gift by packing him off to govern Ireland. Ireland, for once, was peaceful, and the semi-regal role of Viceroy was well-suited to a semi-regal duke like Devonshire; it also offered considerable patronage, and emoluments approaching £20,000 a year – a handy income even for a duke.

In fact the Third Duke performed admirably in Ireland. His duties were not onerous; he was a tolerant, fair-minded man who got on well with everyone, and his 'rough diamond' image did no harm with his Irish subjects – any more than did his fondness for the bottle.

'I think as yet he does not look the worse for his drinking, but he has almost killed his aides-de-camp already', wrote Lord Sackville shortly after the Duke arrived in Dublin Castle. But, despite the drink and the attendant gout which plagued him cruelly with the years, the Third Duke clung on gallantly to this invaluable piece of 'aristocratic outdoor relief' in Ireland, even surviving Walpole's fall in 1742. Three years later he returned to England to the heartfelt congratulations of the Irish Parliament on 'the tranquillity and happiness the nation has enjoyed under His Grace's gentle and prudent administration', and was reappointed Lord Steward of the Royal Household. But back at Chatsworth the Third Duke's own 'tranquillity and happiness' would not endure for long: within a few years this gentle, easygoing man would be engulfed in a bitter family rumpus involving his wife and his eldest son, Lord Hartington, over the girl the young man wished to marry.

It was a very strange affair which rapidly got out of hand, reaching the proportions of a public scandal; and it was all the odder because throughout it all, Lord Hartington acted exactly as a true-born Cavendish should, with all the interests of his family in mind, while his mother turned hysterically against him, finally all but destroying her own marriage in her attempts to thwart him. But then, her own marriage, by strict Cavendish standards, was a somewhat odd affair as well.

His Duchess was born Katherine Hoskyns, the daughter of a solidly middle-class City businessman known to his friends and enemies alike as 'Miser Hoskyns'. The Hoskyns family had owned a manor house and lands at Oxted in Surrey since Tudor times – as well as property at Limpsfield, Chelsham, and Hendon in Kent – and had grown rich in trade; for a period Katherine's father is known to have worked as chief agent and adviser to the Duke of Bedford. No details have survived about the future Third Duke's courtship of the young unaristocratic heiress, but it is clear from letters still at Chatsworth that after his convivial life at Oxford the young man – who was a great gambler – was very short of cash, and borrowed heavily from his cousin Bedford.

As late as 1729, the Duke of Bedford wrote the new Third Duke a very tart request for the final repayment of considerable sums of money he had lent, adding that 'it will be a great inconveniency to me if it cannot be done soon'. And in 1718, when the then Lord Hartington's financial problems must have been particularly acute, marriage to an heiress would have seemed a sensible solution to his difficulties. Miss Hoskyns was at hand, Lord Hartington would have known her father through the Duke of Bedford, rich Mr Hoskyns would have been flattered to have had a future duke as son-in-law, and the future duke, from all we know about his character, was hardly likely to have bothered over any lack of social polish in his bride. For generations, the Cavendishes had married into titled families for land – now one was marrying a commoner for money. This was not unheard of in the English aristocracy, which was far more down-to-earth about such things than its Continental counterpart. Sufficient money sanctioned almost any marriage and nobody at the time appears to have objected to the match as a *mésalliance*.

There was little of the 'polite' social snobbery between the classes that was rampant by the end of the century, and the only criticism one hears of any lack of refinement in Mr Hoskyns' daughter comes much later – and once again from Horace Walpole who considered her 'delightfully vulgar'. But he was always anxious to make fun of the Duchess, just as he did of her husband, and in fact the picture that he gives of how she occasionally entertained her friends is most endearing, showing how little the grandeur of her position in society had affected her.

> [She] complained of the wet night, and how the men would dirty the room with their shoes; called out at supper to the Duke, 'Good, God! my Lord, don't cut the ham, nobody will eat any!' and relating her private *ménage* to Mr. O'Brien, she said, 'When there's only my Lord and I, besides a pudding, we always have a dish of roast.'

A pudding and a dish of roast were obviously exactly to the good Duke's taste, and he and his homely Duchess seem to have enjoyed a close rather simple life together like any bourgeois couple of the period. She bore him seven children, coped with his drinking, nursed him through his gout, and though she was something of a martinet – as one imagines that she had to be with her often fuddled husband – they were a touchingly devoted family. The Duke even gave his children silly nicknames: Mrs Hopeful, Mrs Tiddle, Guts and Gundy, Puss and Cat and Toe. Then suddenly, at the beginning of 1748, their eldest son, Guts Hartington decided to get married, and the peace of this affectionate family was shattered.

Hartington was twenty-eight, his mother's favourite, and clearly a great catch for any scheming female. The Duchess had been considering several potential daughters-in-law already when the young man made his mind up for himself, choosing sixteen-year-old Charlotte Boyle, the second daughter of the extremely rich Third Earl of Burlington. She was pretty, affectionate, intelligent, and she possessed one further virtue which should have made her the perfect bride for any Cavendish: since her elder brother, Lord Clifford, had died in infancy, and her elder sister, Lady Dorothy, had followed him in 1742, Lady Charlotte was one of the greatest heiresses around.

Lord Burlington was more than merely rich. He was a man of extraordinary taste, an inspired collector, and architectural virtuoso, whose mansion in Piccadilly and Palladian villa by the Thames at Chiswick were considered models of their age. At his death, Charlotte would inherit them, together with the Boyle estates at Londesborough and Bolton Abbey in Yorkshire, and a vast tract of land in southern Ireland, crowned by King John's impressive castle at Lismore in County Waterford. The Duke, who appreciated real estate, seems to have approved. The Duchess was outraged.

She would appear to have had no personal objections to Lady Charlotte, except that she was far too young for marriage to her son – 'a baby-face' is how she is supposed to have referred to her, presumably oblivious of quite how many baby-faces her husband's family had married in their time. But as a middle-class outsider, the former Miss Hoskyns had none of the cool Cavendish instinct for dynastic marrying, and the conflict that ensued reflects the very different attitudes to love and marriage held by the English aristocracy and the middle classes in the eighteenth century.

One of the Duchess's chief objections to the Burlington marriage undoubtedly arose from a bad attack of middle-class morality, for as everybody knew, the Burlingtons were decidedly unusual, even by the easy-going standards of the eighteenth-century upper classes. They were descended from the unscrupulous adventurer, Richard Boyle, the self-made 'Great Earl' of Cork who had purchased Lismore and considerable estates in Munster from Sir Walter Raleigh at a knock-down price before his execution. The 'Great Earl's' seventh son was Robert Boyle, the scientist, and Lord Burlington had certainly inherited his fair share of the Boyle intelligence.

But they were a family who attracted scandal. Lord Burlington himself, despite his marriage and his offspring, had for many years enjoyed an emotionally as well as artistically satisfying relationship with his principal architect, William Kent. And Lady Burlington, for as many years, had conducted a blatant and rumbustious liaison with the Duke of Grafton.

But the greatest scandal of the time concerned the mysterious fate of their daughter, Lady Dorothy, who in October 1741 married her mother's lover's son, Lord Euston. Seven months later, barely seventeen, she died, and rumour had it that Euston had murdered her. Pope, who was a friend of Burlington's, certainly believed this, and Lord Burlington himself went so far as to challenge his son-in-law to a duel – which increased the rumours but ultimately came to nothing. Lady Burlington wrote on her daughter's portrait in Chiswick House a brief obituary:

She was married, October 18th 1741, and delivered [by death] from misery, May 2nd 1742.

Lord Euston himself was never charged with his young wife's death, but one version of what happened was held in the Cavendish family for many years –

and finally related by the Fifth Duke's second wife, the Dowager Duchess Elizabeth: in the *Anecdotes* which were published privately after her death in 1822. According to this account:

> Lady Dorothy's fate was singularly unfortunate and dreadful. She was young and beautiful and a great heiress. She married a man she adored and of the first rank, but he was a man of vicious principles and in love with his brother's wife. He promised her, so it is said, that no son of his would inherit his father's fortune and when Lady Euston was with child, he drove her through the worst paved streets of London. He made her walk till exhausted. She had been seen to sit fainting on the steps before peoples' houses. Sir Henry Englefield told me that Mr. Churchill, who is now alive, told him that he had seen her, and my Aunt, Lady Mary Fitzgerald, gave me the same account. When Lady Euston was in labour, be suffered none but the midwife to come and after her death – she died in labour – the same thing. The birth was premature and the child died.

The Duke and Lord Hartington, who must have heard the story, would have concluded, as realistic men of the world, that shockingly though Euston had behaved, it was thanks to him that Lady Charlotte was now sole heir to the great Burlington inheritance. The Duchess, on the other hand, was horrified to think that any son of hers could even think of marrying into such a family, and battle started.

From the beginning she made her opposition clear, and there were scenes the like of which Chatsworth had not seen since the bracing days of Bess of Hardwick. The Duchess was adamant. So was Hartington. And, although the Duchess raged against 'the accurs'd match', the children tended not unnaturally to side with their elder brother. As for the Duke, poor man, he seems to have been torn between his own domestic peace, and awareness that his heir was poised to achieve the marriage of the century. For several weeks he dithered, doing his conciliatory best, like the good Cavendish he was, to make everybody happy. He tried to convince the Duchess. He attempted to dissuade his son. At times, when in his cups, he seemed to agree with everyone, but in the end even he had to come to a decision.

For Lord Hartington was as inflexible by now as his mother; insisting on his right to marry as he pleased, he left for London where the preparations for his marriage went ahead. As wedding presents for his future wife he bought 'a repeating watch on a chain with cameos and brilliants' for £157 10s, 'an etuy set with cameos, brilliants and gold', for £73 10s, and 'brilliants and knots for ear-rings' for £4 4s. In return Lord Burlington promised his daughter a dowry of £30,000, 'pin money' of £1000 a year after her marriage, and assigned Burlington Gardens to her husband for life.

The Duke could presumably still have attempted to forbid the marriage, but by now there was little point, even had he wished to. Instead, he bowed to the inevitable, gave his son his blessing on his brilliant match, and followed him tactfully to London where, on 28 March 1748, at the notorious Lady Burlington's Pall Mall residence, he witnessed the private wedding of Lord Hartington to his 'baby-faced' heiress, Lady Charlotte Boyle.

The embattled Duchess stayed at Chatsworth, but to the very last her amiable husband did his best to smooth things over, even drafting out a letter in his ducal hand and suggesting that she sent it to Lord Hartington on the eve of marriage. A copy of it still exists – unsent – and it speaks volumes for the efforts the good man made to restore harmony within his warring family:

> Believe my dearest child that I never could have a thought that should give you a moments uneasiness and . . . I am determined to believe you never meant the least disregard to me or ever to think of what has passed. My whole concern is for your happyness. I heartily wish this and every thing you engage in may answer your expectations and shall be infinitely happy to find myself in the wrong in having given opposition to your inclinations and hope you will always believe that I have nothing in this world so much at heart as your happyness.

The Duke should have known his Duchess better than to think she would ever sign a letter such as this; and far from accepting the marriage as a *fait accompli*, she vented her anger now in no uncertain terms.

Her husband having failed to calm her down, it was his son's turn to try to pacify her. This he did in a letter written in the spring of 1748, that, if nothing else, provides a fascinating insight into the attitude of a responsible young eighteenth-century aristocrat – and true scion of the House of Cavendish – to love and marriage.

He began by apologizing briskly for having been 'the unwitting cause' of his mother's unhappiness and insisted that he had always regarded marriage as 'the most serious and critical event' in anybody's life.

> I was aware also that in the particular situation of our family, and out of Duty to my Father and you, I was not only merely to consider the dictates of my own passion, but was to have a regard for what was for a Benefit for my Family. This, and this only, I do assure you, was what first made me think of L.C. I endeavour'd to persuade myself to like her because I flatter'd myself that it would have been agreeable to every body, when perhaps had I thought only of pleasing myself my inclinations might have led another way as the difference in our age in all probability would have prevented me from being acquainted with her. While I have said this it is not to endeavour to prove whether I have made a good choice or not. All I mean and all I wish is to persuade you that it was my desire to do what was right and what might please you, and that I never harboured a thought in any one action of my whole life of the least disrespect or disesteem of you. I do assure you Madam, that it is not possible for a son to have a more sincere and real love for a mother than I have for you. . . .

There was a good deal more in this letter about the respect and the undying sense of gratitude he felt towards his mother, but not the faintest hint of any feeling or affection that he had for his child bride. He had married her to enrich his family. He had done his duty as a Cavendish, and that should have been the end of it.

To his mother's credit, it was this calculating and profoundly unromantic attitude that upset her most of all; but then, she was not a Cavendish herself and failed to understand that for the members of a great Whig family, in marriage as in politics, property was paramount. Instead, in her emotional, middle-class way, she believed that marriage was concerned with something else. It was, she replied in a forthright letter to her son,

the event upon which the happyness or misery of our whole life depends . . . and you can never perswaid me that the thoughts of happyness in that state ever had a moment of your attention or you could never have made choice of a child for a companion. I know very well what was the inducement and could say a great [deal] upon it.

Out of respect for his father, she promised to restrain herself, but the unhappy Duchess had always found it hard to control her feelings; she was a dramatic lady with strong veins of self-pity and self-righteousness, and she was soon obsessed with the idea of the wrong her son had done to *her* and all she stood for, by his monstrous marriage. The Duke was still in London – the unpleasantness and worry had brought on a bad attack of gout – and she informed her son that, thanks to his behaviour, she could not think of any way 'to produce ease to the family and to my self but to live hear aloan for grief and solitude are fittest companions for each other.'

She meant exactly what she said and, before the Duke could return to Chatsworth, the Duchess had decamped in dudgeon to the nearby Cavendish rectory at Eyam. Since the Duke had sided with Lord Hartington, she could no longer live with him – as she explained in an anguished letter that she wrote him a few days later:

My Lord,

'Tis impossible for me to speak to you upon so unhappy a subject so must take this way to tell you my life in your family is more miserable than I am able to endure any longer and the only expedient I can think of is that you give me leave to retire from it. This is no sudden thought for I saw but to plainly from the first of this Match of your Son's that it would be impossible for us to live together and if you pleas to recolect your self I have more than once desired you to turn me out of dors and before your Brother went last year did upon my knees beg of him to tell you that as we could not live in friendship we might part with civility but could not prevail with him and he is the only one in the world I ever mentioned this to and my most humble request now is that I may go quietly and say no thing to any body. You may be very sure I can have no Tongue to utter so dreadful a word as that I have left you for ever. But to live in your family and do the office of the Clarke of your Kitchen and have leave to sitt and spin I have don as long as I can for my affection for you is to great to live in that manner with you and not only with you but with all my family without a possibility of its ever being better as my abhorence to this most Cursed Match increases more and more every day I live and has made such unhappy differences amongst us.

It has been the business of my life to instill all the Duty and regard that was possible into all your children for you and I have done it so effectively that they have none for me. But that I do not wonder at as they to plainly saw you had none but they are my Children as well as yours and how dearly I have loved them none but myself can tell (and have denied myself every thing for their sakes). How I have so entirely lost myself with you I cannot imagin for I do most solemnly sware that I never in my life did any thing that I could think would offend you and have imployed all my thoughts and attention to do every thing I could for the servis of you and all your family and most sincerely hope and pray that you and all in it will be happyer when I am out of it. . . .

What will become of me God knows but this I most faithfully promise that you will never be troubled with me more for my Dear Wise and good Father took care I would not want bread and in my most miserable circumstances I am sure I can want nothing but to drag out the remains of life in quiet and peace where ever I am. I shall dayly pray for your happyness for tho I am so unfortunate as not to be able to live with you I can never remove you from [my] heart. Pray God all mighty send you all the blessings and comforts this world can give and not only the blessings of this life but what is greatly to be prefered those of a better. This will be the constant prayer of her who always has been and ever shall be

Most faithfull and most affectionate
K Devonshire

Throughout the crisis, the Duke's gout can have done little for his temper, and one can but admire the way he handled things. One of the Duchess's few close friends was the Bishop of Kildare, and the Duke employed him as a go-between, tactfully explaining that all he wanted was to forget the past and have his wife return to him at Chatsworth.

This was the message that the Bishop took to Eyam Rectory, but he found 'My Lady Dutchess' still nursing her grievances and difficult to deal with. She was miserable and lonely and assured the Bishop that

she would be exceedingly glad to return to His Grace and live with him for the remainder of my life. . . . But as to those of my children who have made me so miserable, I cannot think of returning to see and receive them, while the remembrance of their behaviour is so fresh upon my mind; nor can I be sure whether I shall ever be able to prevail with myself to submit to that: tho' possibly Time and Kind Treatment may effect more than I can venture to answer for at present.

The Bishop urged the Duke to take the initiative and plead with her in person to return; which he did, apparently to no avail, for in June 1748, another pacifying cleric, Dr Thomas Cheyney was writing to the Duke advising patience and suggesting that with tactful handling Her Grace might still be persuaded back to Chatsworth if the Duke could convince her that he needed her.

Possibly such an act of kindness might bring Her Grace silently back with you and without one word's being said of the reasons that had induced the separation . . . But whether the happiness either of your Grace or Herself would be much advanced by such a return, I must own, I very much doubt, unless Her Grace could be brought to some better temper with regard to Lord H – and his new alliance.

But the Duchess was sticking to her guns and throughout that summer stayed at the Rectory in a state of virtual siege, refusing to compromise or return to Chatsworth.

She must have been an immense embarrassment to her noble family, for she was clearly starting to become unhinged by her obsession – and inevitably the gossip started. It soon reached London and, in September, urged on by his father, Lord Hartington himself wrote to his mother, begging her forgiveness and asking for a reconciliation. In a letter which she wrote from Eyam on 10 September 1748, she angrily refused:

> Your friendship was the greatest comfort I proposed to myself in this world . . . but as I never can or shall be reconciled to your match or concern myself with any body or any thing that relates to it, that is impossible.

Instead she was set on martyring herself to her ungrateful family.

> I have made it my most humble and earnest request to your father that he will let me remain here. If he will not, he must turn me out of doors which would be a terrible shock to me, but what I must submit to, for I would infinitely rather beg my bread than return to London to suffer what I did before I left it. . . . Henceforth I shall in silence and sorrow patiently wait till Almighty God in His infinite wisdom shall think fit to take me to Himself or deliver me from all my suffering.

Stalemate ensued, with the Duchess determinedly holed up in Eyam Rectory 'with her two maids and a weekly visit from the local curate'; and there she was to stay for nine months more, with the Duke regularly pleading with her to return, and she as regularly insisting on her own unyielding terms. Finally the Duke gave in.

The invaluable Horace Walpole revealed the terms of his surrender in a letter that he wrote early in June the following year to his friend, Sir Horace Mann in Florence:

> The Duke of Devonshire has at last resigned [as Lord Steward of the Royal Household], for the unaccountable and unenvied pleasure of shutting himself up at Chatsworth with his ugly mad Duchess; the more extraordinary sacrifice, as he turned her head, rather than give up a favourite match for his son. She has consented to live with him there, and has even been in town for a few days, but did not see either her son or Lady Hartington.

Like everybody, Walpole was puzzled over why the Duke had sacrificed his place at Court simply to return to such a termagant. Why should he have bothered? Was he impelled by love for the dominating lady, or desire for domestic peace, or was he worried by the fear of further scandal she might cause?

Any or all these motives may have played their part in the Duke's decision, but Walpole himself was sharp enough to have discovered one further fascinating reason which lay behind the Third Duke's resignation: In an unpublished passage in the original manuscript of the *Memoirs of the Reign of George II*, Walpole wrote the following about the Duke:

> He, the D. of D. loved gaming, drinking and the ugliest woman in England, his Duchess, on whose account he had resigned his employments to retire with her, after having parted with her and turned her head, by breaking a promise he had given her of not marrying her son to Lady Burlington's daughter.

So Dr Johnson had been particularly acute when he noted that the Duke was 'so unconditional in keeping his word'. During those emotional scenes at Chatsworth the Duke must have assured his wife that he would never sanction the marriage. Finally, of course, he had no choice, for his son was a grown man and intended to marry as he wished. But the promise had been made – and as a man of honour the Duke felt bound to pay the price for breaking it. He was a gambler and a drunkard, but he was also a gentleman who kept his word, and in return for sanctioning what proved to be the greatest enrichment of the House of Cavendish since the marriages of Bess of Hardwick, he condemned himself to pass the remainder of his days away from Court and out of office, a virtual prisoner at Chatsworth of his unforgiving, intolerable wife.

Strong in her self-righteousness, she refused ever to be reconciled with her daughter-in-law although, ironically, young Lady Charlotte gave her husband all that 'happyness' in marriage which the 'Lady Dutchess' had insisted he could never find with her. But the irony did not end there. In the midst of their idyllic life together, pretty young Lady Hartington presented her now devoted husband with four children – including the all-important male heir to their joint possessions – and then, after an ill-advised game of shuttlecock while pregnant at her mother's house at Uppingham in Rutland, she succumbed to smallpox and was dead within a week.

By her death in 1754, Lord Hartington gained instantly that great 'Benefit' to his family that he once said had been the motive for his marriage, so almost doubling the Cavendish estates, – but none of the great Burlington possessions which now belonged entirely to him and his successors was any consolation for his loss. And when, within a year, his father died as well, making him as Fourth Duke one of the richest, most extensive land-owners in Britain, he could only mourn the fact that his wife had never lived to be Duchess of Devonshire herself. He would go on to achieve a political success which no other Duke of Devonshire would reach, but his private life was blighted; and many years after he was dead, his son, the Fifth Duke, discovered a secret drawer in his father's desk and opened it. Inside, carefully preserved, were a woman's comb, a small silk bag and a handkerchief – all the possessions Lady Hartington had had on her on the day she died.

But the greatest irony of all concerned the 'ugly mad' old Duchess, who had been the cause of so much trouble to her family. She survived everyone – her daughter-in-law, her husband and her son – and lived on at Chatsworth into extreme old age, dying there at last in 1777. Before then she grudgingly made peace with her son, the Duke, and ended by being rather proud of the vast possessions he had brought into the family.

The last sight we have of her comes appropriately from Horace Walpole who finally deigned to visit Chatsworth, where he had never been before, in August 1760. He was surprised to find that he actually liked the outside 'which ever since I was born, I have condemned – it is a glorious situation. . . . The principal front of the house is beautiful.' On the other hand; 'The inside is most sumptuous but did not please me. The heathen gods, goddesses, Christian virtues and allegoric gentlefolks, are crowded into every room, as if Mrs Holman had been in heaven and invited everybody she saw . . . The great apartment is trist . . . the tapestries are fine, but not fine enough.'

But there was one thing to alleviate his disappointment – the old Duchess. 'Would you believe that nothing was ever better humoured than the ancient Grace?' he told George Montagu.

She stayed every evening, till it was dark, in the skittle-ground, keeping the score; and one night, that the servants had a ball for Lady Dorothy's birthday, we fetched the fiddles into the drawing-room, and the Dowager herself danced with us!

8. Crown Prince of the Whigs

The Fourth Duke, William (1720–1764)

THE Fourth Duke was thirty-four at his accession and, thanks to the combined Burlington and Cavendish inheritance, by far the grandest and the richest of the Dukes of Devonshire to date, owning ten great houses and four immense estates. He should have been a happy man, for besides great wealth he had considerable intelligence and taste. 'Universally respected', and with political ability 'higher than that of many great noblemen who held office in eighteenth-century England' he had reached what seemed an unassailable position in society and politics.

Princess Amelia called him in all seriousness, 'the Crown Prince of the Whigs', and there is an undoubted air of quasi-regal ease and dignity about the Duke which none of his predecessors had enjoyed. There is also something sad about him; his young wife, had she lived, might have brought him more straightforward zest and relish for his earthly blessings. Perhaps he simply owned too much, and life presented nothing else to strive for. He may have been a little bored. For, despite the great 'Benefit' his calculated marriage bestowed upon his family, his dukedom in many ways foreshadows the changing status of the House of Cavendish – and the crisis beginning to afflict the great Whig monopoly of power as the century was moving to its close.

The Fourth Duke had always had a strong dose of the caution of the Cavendishes, and became if anything more cautious and withdrawn with the years. Garrick, who knew him well spoke of his 'great prudery in dress and detestation of approaching within a mile of the *bon ton*' – as one would guess from his portraits with the wistful, rather distant face offering no concessions to the vulgar world around him. Lacking his father's easy-going *bonhomie*, he always was a vulnerable man who never found anyone to take his dead wife's place, and who was never particularly close to any of his four young children.

On the other hand, he was a very ornamental duke; again unlike his 'unpolish'd' father, he had perfect manners, did not drink excessively, and took his social duties seriously – as one sees in a contemporary account of him in the diary of Caroline Girle, the daughter of a London surgeon, who visited Chesterfield with her parents in 1757:

> About ten we went to the Assembly Room, where the Duke of Devonshire always presided as Master of Ceremonies, and after the Ball, gave an elegant cold supper where, by his known politeness and affability, it would be unnecessary for me to say how amiable he made himself to the company.

The middle-class surgeon and his wife invited the Duke back to take tea with their hosts, and His Grace obliged, charming everyone again with his 'condescension' and his faultless manners.

At this period the rapidly expanding and 'polite' middle classes were just starting their great love-affair with the English aristocracy which was to have such curious and far-reaching consequences in the century to come. A celebrity like Garrick would do almost anything to get an invitation from the Duke to stay at Chatsworth – making absolutely sure his friends knew when he did – and it is now that public interest in the house began in earnest.

From the beginning of the century, the Dukes of Devonshire had all been hospitable possessors; occasional visitors to the house would sometimes unexpectedly find themselves invited to stay on for dinner with the Duke when the family was in residence. But now, as the general public curiosity about the house began to grow, its role inevitably changed as well. The First Duke's Chatsworth was essentially a place of power from where he could rule the county and if required, defy the King. But this semi-feudal role was fading now as Chatsworth increasingly became one of the established 'sights' of Derbyshire, where middle-class visitors could come to marvel at the riches of the Cavendishes and dutifully learn to ape their betters. The house was one of the earliest of Britain's 'stately homes' officially opened to the public. Monday was called the 'Public Day' – and by the Fourth Duke's time a constant stream of visitors was walking through his gardens and the State Apartments much as they do today.

The Fourth Duke's changes at Chatsworth all reflect this new attitude towards the house. He was not particularly concerned with altering the interior, nor with adding to the treasures it contained. There were more than enough by now, and space would eventually be needed for Lord Burlington's extensive library, and many of his pictures which were added to the Devonshire collection. For that matter, the Duke was in no sense a collector or a connoisseur. When Garrick wrote to him from Venice, offering to buy on his account, he rapidly wrote back, 'I am much oblig'd to you for your offer in purchasing Pictures and Statues, but I have no money', an odd excuse from somebody with £40,000 a year.

Instead, the Duke spent lavishly on what did interest him – changing the whole setting of the house, so that by the time he finished, Chatsworth appeared transformed from that solidly entrenched great bastion of ducal power the First Duke had created.

This change was already in the air. The Third Duke had realized that the natural front of Chatsworth was its splendid west façade, facing the valley of the Derwent, (which the First Duke had treated as its rear) and had cleared away the office and stables partly obscuring it. The Fourth Duke now carried on his father's work, employing the architect James Paine to design an impressive new stone stable-block to the north-east of the house, and an elegant bridge across the widened river. But his most important change of all was to call in the famous landscape gardener, the indefatigable Lancelot 'Capability' Brown, to sweep away the First Duke's formal gardens round the house and to surround it with a carefully planned and planted lush romantic landscape.

Chatsworth's formal gardens had always played a crucial part in the impression it conveyed to visitors, making the great house with its geometric alleys and parterres stand rigidly aloof from the untamed countryside around. Early travellers were constantly amazed at the sudden contrast between this regal palace with its regimented gardens and Defoe's 'houling wilderness' beyond. For Charles Cotton, Chatsworth had been a diamond 'set in a vile socket of ignoble jet' which was exactly as the First Duke had intended.

Now this was swiftly being changed, thanks to Mr Brown's unrivalled skill at creating an illusionary landscape, and the Fourth Duke's unrivalled ability to pay for it. At a cost of something over £40,000 the surrounding valley and the hills beyond were being tamed and planted, and a fine new bridge and stable block built to James Paine's classical designs. Chatsworth was being elaborately set within a pictured harmony with nature. It would no longer be that sudden foursquare symbol of the strength and independence of the Dukes of Devonshire which the First Duke had left to his successors. As the new woodlands grew, it would increasingly appear like some fabled palace from the distant past floating within a sylvan paradise while the deer grazed contentedly beneath the ancient oaks of this Derbyshire Arcadia.

Mythology was taking over from reality and, while Sheffield barely fifteen miles away was growing as a rich industrial centre and a brutal portent for the future, Chatsworth was entering the past. But for the Fourth Duke with his great houses and enormous fortune it must have seemed as if this paradise – like the great Whig settlement established by his ancestors – would last for ever.

The only area within the Fourth Duke's world that can have given him serious concern was politics, where he always did his conscientious best to play the proper part expected of a Whig Crown Prince. In 1755, in accordance with the eighteenth century's customary adherence to the biblical 'to them that hath shall be given', he was despatched to enjoy the lucrative and not particularly taxing Governorship of Ireland, as his father had before him. He was a widower by now – his wife having died the previous December. He ruled sagaciously, and the Irish seem to have been grateful to have somebody in Dublin Castle who, as lord of the Boyle estates and Governor of Cork, had a personal stake in Ireland's future. He proved, in the words of his biographer, 'a suave Viceroy' and was more valued for his intelligent diplomacy than for the convivial qualities which had endeared his father to the Irish.

The Duke's role in Ireland in no way interfered with his importance in English politics, which had increased with the Burlington inheritance. Namier calculates that by now he directly controlled at least twelve seats in parliament, four of which were held by members of his family, making the Cavendishes, as Horace Walpole put it, 'almost a political party of their own'. Since Robert Walpole's death, the supreme manipulator of the whole corrupt parliamentary system on which the political power of the great Whig families depended was Thomas Pelham-Holles, Duke of Newcastle. He was a close friend and ally of the Duke of Devonshire and, although the Fourth Duke was very much aware of Newcastle's personal failings – among them obsessional vanity, incompetence and indecisiveness – he valued him for what he was, the lynch-pin of the great Whig *status quo*.

For the Fourth Duke's view of politics was really very logical and simple –

the calm continuation of this best of all possible worlds for the English aristocracy. For him as for his father and grandfather before him, all the great questions that had once bedevilled English politics had been settled for ever by the 1688 Revolution and the sacred and unchanging English Constitution. And, as a politician, the Fourth Duke is the supreme example of the sort of Whigs described by Sir Lewis Namier as 'unromantic latitudinarians tinged with a tolerant liberalism such as most men acquire in the practice of government.'

He was all for a polite acceptance of the rising middle classes, provided they posed no threat to the men of property who ran the country. His attitude towards the House of Hanover was not dissimilar. What we would term 'parliamentary corruption' would have struck him as an inevitable and quite legitimate extension of the rights of property. And in overseas affairs he was, like all true Whigs, a dedicated 'Little Englander', firmly and totally against foreign adventures, expensive wars and unnecessary empires. He was a man of harmony and peace, and in 1756 almost all he stood for was threatened by two unforeseen events – the outbreak of the Seven Years' War with France and the rise to power and unrivalled popularity of William Pitt.

Indefatigable, incorruptible, and the greatest war minister Britain has produced, Pitt was a thorn in the comfortable backside of eighteenth-century English politics. The Fourth Duke inevitably disliked him, but he could not ignore him, any more than could the rest of England, for the war was going badly. The French had taken Minorca and the execution of poor Admiral Byng would never bring it back. Calcutta fell, the American colonies were threatened and, on the Continent, Britain's one remaining ally, Frederick of Prussia, seemed overwhelmed by the unstoppable coalition of France and Austria. The Whig government was rightly blamed for these calamities; the country was clamouring for Pitt to lead them, but Pitt refused emphatically to serve in any government containing that arch apostle of incompetence, the Duke of Newcastle.

Impasse ensued with a world war waging. The country wanted William Pitt; the great Whig magnates wanted to preserve their parliamentary power; and King George II, with his beloved Hanover threatened by the French, wanted someone to construct him an effective government.

The Crown Prince of the Whigs' great hour had come. Unlike the Duke of Newcastle he was a man of considerable diplomatic subtlety, known for his incorruptibility; and unlike William Pitt he was more than acceptable to the old guard Whigs in Parliament. He, and at this juncture he alone, held enough prestige and parliamentary power to paper over all the cracks between Pitt and his followers and the old Whigs who still clamoured for their places in the administration.

Supremely unambitious, he took considerable persuading but, in October 1756, he returned from Ireland. A few weeks later, Newcastle resigned, and on 16 November the Fourth Duke was appointed Prime Minister in his place with Pitt as his Secretary of State effectively responsible for the conduct of the war. It was, as George II himself said later, 'a very disagreeable situation' for the Duke, with Pitt in the House of Commons effectively in charge of policy and stealing all the thunder, as he launched a war of which the Duke at best faint-heartedly approved.

The Duke endured six months. During his prime ministership Pitt had laid the foundations of the great victories of the Seven Years' War, but the Duke's own usefulness was over. Pitt made his peace with the Duke of Newcastle, to become Prime Minister himself, and in May 1757, the Duke of Devonshire exchanged the First Lordship of the Treasury for the more appropriate position of Lord Chamberlain. The most reluctant and uncomfortable Prime Minister in English history had had his day; but his political misfortunes had only just begun.

Wolfe took Quebec, Clive won India, and Fort Duquesne, captured from the French, was renamed Pittsburgh. But the Fourth Duke, like his friend the Duke of Newcastle, wanted peace, for the war was an increasing burden on the landed interest, and Pitt's immense popularity threatened the power of the old Whig aristocracy. Then, in 1760, the two Dukes discovered what might have been an unexpected and unasked-for ally. George II died, and his grandson and successor, the young George III, disliked Pitt and his warlike policy even more than they did. With anyone but George III, this might have led to a useful community of interests. But George III, an ignorant and autocratic twenty-three-year-old, hated the Whigs as firmly as he hated war and William Pitt. The result was a most unseemly muddle, which in the end destroyed the Duke, and most of the Whig political system he stood for.

The first victim of the new King would be William Pitt himself, who by 1761 was demanding harsh terms for peace with the defeated French – or a continuation of the war. The King refused to back him; so did Newcastle, and 'with him, tied by every bond of class tradition, went the Duke of Devonshire.' 'I wish to God some expedient may be found out, to prevent the continuance of the war,' the Fourth Duke wrote to Newcastle, 'if the war is to continue, I for my part see no day light'.

There was not much daylight anyhow for the political future of the old Whig families. Pitt resigned that autumn, to be succeeded as prime minister by Newcastle. But power was in the hands of George III's former tutor, the incompetent Lord Bute. Negotiations started for a feeble peace with France, and Bute and his 'royal friends' were soon picking up the plums of office. Bute and the King were intent on humiliating prickly old Newcastle – which was not difficult – and the Fourth Duke, alarmed at the rapid disappearance of traditional Whig power and influence in Parliament, was soon begging him, like some exasperated nanny, to *please* be sensible and try to stay friends with Bute and George III:

> Never was a time when it was more necessary for two persons to agree than it is for you two at present. And therefore for Godsake keep your temper. . . . It is very hard that I can't be gone four and twenty hours but you must all be quarrelling. *Pray be friends*, for the public will suffer if you are not so.

But by now it needed more than Devonshire's emollient influence to keep the old political order intact. For, having disposed of Pitt, the King and Bute were now intent on sweeping away the monopoly of political power enjoyed by the old Whig families. In May 1762, Newcastle was finally winkled out of power, and the Fourth Duke, who as Lord Chamberlain was still officially a member of the government, had to consider what on earth to do himself.

The Duke had no intention of allowing a young, bad-mannered member of the foreign family his own ancestors had helped hoist onto the throne of England to treat him as ignominiously as he had the Duke of Newcastle. On the other hand, he could hardly see himself continuing in office with a prime minister like Bute. Horace Walpole described him now as 'fluctuating between his golden key [his symbol of office] and disgust', and he continued to fluctuate all summer, staying determinedly at Chatsworth in a huff, and refusing to play any part in the government of which he was a member.

He knew quite well the absurdity of his position, as he makes clear in a letter that he wrote his friend Bishop Newcombe that September.

> Having declined attending Councils all this summer, how long I shall be able to remain in office is uncertain. I should rather think my continuance will be short, for if I should appear to be one of the present Administration, I should lose the little credit I have in the world. At the same time I detest opposition, and therefore am determined to keep myself free and enter into no engagements.

To make matters worse, he was not well.

> My health has for some time been rather shatter'd, the Physical people say that the fever I had last year did not go off as it should have done, and has left some little foulness in my blood. I eat, drink and sleep as well as ever in my life, at the same time I am scarse ever 24 hours well [and have] strange unpleasant sensations all over my body attended with lowness of spirits.

His reign as the Whig Crown Prince was drawing swiftly to a close, and with it the position he had long enjoyed above the vulgar cut and thrust of politics.

On 2 October the flexible Lord Egremont – who, once a Tory, then a devoted beneficiary of Newcastle, had now taken on the post of Secretary of the Southern Department, responsible for negotiating peace with France – wrote a decisive letter to the Duke.

> Notwithstanding your having of late declin'd attending the Cabinet Council, yet, as the final Decision on the Peace is to be taken at one that will soon meet, on which the fate of the Country may depend, His Majesty has no doubt that you will give your personal attendance, and your advice freely on so great a point. And to that end the King has ordered me to desire Your Grace to come to Town as soon as you can.

Even now the Duke had no intention of being hurried by anything the unmannerly young King 'desired', so instead of following the royal summons up to London, he took his time and went to Bath instead, hoping the waters might provide a cure for his 'lowness of spirits'. The peace of Europe and the King of England could wait while the Duke of Devonshire took the waters.

Then at last, purged and rested, the Duke did deign to meet his monarch, having made up his mind to have done with all the nonsense and resign. The best description of what happened then is in the distinctly shocked account written by the Duke of Newcastle.

> The Duke went to the Court as usual, and told the page as usual that he was there to attend His Majesty. The page stayed some little time in the lower closet, and came out very much embarrassed, and said *that he had the King's orders to tell* His Grace that he would not see him. Upon that the Duke desired the Page to present his duty to His Majesty, and to desire to know *to whom he should deliver* his staff of office? The same page came out, and acquainted the D. of D. that the King would send His Grace his orders.
>
> Upon this the D. of D. went to my Lord Egremont and delivered his key to him, and desired his Lordship to deliver that and his staff to the King, and there it ended. And the D. of D. is gone this day to Chatsworth.

The news was soon round London. It was, wrote Horace Walpole to his friend George Montagu, 'something that will make you stare' – and he went on to relate how, when the Duke had gone, the King was in such a fury that he called for the Council book, and personally dashed out Devonshire's name. 'If you like spirit,' wrote Walpole gleefully, '*en voilà!*'

Low comedy apart, this extraordinary scene of royal bad temper was of considerable significance, for it dramatically marks the end of an important era for the Dukes of Devonshire. Until now they had always had an automatic place in government because of their prestige and their wealth and influence within the country. Now this prescriptive right to a place in government was over and would never be regained. For the King – however inelegantly – had called the Duke's bluff, and the Duke – however reluctantly – had bowed to the power of the throne.

The Duke received a lot of sympathy. His brothers and Lord Rockingham resigned their places in the administration in disgust at the King's behaviour, and the most comforting, and interesting, letter of condolence that the Duke received came from a member of the royal family, the Duke of Cumberland, the 'Butcher of Culloden':

> The pittyful way in which your rank and Imployment was attacked falls only on those that advise their Master merely from Interest or Passion, but cannot affect you, and I own on this occasion I must pity the poor young King that has bereft himself of the most useful and zealous subject for the present through the instigation of the most dangerous and wicked advisers that a young King had.
>
> I know your good sense and zeal for your country too well not to hope that how ever warmly you do, and indeed ought to feel, the undeservedly ill usage you have met with, will not lead you to resolutions that would be very unfortunate for all your friends and that whenever the vermin that the Court is now so full of be swept away, we may see you there again at the head of

your real friends, for our family must not be left long without a Duke of Devonshire in the Administration.

But this was not to be. The 'foulness in the blood' seems to have got steadily worse, and the Duke's health was not improved by the disgust he felt at the 'vermin' who had taken over the King's government – and the way he had been treated by the King himself. Troubled to see the great Whig settlement of his ancestors destroyed, he felt instinctively that there was little hope left for his country, 'govern'd by the mob or by an authoritarian king' using 'methods entirely destructive of and contrary to the principles of the Constitution'.

The Great Whig Settlement was sick – and so was he. Early in the autumn of 1764 he went to the fashionable resort of Spa in the Ardennes, hoping the waters there would cure him, but nothing could save him now. In October, Charles Townshend wrote to Earl Temple that he had just heard 'a most melancholy account of the Duke of Devonshire, who has suffered another stroke of the palsy, by which he has entirely lost the use of one hand and one side . . . .' A few days later he was dead, and once again, as so often with the Cavendishes, it was Horace Walpole who was to have the final word.

'There's a chapter for moralizing!' he wrote to Lord Hertford when he heard the news, 'but five-and-forty, with forty thousand pounds a year, and happiness wherever he turned him! My reflection is, that it is folly to be unhappy at anything, when felicity itself is such a phantom!'

9. The Genius of Clapham

Henry Cavendish (1731–1810)

That philosopher, the man who weighed the world and buried his science and his wealth in solitude and insignificance at Clapham.

The Sixth Duke, Handbook of Chatsworth

THE premature departure from the scene by the Fourth Duke in 1764 was a disaster for the House of Cavendish, for the new Duke was no 'Crown Prince' but an unknown fifteen-year-old youth: the political ascendancy of the old Whig families had more or less collapsed, and the importance of the Dukes of Devonshire seemed to have crumbled too. The great fortune and possessions were still there to be enjoyed, the honoured position waiting to be filled, but the dukedom was effectively in mothballs until the new incumbent came of age.

In the meantime the massive income accumulated, the great houses, except for Devonshire House in Piccadilly, were closed up, and the fledgling Duke was soon to depart on the grandest of Grand Tours of France and Italy to anxious warnings from his former tutor, the clergyman, John Hinchcliffe:

> Tho' there is not a Duke in Christendom that I have more confidence in than your Grace, yet in that climate, from eighteen to eight and twenty, the odds are certainly on the side of passion against prudence.

From what one knows of the Fifth Duke's later life, one must imagine that the Italian climate had the usual dire but enjoyable effects upon the young man's morals. In Rome, he was painted by the fashionable Batoni, looking elegant in a gold and scarlet coat, but also effete and rather bored, a condition which prevailed, with occasional exasperated intermissions, for the remainder of his life. A kindly but somewhat wooden youth, he was a good classical scholar, but he showed little of the virtuosity of the Burlingtons, or the shrewd caution of the Cavendishes. No one could guess as yet what use – if any – he would make of his great inheritance on reaching his majority.

Nor were his three politician uncles, Lord John, Lord George and Lord Charles Cavendish of any great account during this period of crisis for the Whigs. But there was one member of the family who was just beginning to make a name which would outlast them all. Few could have guessed this at the time, for the new Duke's second cousin, Henry Cavendish, must have appeared distinctly odd by Cavendish standards: a gangling, painfully unsociable thirty-four-year-old bachelor with a high-pitched voice, eking out a meagre income in the absolute obscurity of his father's house in Great Marlborough Street.

He was totally uninterested in any of the things the Cavendishes traditionally believed in – politics, land, wealth or marrying. He was unconcerned with what he wore or what he ate. He was pathologically shy and often at a total loss for words. Yet he was more important than all his Cavendish contemporaries put together – for threadbare Henry Cavendish was a scientific genius, and the most original, wide-ranging British man of science since Isaac Newton.

In fact there was a fairly long tradition of mathematical and scientific interest among the Cavendishes. In the 1640s there had been Newcastle's younger brother, deformed Charles Cavendish, the enthusiastic mathematician and friend and correspondent of Gassendi and Descartes; then came the powerful influence of Thomas Hobbes upon three generations of the family; and the Third Earl and the First Duke were both important early Fellows of the Royal Society. But it was with the Second Duke's younger son, Lord Charles Cavendish, that this scientific bent emerged as something more than mere dilettante interest. Lord Charles managed somehow to combine Whig politics and social position with an extremely practical concern for science and mathematics. He married a younger daughter of the Duke of Kent, but also found time for experimental work in electricity and meteorology, and was awarded a medal by the Royal Society for inventing a maximum and minimum thermometer.

His wife's health was far from good, and it was while on restorative stay in Nice that she gave birth, in October 1731, to their first son, Henry. Her second son, Frederick Cavendish was produced in England two years later, and she died soon afterwards, thus condemning both her sons to a secluded childhood which undoubtedly contributed to later shyness and problems of communication, even between themselves.

They are the subject of the story which illustrates well the verbal caution of the Cavendishes. As young men they were travelling through France and, staying at an inn, they passed an open door on the way to bed. Inside the room they saw a dead body laid out for burial, but neither of the brothers spoke, and it was not until next morning that Frederick finally remarked, 'Brother, did you see the corpse?' 'Brother, I did,' Henry Cavendish replied – and that was that.

Both brothers went to Peterhouse, then as now one of the more intellectually distinguished of the smaller Cambridge colleges, where Frederick's oddities were possibly made worse by falling from an upper window into the college court. Although his head was permanently dented, this did not stop him from beginning a lifetime's interest in botany and poetry – Thomas Gray, author of the *Elegy*, was a fellow of Peterhouse in their day. But nothing is known of Henry Cavendish's studies, except that he left Cambridge in 1753 after four years in residence without taking a degree. As a nobleman in unreformed Cambridge nothing as vulgar as failure in an examination would account for this, so perhaps Henry Cavendish, as a lifelong non-believer, jibbed at the necessary religious test. On the other hand he may simply not have bothered. Honours and ceremonies always bored him, and it was after Cambridge that he more or less retired from the world to dedicate himself to the one thing that really roused his interest – the systematic study of scientific phenomena.

Living under the paternal roof – he was to stay contentedly at Great Marlborough Street until Lord Charles's death in 1783 – it is certain that his father's scientific interests guided his own researches to begin with. As well as designing thermometers, Lord Charles was an acknowledged expert on other meteorological instruments such as barometers, hygrometers and rain-gauges, and he and his son were occasionally observed conducting experiments together in the garden. Lord Charles was also involved in studying the measurement of heat, electricity and the earth's magnetic field – all of which engaged his son's attention too.

Henry's late twenties coincided with the Fourth Duke's period of greatest wealth and splendour, but there could hardly be a greater contrast than between these two cousins' lives: where the Fourth Duke had his £40,000 a year, Henry existed uncomplainingly on five shillings pocket-money a day from his father, and while the Duke was becoming Prime Minister, his cousin was patiently developing that 'combination of mathematical precision with exact experiment' which was to form the basis of an astounding range of the most profound discoveries.

But Henry was as reticent as the Duke was famous. It is now accepted that, some time after leaving Cambridge, his interest in Newtonian mechanics and his researches into heat 'led him to make the first precise statement of the principle of the conservation of energy, specifically including the transformation of mechanical energy into heat'; but he seems to have mentioned this to no one, let alone risked publishing it, and it was not until 1921 that Larmor brought it to general notice in his full edition of Cavendish's scientific papers.

By an odd coincidence it was in 1764, the year the Fourth Duke died, that Cavendish did summon up the courage to produce his first privately circulated account of one piece of advanced research – what one writer has somewhat alarmingly described as his 'Notes on some experiments with arsenic for the use of friends'. In fact this was his first known attempt at sustained chemical research in which with extraordinary skill and intuition he produced and described arsenic acid a full ten years before the Swedish chemist Scheele was publicly credited with its discovery. But although his method of preparing the acid was superior to Scheele's – and the one still in use today – it was typical of Cavendish to lay no public claim to it. All his life he was to work with this strange and often self-defeating combination of secretiveness and diffidence. This may have been caused by his shyness, or aristocratic indifference, or have even been an exaggerated form of Cavendish caution. It was certainly a useful way of avoiding wasting time and energy on professional controversy, but it does make Henry Cavendish one of the most baffling distinguished men of science. It also helped to cut him off from his great scientific contemporaries of the early Industrial Revolution – men like Black and Watt and Joseph Priestley – as well as from the new innovative industrialists like Boulton and Wedgwood who, as J. G. Crowther has suggested, might 'have provided conditions in which his genius would have been more efficiently employed for the benefit of mankind'.

As it was, in 1766 even he felt impelled to publish the results of some recent chemical research which alone would fix his name in history. This was his discovery of hydrogen, for which he was honoured by the Royal Society. But this did little to affect his way of life. He began attending the dinners of the Royal Society – for which his father somewhat grudgingly paid each time he went – and he seems to have enjoyed the conversation of his fellow scientists despite his shyness.

The remainder of Henry Cavendish's long and increasingly reclusive life – he died in 1810 at the age of seventy-nine – was outwardly uneventful. He shunned honours; when a distinguished Austrian announced to a gathering at Sir Joseph Banks's house that he had come there specially from Vienna in the hope of conversing with Mr Cavendish, 'one of the most illustrious philosophers of the age', Henry fled the house in horror. He continued to shun women, although he did once save a lady from an enraged cow on Clapham Common. When his father died, in 1783, he moved first to Bloomsbury, and then to a house in Clapham which was converted in almost its entirety into one big laboratory. Thanks to several legacies, and shrewd investment by his bankers, he became extremely rich; 'le plus riche de tous les savants, et probablement aussi, le plus savant de tous les riches', as his French biographer, Biot, put it. But, despite his wealth, he continued to live austerely, dining invariably off a leg of mutton left for him by his single servant, and dressing in the style of his youth. His only luxury was a splendid library, containing the classics as well as the latest scientific works, which he kept in a separate house in Soho Square and generously made available to other men of learning. The older he got, the more eccentric and withdrawn he became, until Thomson could describe him, shortly before his death, as 'shy and bashful to a degree bordering on disease'.

But his work and achievements were prodigious. They ranged over every known branch of the science of his day, and his published work alone was enough to make him, as Sir Humphry Davy said, 'an immortal honour to his house, to his age, and to his country'.

His researches on the composition of air provided 'the first adequate proof of the constancy of the composition of the atmosphere' – and incidentally led to his interest in aeronautics, and balloonists such as the Montgolfiers. He invented a technique for the analysis of water which was to have considerable importance for public health. He discovered the nature of nitric acid, and of the gas later known as argon. Working quite separately from Watt and Lavoisier, he almost certainly preceded their discoveries on the compound nature of water. His research on electricity was equally important and ingenious, anticipating the idea of electrical voltage, of positive and negative charges and the accurate measurement of electrical resistance. But in his own day his most celebrated feat came in 1798 when, at the age of sixty-seven, after years of research and mathematical calculation at his house in Clapham, he announced the solution of the problem left by Newton by measuring the force of gravity, and calculating that the average density of the earth was 5.448 times that of water.*

---

*In fact, after much accurate and painstaking research, Cavendish made an elementary mathematical slip in preparing his results. The correct figure should have been 5.505.

But it was Henry Cavendish's unpublished work which years later would reveal his even greater stature as a man of science. Clerk Maxwell and Larmor, on working through his papers, found that time and time again this solitary genius in Clapham had anticipated many of the crucial discoveries and scientific laws of the nineteenth century.*

Because of his appearance and his solitary eccentric way of life, Henry Cavendish has always been pitied, particularly in contrast to the other contemporary members of his family, with their resounding honours and glittering social life, their love affairs, political ambitions and immense possessions. 'There is', writes Bickley, 'something pathetic about such an existence as Henry Cavendish's, so fruitful, and yet so utterly barren.'

On the contrary, the more one learns about him, the more enviable and admirable he seems, and the more to be pitied those around him. For Henry Cavendish was really the most fortunate of men, possessed of a great mind, unceasing curiosity, and mental powers that lasted till his death. He was fortunate in being able to stay free from the cares and passions that enslave most lesser men. He had material freedom, and was lucky to have lived in a period when a dedicated aristocratic amateur like him could make discoveries on such a scale and over such a range of subjects.

Against the unlikely background of the eighteenth century, he appears a sort of Merlin figure, discovering the secrets of the world around him for his private satisfaction; and if he ever did regret the human pleasures he was missing, he always had the consolation T. H. White describes Merlin offering the young King Arthur as his personal antidote to melancholy:

> The best thing for being sad is to learn something . . . Learn why the world wags and what wags it. That is the only thing that the mind can never exhaust, never alienate, never be tortured by, never fear or distrust, and never dream of regretting.

Henry Cavendish must have known this, and other members of his family might have learned by his example.

---

*According to J. G. Crowther, 'Besides his unpublished formulation of the conservation of energy, Cavendish also made an extraordinary series of unpublished electrical discoveries, including Ohm's law and specific inductive capacity. He anticipated Kirchhoff on the flow of electricity in divided circuits, and some of Kohlrausch's work on the electrical conductivity of salt solutions. He conceived the idea of electromotive force, or electrical "pressure" as he called it, and the idea of potential, foreshadowing the thought of George Green.' He also anticipated Charles's Law of gases, Dalton's Law of Partial Pressures and Bunsen's work on the effusion of gases, as well as 'some of the work of Kelvin and G. H. Darwin on the effect of tidal friction on slowing the rotation of the earth, and Larmor's discovery, published in 1915, on the effect of local atmospheric cooling on astronomical observations; the work of Pickering on freezing mixtures, and some of the work of Roozeboom on heterogeneous equilibria. He had a clear understanding of neutralization in chemistry, and its implications of chemical equivalence, giving accurate quantitative measurements of chemical equivalents. He anticipated Richter's law of reciprocal proportions.'

10. 'Racky', 'Canis' and 'Mrs Rat'

The Fifth Duke, William (1748–1811)

Perhaps no set of men and women since the world began enjoyed so many sides of life with so much zest, as the English upper class at this period.

G. M. Trevelyan, English Social History

WITH the Fifth Duke of Devonshire, most of the qualities that had made the earlier Devonshires exceptional seem to have conspired from the start to ruin his life, for he did badly out of the genetic lottery, and in him almost all the dominant Cavendish characteristics turned out slightly wrong. The family caution was transmuted into chronic lethargy, tolerance to icy unconcern, persistence to obtuseness, and learning to pedantry. The loss of his mother when he was barely six, and of his distant father at fifteen, cannot have helped his character. He might still have made a slumbrous eighteenth-century country parson, or a forgettable, deep-drinking fellow of an Oxford college, but as the greatest inheritor in England a suitable vocation was impossible, and most of his unhappy qualities were made worse by his inheritance.

His misfortune was that nothing really mattered. Anything he wanted could be bought, anyone he liked would flatter him, and there was no one with the presumption to correct him. Once back in England after his tour of France and Italy, he inevitably fell in with several of the richest and most dissolute young bloods in London, from whom he rapidly picked up further habits, most of which plagued him for the remainder of his life – compulsive gambling, heavy drinking, and a nocturnal existence which began when he emerged from bed sometime in the afternoon: he dined at seven, drank until eleven, and for exercise walked back up St James's Street to Devonshire House as dawn was breaking, having gambled the night away at Brooks's Club. There was nothing wrong with this – except that he never gave the faintest hint of actually enjoying this expensive, very wearing way of life. He had not an atom of that gusto which had led his friend, Charles James Fox, to gamble off an unlamented fortune by the age of twenty-four. His drinking gave him gout at twenty-six, but never seemed to raise his spirits. 'Constitutional apathy', wrote Wraxall, 'formed his distinguishing characteristic.' And even his amours, although determined, seem distinctly dull. Scandal credits him with having crowned his grand tour of the Continent, by slipping into bed with Madame du Barry during his time in Paris, but if he did enjoy the delicious mistress of the ageing King of France, he was to follow this, on his return to London, by setting up with a tarnished Mayfair milliner called Charlotte Spencer,* whom he finally made pregnant but naturally could never marry.

---

* It is a pure coincidence that she had the same surname as the Duke's eventual bride.

One contemporary described him as 'an image for a wintry day'. Another, more perceptively, remarked that the trouble with the Duke was 'that he seems to want *spring* rather than sense'; for throughout his life, the Fifth Duke, who was later to reveal surprising virtues in unenviable circumstances, always seemed like a man who was simply crushed beneath the sheer weight of the importance and possessions he was saddled with.

Nowhere is this clearer than in the long strange saga of his first marriage, which was both the most important and the most ill-advised decision of his life. He took it in the spring of 1774 when he was twenty-five. Miss Spencer was in the late stages of her pregnancy, and it may well have been her state, by reminding him of his powers of generation, that prompted him towards this uncharacteristically decisive act.

He was easily the most eligible young bachelor in England but, as with royalty, his actual choice of appropriate bride had always been strictly limited. Several ambitious mothers had inevitably pursued him with their daughters, but with his lethargic nature he had never found much difficulty ignoring them; and, now he had made his mind up, he acted with all the cool formality of his very cool and formal nature. He clearly had to make a sound dynastic marriage, and without overstraining his imagination, or pretending to a passion which he did not feel, there was one obvious choice at hand.

The Spencers of Althorp in Northamptonshire, though nowhere near as rich or distinguished as the Cavendishes, were one of the tiny group of acceptable families towards the top of eighteenth-century Whig society. The family emerged from the peasantry under the early Tudors, were created Earls of Sunderland by Charles I, and when the Third Earl married a daughter of the great Duke of Marlborough, he finally (thanks to the death of Marlborough's son and a special Act of Parliament) inherited Blenheim and the ducal title in addition to his earldom. As a consolation prize at the Duchess's death, his younger brother, John, received the family house at Althorp, Spencer House in London, and the Duchess's former country house, Wimbledon Park in Surrey. The senior branch of Spencers (having changed their name to Spencer-Churchill) have continued to the present day at Blenheim as the Dukes of Marlborough, and the Althorp Spencers were soon on the busy road to rank and ever greater wealth themselves, with the present Earl's daughter now in line to be Queen of England.

This branch of the family was soon closely associated with the Cavendishes. For John Spencer's son – also christened John and known in his day as 'the richest commoner in England' – had the sense to find and wed a solid heiress, Georgiana Poyntz, the daughter of a self-made London businessman (and son of an upholsterer) called Stephen Poyntz. Poyntz *père* was not merely very rich: he was also a man of culture and distinction, having been tutor to the Duke of Cumberland, a Privy Councillor, and friend for many years of the Dukes of Devonshire. The widowed Fourth Duke may even have considered marrying Stephen Poyntz's formidable sister, Louisa, but this came to nothing. However, the families stayed close, particularly after Spencer himself was raised to the peerage in 1761, as Baron Althorp, and given an earldom four years later.

The Spencers had three children, Georgiana, born in 1757, her younger sister Harriet, and a son and heir, known by the courtesy title of Lord Althorp. These children were slightly younger than the Fourth Duke's brood, but they inevitably knew each other. After his father died the young Fifth Duke would occasionally stay at the enormous house Lord Spencer was busily rebuilding at Althorp; and the former Miss Poyntz, now Countess Spencer, would have been less than human had she not thought of marrying off her eldest daughter to the richest duke in England.

It is impossible to know how far she engineered the match. The Countess was a clever woman, energetic, well-read, firmly in touch with what was happening in society, and a great practitioner of workaday Christian piety. She would certainly have been aware of the young Duke's personal deficiencies – and some of his escapades – and is unlikely to have approved of them. On the other hand she was ambitious for her family, her own marriage made for dynastic reasons had proved happy, and the prospect of her daughter as a Duchess must have been irresistible. When twenty-four-year-old William Cavendish asked for the hand of sixteen-year-old Georgiana Spencer, the Spencers gave him their assent – with reservations.

Georgiana was a very giddy girl, a fresh-faced, tall, red-headed creature who was already almost everything the Duke was not – extrovert, emotional and impulsive to a degree. Where he was congenitally bored with life, she was an enthusiast in everything; where he was withdrawn, she loved company, the more the better; where he was the most formal of young aristocrats, she made her rules to suit herself. Frigid eighteenth-century Classicism had come face to face with a foretaste of the Romanticism which was to succeed it – and was formally proposing marriage.

The Spencers, not unreasonably, suggested a delay before the wedding. Georgiana was extremely young, and needed to be schooled in the duties expected of a Duchess, but the Duke, who had always had his way in everything, would not hear of this. Nor would Georgiana; marriage to the Duke must have seemed to offer all the freedom and excitement her exuberant teenage nature craved. The Spencers bowed to the inevitable, and acceded to His Grace's wishes. But there was one subject on which everyone agreed – the need for secrecy. The Duke was a favourite subject for the gossip-mongers, and rumours of the impending match were flourishing. The vulgar throng – which could easily get out of hand in the days before the regular police – must at all costs be avoided.

On Saturday, 4 June 1774 the Duke made a public show of partnering Georgiana at a London ball in honour of the royal birthday. They danced late. Afterwards the Duke returned to Devonshire House, and Georgiana to her parents' house at Wimbledon. Then on Sunday morning she was woken early, told by her mother her wedding day had come, decked in her wedding dress, and driven off in haste to Wimbledon Parish Church where, shortly after matins, and in the presence of a few close members of her family, her uncle, the Rev. Charles Poyntz made Georgiana in the eyes of God and man the wife of William Cavendish and Duchess of Devonshire. Two days later she was seventeen.

Georgiana was undoubtedly in love with her impassive Duke. There is one surviving note he scribbled her during the first months of their marriage, which is typically brief and to the point: 'I am going to sup in St James's Place and have sent you the carriage that you may come in it if you like it.' But on the back, in Georgiana's writing, is the poem she wrote him in reply in her best schoolgirl French:

> *J'aime, je plais, je suis contente,*
> *Tout se joint pour mon bonheur.*
> *Que peut on plus, je suis amante*
> *Et mon Amant me donne son cœur.*
> *Il est si digne de ma tendresse,*
> *Il est mon amant, mon ami.*
> *Loin de lui rien ne m'interesse*
> *Et tout m'enchante auprès de lui.* *

The duke must somehow have aroused himself from his customary torpor to have produced such feelings in his passionate young bride, for the unfortunate Miss Spencer had been generously pensioned off and, for a while at least, discarded. Her child, a girl, was christened Charlotte and the surname she was given made only the most discreet allusion to her paternity: it was 'Williams', a tactful adaptation of her father's Christian name, but at this stage it is unlikely that Georgiana was aware of the child's existence, or her mother's.

As for the Duke, he must have felt that he had done his duty by his family and his position in society by marrying Georgiana. Whether she was as satisfactory sexually as the experienced Miss Spencer was another matter, but dynastically he had made an entirely appropriate match and given the cautious house of Cavendish something it had never really had before – a touch of glamour.

From the beginning of her reign, his radiant young Duchess proceeded to bowl London over with her presence and her personality. A fortnight after she was married she was formally presented, and even that unforgiving antagonist of the Devonshires, George III, had been patently impressed. It was the first of Duchess Georgiana's many public triumphs as she swept into that unfashionable Court, and, although barely seventeen, outshone everybody as she made her curtsy.

What makes her early triumph remarkable is that by the standards of the not over-generous society she moved in, Georgiana was not conventionally beautiful. She was too tall for current tastes, and her face lacked the classical

---

*I love, I please, I'm full of joy,
  All things conspire towards my happiness.
  What else is there to do? For I'm in love,
  And my beloved gives his heart.
  He is so worthy of my tenderness,
  He is my lover and my friend.
  I care for nothing when away from him
  And everything charms me when with him.

refinement of the age. But as Horace Walpole – who was not disposed to flattering the Devonshires – explained, 'The Duchess of Devonshire effaces all without being a beauty; but her youth, figure, flowing good-nature, sense, and lively modesty, and modest familiarity, make her a phenomenon.' Garrick felt no restraint at all in praising her. 'Were I five and twenty,' he told Henry Bate, 'I could go mad about her. As I am past five and fifty, I would only suffer martyrdom for her.'

This was all very flattering, and Georgiana would have been less than human had she not relished her success. But to start with, the success she really wanted was with her husband, and she did her best to live up to that sentimental poem she had written him, particularly when they were together during the first autumn of their marriage up at Chatsworth. It should not have been too difficult in that great house set in its romantic park. Georgiana loved it and the surrounding countryside. She did her social duties, gracing a ball at Chesterfield, and visiting the local poor as her mother would have wished. Soon her parents came up from Althorp, and everyone got on splendidly.

When they departed, Georgiana and her Duke continued their apparently idyllic life together, riding and walking together in the park, and listening to music after dinner – Giardini the celebrated violinist had been specially hired from London, although the Duke, like almost all the Cavendishes, was quite unmusical. He was equally impervious to religion, but here again Georgiana did her energetic best to improve him. 'The Duke of his own accord beg'd Mr Wood to read prayers in the Chapel which has not been done for many years,' she triumphantly told her mother.

But the Duke did not want to be improved. His former way of life had suited him quite well, and when the Devonshires returned to London for the winter, he was soon back at Brooks's every night and breakfasting as usual off cold mackerel when he returned to Devonshire House each morning. Georgiana was increasingly left to make her triumphant progress through society alone.

There was still a chance that these two extraordinarily ill-matched beings might have built a tolerably happy marriage. In the spring of 1775 they were off to Spa for a few weeks holiday with the Spencers. The waters, the cosmopolitan company, and the amusements of that fashionable resort made the stay a great success. The Duchess enjoyed herself; the Duke was positively human; and shortly after her eighteenth birthday Georgiana discovered to her joy that she was pregnant. Summer was spent again at Chatsworth with the Duke, but once again their stay would end in failure. At the beginning of October Lord Spencer, who was now in Paris, wrote his daughter a short consoling letter when he heard she had miscarried. He told her how sorry he was 'that you have fail'd making me a grandfather; however what has been may be again, and you will succeed better another time if you will have a little patience.'

Patience was one virtue Georgiana lacked. 'La Duchesse fait des paroles, mais non pas les enfants,' wrote one observer, as she impetuously set out to enjoy herself as only someone of her energy and position in the beau monde could. With dowdy Queen Caroline wilting on the throne, the role of social queen of London was there for the taking – and Georgiana took it.

It was a fascinating period, for Whiggism, which had previously been the solid political expression of the down-to-earth inheritors of the 1688 Revolution, was in the process of becoming something very different. The so-called 'New Whigs' with Edmund Burke as their philosopher, Charles James Fox their most impressive spokesman, and opposition to the King's treatment of the American colonies their primary concern, were radical, libertarian and passionately ranged against the new power of the Court in a way that would have been unthinkable to an old-school Whig like the Fifth Duke's father.

At the same, time, Whig society itself had developed into something infinitely more refined and fashionable than the masculine, hard-drinking gatherings of the political families who ruled the country under Robert Walpole. It had grown softer, more civilized and more extravagant. Shorn of their old political power, the great Whig families had switched their energies to the undisguised pursuit of pleasure, and briefly attained a sort of civilized perfection which England had never seen before – or since.

'As types of distilled civility,' Harold Nicolson has written, 'the Whig aristocrats of 1770–1830 have never been surpassed or equalled,' and he went on to rejoice that 'before respectability came to dull the skies of England, they were there, like fallow deer, to sparkle in the sun.' Few sparkled more entrancingly and with less regard for drab respectability, than did Georgiana.

She was ideally suited for her role as queen of this frivolous yet highly civilized society. She obviously possessed that subtle combination of style and magnetism which we would classify today as 'star quality', and like most stars she seems to have been slightly larger than life when encountered face to face; Elizabeth Sheridan remarked that, whenever the Duchess entered a room, there seemed 'a little too much of her' as if she were larger than 'full length'. While not an intellectual, she had inherited sufficient of the Poyntz intelligence to match the conversation of a Sheridan or Fox and to soften up the 'cynical moroseness' of the aged Dr Johnson when he came up to Chatsworth. 'He din'd here,' she reported, 'and does not shine quite so much in eating as in conversing, for he eat much and nastily.' She even visited Henry Cavendish at Clapham, until her husband forbade her with the unanswerable argument, 'He is not a gentleman – he works.' She was a loyal friend, with an insatiable appetite for human beings; she had wit, a sometimes excessive sense of fun, and she adored the social whirl. Above all, she had that slightly suspect but unstoppable quality – outrageous charm. For a while it must have seemed that she could get away with almost anything.

Her one potential rival, Lady Melbourne, had the sense to seek her friendship and, once Georgiana was really in her social stride, her husband never stood a chance. It was as if she had become the Duke herself and recreated the power of the Devonshires in her female image. The real influence of the Devonshires was no longer seriously political but social, and it belonged to her.

She quietly took over Devonshire House and made it something it had never been since William Kent rebuilt it for the Third Duke after the First Duke's original building was destroyed by fire in 1733 – the most fashionable and influential great house in London. Burlington House, nearby, had been leased off by the Fifth Duke to his brother-in-law, the Duke of Portland, and although there is no evidence of any break between them, the two dukes never seem to have bothered to communicate. But then, the Fifth Duke's *forte* never had been communication, and the more sociable his wife became, the more withdrawn he appeared. In London he was most at home at Almack's or Brooks's, where he could gamble or pronounce on Shakespeare or his favourite Latin authors with a group of ever-faithful cronies who included Fox, Fitzgerald, the poetry-loving Secretary of State for War, and the melancholy James 'Fish' Craufurd.

But in Devonshire House, with its sumptuous Kent reception rooms, its spacious gardens and its high wall guarding it from any danger of the mob outside, there 'flowered the female aspect of Whiggism. . . . Here in the flesh was the exquisite eighteenth-century world of Gainsborough, all flowing elegance and melting glances and shifting silken colour.' For the house was rapidly becoming a unique institution, part Georgiana's private salon, part fashionable show-place for the *ton*, and partly too the effective headquarters of the Foxite Whigs, who had adopted the colours of General Washington's army to show their support for the American Revolution, and were intriguing endlessly but ineffectually for power themselves. Although the most unlikely of revolutionaries, the Fifth Duke – both as a friend of Fox and as hereditary grand master of the Whigs – had roused himself to give the cause his vague but invaluable support. Politically Georgiana was just as vague, but more passionately involved, and all her social influence was at Charles James Fox's beck and call. It was a strange phenomenon, this uncomfortable combination of high fashion, great wealth and pseudo-revolutionary politics, and the earliest example history offers of what Tom Wolfe would one day scathingly describe as 'radical chic'. It reached its height, of course, in the notorious incident of the 1784 Westminster election, when Georgiana and her sister – by then Lady Bessborough – campaigned in all their finery for Fox, and were said to have helped him win the seat by kissing the butchers of Long Acre in exchange for votes.

One result of Georgiana's notoriety was that she inevitably became the butt of endless gossip, much of it malicious. With her flowing dresses and immense coiffure – she once startled London by wearing an ostrich plume four feet high – she was out to attract attention. And she got it, especially from the caricaturists in the hostile press. But what was the truth about her private life? Was it really as outrageous as the gossip-mongers claimed, or as carefree and as brilliant as its surface would suggest? What did go on behind the elaborate wrought-iron gates of Devonshire House when the balls were over and the sparkling conversation ceased?

It was a question which fascinated London for, scandal apart, the Devonshires would go on playing an important and complicated role in the socio-political life of London for over thirty years. Much of the evidence was hushed up at the time, and more of it carefully destroyed by later members of the family, but looking back at what he called the 'private history' of Devonshire House during Georgiana's reign, the diarist, Charles Greville, who had talked to most of the survivors, summed it up as follows. It was, he wrote 'very curious and amusing as a scandalous chronicle, an exhibition of vice in its most attractive form, full of grace, dignity and splendour, but I fancy full of misery and sorrow also.' To understand the truth of this, one must return to the source of most of the 'misery and sorrow', that strangely unsatisfactory marriage between Georgiana and her husband.

Early in 1777, barely a year after Georgiana's miscarriage, an article appeared in the lively *Town and Country Magazine* about the long-standing friendship between 'the D—e of D—e and Miss C—e S—r'. It went on to describe how the D—e had 'married a nobleman's daughter, a universal toast, still in her teens, who gives the *ton* wherever she goes,' but added that he was still fond of his 'antiquated' mistress. 'There is a caprice in mankind, it is true . . . but that the blooming, the blythe, the beautiful D— should be neglected for C— S—r really is astonishing.'

By now Georgiana was almost certainly aware of the existence of Charlotte and her child. She may even have known the Duke still visited her, and may not particularly have cared. But for someone in Georgiana's position, it must have been exasperating, to say the least, to have had her husband's continuing affair proclaimed in public.

As she was so much in the public eye herself by now, there was little she could do. (She may even have been made pregnant by the Duke again around the time the article appeared, but if so she rapidly miscarried yet again.) She and the Duke went off to Chatsworth for the summer, and appearances were rigidly maintained. The following year, when war was declared with France and the Duke, as Lord Lieutenant, heroically led the Derbyshire militia to Kent, the Duchess accompanied him as far as Tunbridge Wells. And while the Duke prepared to face the French, the Duchess planned her very feminine revenge on Charlotte Spencer.

Fanny Burney's anonymous novel, *Evelina*, had just appeared and was enjoying great success; Georgiana, with time heavy on her hands away from the joys of London, decided to copy her example, and with typical impetuosity dashed off a novel of her own in eight weeks flat. It was called *The Sylph*. She sent it to Fanny Burney's publisher, and it appeared anonymously in 1779 to considerable interest and acclaim. For, despite the absence of an author from the title-page, it was a fairly open secret who had written it. The main characters were all too easy to identify, the dialogue – and there was a lot of it – was obviously culled from life, and the subject-matter, for a close, scandal-loving society such as London now possessed, was irresistible. Twaddle it may have been, but *The Sylph* was *authentic* twaddle, for during her eight creative weeks in Kent, Georgiana had poured out her heart on all the unspeakable subjects that obsessed her – marriage, husband, friends and, most of all, herself. Soon *The Sylph* was being advertised alongside *Evelina*, and Fanny Burney, much to her annoyance, was being credited with its authorship.

What makes the book absorbing reading even now is the sense one has of someone compulsively lifting up the lid of a tightly battened-down society, and showing what is really underneath. It may not be completely true, it was probably not entirely fair, but *The Sylph* was undoubtedly what Georgiana *felt* about herself and the brilliant world she lived in.

She composed it, according to the model of the day, in the form of a series of intimate letters, written by and to her ingenuous young heroine Julia, who, exactly like Georgiana, came from the country at sweet seventeen to marry a rich man of fashion, Sir William Stanley. And the first sight we have of her, on the eve of marriage, is exactly that of the freshly-wed Georgiana who wrote her William that effusive little poem in French.

All my hopes are that I may acquit myself so as to gain the approbation of my husband. Husband! What a sound has that when pronounced by a girl barely seventeen . . . and one whose knowledge of the world is purely speculative.

She accepts that it is her duty 'to comply with everything he judges proper to make me what he chuses' and although with her youth and beauty, Julia/ Georgiana is soon 'the whim of the day', all that she really longs for is her husband's adoration. At a ball, 'I saw [his] eyes were on me the whole time; but I cannot flatter myself so far as to say that they were the looks of love; they seemed to be rather the eyes of scrutiny, which were on the watch, yet afraid they should see something unpleasing.'

To please her husband, she endures 'the disorder of this great town, and with blushes I write, have too frequently joined in some of its extravagances and follies.' These include gambling, which she resorts to when she feels her husband is bored with her, although she admits that 'the gloomy pallidness of the losing gamester ill accords with female delicacy'. As for her husband's gaming, 'the more he loses the more impetuous and eager he is to play'.

But her chief complaint against her husband is the lack of all romantic love.

My person still invites his caresses . . . but for the softer sentiments of the soul . . . that ineffable tenderness which depends not on the tincture of the skin . . . of that, alas, he has no idea. A voluptuary in love, he professes not that delicacy which refines its joys. He is all passion; sentiment is left out of the catalogue.

He is unfaithful to her, and worse still, seems unconcerned when one of his friends attempts to make love to her. Very well, she concludes, 'if *he* is indifferent about my morals and my well-being in life, it will more absolutely become my business to take care of myself.'

In Julia's case this did not mean a lover – nor is there any evidence that it did for Georgiana at this time in her career. Both made a point of staying faithful to the unromantic husband whose embraces they despised, for neither as yet had done her duty, which was to produce an heir. But the Duchess, like her heroine was proclaiming social independence; like Julia, it had become her business to 'take care of herself'. As for marriage, Julia/Georgiana writes, 'I have tasted of the fruit, and have found it bitter to the palate and corroding to the heart.'

At the conclusion of the book, Georgiana solves her heroine's problems by having her husband kill himself, but in her own case there was no such convenient way out. Her marriage was unhappy, but appearances had to be maintained. She had poured her heart out in *The Sylph*; he gave no sign of having read it. And in London their separate 'dissipated' lives continued; so did Georgiana's gambling – so did her losses. In the end the Duke would generally pay, and if she thought he would refuse, she could always borrow.

But despite the note of petulant despair Georgiana sounded in her book, her marriage was to find a curious salvation. It was more novelettish than anything she wrote, and it was what Greville was referring to when the spoke of 'vice in its most attractive form'. For it began with the appearance on the scene of a feline, highly intelligent adventuress called Elizabeth Foster. Deserted by her drunken Irish husband, she was an object of compassion. The Duke and Duchess were at Bath when they met her in the spring of 1782, and both, in their different ways, were powerfully attracted to her.

For Lady Elizabeth of the soulful eyes and the deceptive air of fragile femininity was a creature of considerable allure. She was twenty-four, the same age as Georgiana, and her father, Frederick Hervey, 'the Earl-Bishop', was one of the great eccentrics of the eighteenth century. Son of the notorious Lord Hervey, who was hated and immortalized by Pope in the character of 'Sporus', he became Bishop of Derry, inherited the rich Earldom of Bristol when his elder brother died, and spent so much time travelling in splendour on the Continent that he is still remembered by the countless 'Hotels Bristol' named after him. He had little time for flock or family; Elizabeth, deprived of her children and unsupported by her husband, needed help. The Duchess and the Duke, both bored with one another, were delighted to supply it.

She was one interest they could share, an object for their mutual kindness, and soon they had adopted her. From Bath they went on to Plympton for the summer and they got on wonderfully, for the ill-matched couple had become the perfect threesome; the Duke no longer bored, the Duchess with the confidante she wanted, and pitiful Elizabeth in the niche she needed. She was a sort of human catalyst, creating harmony and happiness where none had been before. Humour had never been the Duke's strong suit, but he was soon laughing when Elizabeth called the Duchess 'Mrs Rat'. He became 'Canis', because of the way he loved his dogs, and Elizabeth, with that worrying cough of hers, was christened 'Racky'. 'Canis', 'Mrs Rat' and 'Racky' they would remain until the end.

Another of the Duke's deficiencies, according to *The Sylph*, had always been his lack of soft romantic feeling, which had almost ruined his marriage. Here again Elizabeth's influence was felt. She was a romantic heroine made flesh – at least on the surface – all yielding sentiment and high-flown feeling, and in the evenings she would read to her friends from two books she particularly enjoyed, Laclos's immensely daring novel of refined seduction, *Les Liaisons Dangereuses*, and that great gospel of Romanticism, Rousseau's *Confessions*.

This must all have immeasurably enriched what would otherwise have been for both the Duchess and the Duke a basic but very necessary sexual chore. For the fact was that, miscarriages and misadventures notwithstanding, it had become essential to produce an heir. The Duke's younger brother, Lord George Cavendish, was about to become a father, and should Georgiana continue childless, the Dukedom and the Devonshire possessions might well pass down to brother George's family.*

So the labours of conception had to go ahead. A fashionable expert in such matters, the physician Dr Moore, was consulted for medical advice. But the gentle influence of Lady Elizabeth was probably more telling. Thanks to Rousseau, thanks to her personal example, she was beginning to complete the Fifth Duke's sentimental education – and probably Georgiana's too. Georgiana had previously longed for 'the softer sentiments of the soul' along with the Duke's perfunctory caresses. After a summer spent with Rousseau and Elizabeth he could hardly continue to forget them. He was presumably still 'all passion' making love, but had no excuse if sentiment was now 'left out of the catalogue'.

Certainly Elizabeth, who knew what was at stake, was an interested party to these serious endeavours, and gave her 'brother' Canis and dear 'Mrs Rat' sisterly encouragement. Success ensued. By the end of that summer by the sea at Plympton, Mrs Rat was well and truly pregnant, and the three devoted friends were closer now than ever, united by the unborn child which all three in their very different ways had helped produce. Inevitably they returned to Devonshire House together, for Lady Elizabeth's self-appointed task was to see Georgiana through the perilous early stages of her pregnancy.

But much as the Devonshires both loved her, she could not stay there for ever; and as a way of keeping her in the family, and silencing potential gossip, it was decided to send her on an extended tour of Europe as well-paid governess to another source of possible embarrassment during Georgiana's pregnancy – the Duke's eight-year-old illegitimate daughter, Charlotte Williams. The pair left for Nice at the end of 1782, and an extraordinarily emotional correspondence between Georgiana and her 'Dearest, dearest Bess', began.

At this stage it is unlikely, although not impossible, that Bess and the Duke were lovers. It is even more unlikely – and this too was rumoured at the time – that Bess and Georgiana were in the throes of some lesbian crush on one another. For up to now the overriding purpose of all three participants had been the procreation of an heir; once it seemed possible, the floodgates of 'feeling' and emotion opened, particularly for Georgiana, and gratitude and overwhelming sentiment came gushing forth.

'Dearest ever ever dearest Love,' she wrote to Bess who by the spring of 1783 had moved on to Italy, 'why have I no letters from you? I cannot express nor describe the anxiety I feel from it, nor how my peace depends on everything that concerns you . . . how necessary you are to my heart.'

This sort of feeling reached its height in July when Georgiana successfully gave birth – to a healthy daughter who was christened Georgiana Dorothy. It was still not the necessary heir to the dukedom, but sons could follow now that Georgiana had proved herself capable of motherhood. This was a triumph for the three of them to share, just as they would share the child, and

---

*Lord George Cavendish had not done badly already. Thanks to a sound Cavendish-style marriage to the heiress Betty Compton, he had gained extensive lands at Eastbourne for his family, and would inherit Henry Cavendish's great fortune on the scientist's death.

Mrs Rat could hardly wait to see her wise sister Racky and thank her properly. 'You have saved your brother Canis and dear Canis's child,' she told her.

The Devonshires themselves were on better terms than they had ever been, but they needed to be patient before being reunited with their 'sister'. For Bess was travelling Europe, at the Duke's expense, with almost as much gusto as the old Earl-Bishop, and the vague presence of nervous, forgettable little Charlotte Williams never did anything to cramp her style. From Turin she went down to Rome and Naples, flirted a little, saw Pompeii, stayed some time in Switzerland on her journey home, had Gibbon on his plump knees in adoration before her in Lausanne, and she was not to see 'her' child, Georgiana Dorothy, until the summer of 1784, when she arrived at Chatsworth.

It was a golden memorable summer. Chatsworth was full of fascinating guests, and Georgiana wanted Bess to see the private apartments she and Canis had been having redecorated in the latest French fashion. For they had both been influenced by current trends to make the great country house a place of pleasure. Thanks to new turnpike roads, Chatsworth was no longer so inaccessible from London, and the Duke had nearly completed an interesting piece of fashionable speculative building on his own account, the construction of a magnificent new crescent, to designs by Carr of York, at the small resort of Buxton, eighteen miles from Chatsworth. The medicinal waters had been famous there since Tudor times, and with the splendid crescent and an elegant new pump-room, there seemed a chance that Buxton might even one day rival Bath.

With so much to see and to enjoy Georgiana wrote of her happiness 'that my dearest loveliest friend and the man whom I love so much and to whom I owe everything, are united like brother and sister.' For Bess's long absence had in no way changed their friendship: in Derbyshire, then back in London at Devonshire House, they were as close as they had ever been at Plympton. Once more the time had come for 'Mrs Rat' to attempt the production of a Cavendish heir, and by Christmas she was pregnant. But there was one important difference from the carefree time two years before beside the sea; dearest 'Racky' was expecting too. And the Duke, for once manifesting more 'spring' than 'sense', was responsible for both almost simultaneous conceptions.

It was now, as this curious *ménage à trois* descended – or ascended – from the realms of sentiment to uncomfortable reality, that unsuspected qualities in the main participants started to appear. This happened first with Bess. She had already made arrangements to winter on the Continent and, undeterred and uncomplaining, she set out for France and then for Italy, alone. As before, the Duke was paying for her travels, but they could not write freely to each other, and this wilting, soft, romantic creature showed extraordinary toughness as she concealed her condition from her friends, stayed on at Naples through the summer, resolutely refused to blame the Duke for what had happened – 'his nature is noble, tender, honourable and affectionate' she wrote in her diary. 'Passion has led us both away' – and in early August 1735, in the house of a backstreet accoucheur outside Salerno, Bess produced yet one more healthy daughter for the Duke.

She was to be called Caroline St Jules, and her mother showed remarkable efficiency in getting her temporarily adopted, before stepping back herself into the swing of Neapolitan society. Georgiana's brother – he had now inherited the Earldom – and his disapproving wife were there, but although they met and inevitably discussed dearest Georgiana, neither Spencer got a hint of what had happened. Georgiana was missing her friend badly now: 'I am terribly in want of you here, Mrs Bess,' she wrote to her from Devonshire House; and two weeks after 'Racky' bore 'Canis' a daughter in Salerno, 'Mrs Rat' in London, did the same. The child was christened Harriet.

Throughout this period the Duke was being very wary in his letters to his far-off mistress. 'I am very much surpriz'd and very impatient at not having heard from you upon a subject I expected to have heard something about by this time [i.e. her confinement],' he wrote at the end of August. With a touch of the old Cavendish caution, he went on to advise her not to use thin paper which anyone could read from the outside. 'For the future in your letters to me and the Rat, you had better put all the secrets you can think of into some one, and let the generality of them contain nothing that you would not mind being seen.'

This letter makes it clear that Georgiana was certainly in on Bess's guilty secret before Caroline St Jules was born, and did not outwardly object. As for the 'wintry' undemonstrative Duke, he was now patently in love – with Bess. Since his wife and his mistress still adored each other as sentimentally as ever, there must have seemed no reason to prevent them all living sensibly and happily together as they had always said they would – except for the power of outside gossip. This still concerned the Duke. Also, his health was far from good. He had recently been consulting the Wedgwood family's famous doctor, the great Erasmus Darwin, and his prognosis goes some way towards explaining the Duke's lethargy and failure to register emotion.

My Lord Duke,

In some constitutions this inflammation of the liver, occasion'd originally by drinking much spirituous or fermented liquor, is removed upon the joints, and causes the gout. . . . In other constitutions it is removed upon the face, and either a number of pustules are produced, called *gutta rosacea* – or a permanent redness, as was the case with Your Grace. I am of the opinion that the use of the solution of sugar of lead was the remote cause of the disability of the muscles of your face . . .

The Duke was not yet forty but, as with so many of these eighteenth-century 'fallow deer', the life he lived had almost wrecked his constitution. (Darwin's advice was 'calomel, regular stools, and about half the quantity of spirituous liquors you have been used to.') Georgiana's health was also far from good: she had already had trouble with her eyes, and her liver too was seriously at risk.

The one member of the trio whose health remained invincible was Bess, and she was the one with all the energy. She must have been immensely resolute and tough to have coped with the squalor and worry of her baby's birth, and to have acted as she knew she must. To keep the gossips off the scent she put the baby out to nurse and spent a year travelling Italy and Spain before it was considered safe for her to leave Caroline with a family in Toulon and return to England. In July 1785, in the freshly gilded privacy of Chatsworth, the trio was rapturously reunited.

It is interesting that, with her return, all the practical problems there must have been about finally setting up a regular *ménage à trois* appear suddenly to vanish. The Duke, previously so concerned about appearances, becomes positively brazen as he takes both his women back to Devonshire House. Both have a call on his attentions, Bess because he is physically in love with her, and Georgiana because she and she alone can still produce an heir. He is quite happy with this supremely rational arrangement. So is Bess, since she is firmly in command. And so in theory is Georgiana. She has her 'dearest Mrs Bess' back with her at last. Canis is content, and there seems no reason why all his children, legitimate and illegitimate alike, should not soon come beneath the loving roof of Devonshire House. After all, there is wealth and room for all of them, and if gossip starts, why worry when they know they love each other?

But however rational a *ménage à trois* may seem, and however much its members talk of mutual love, it is actually a very difficult arrangement to maintain. There is bound to be a dominating partner; there is almost certain to be jealousy; one member will inevitably be left out in the cold, and with the personalities involved at Devonshire House, this was unlikely to be Bess.

Georgiana was described by her discerning fellow-novelist Miss Burney around this time. 'She seems by nature to possess the highest animal spirits, but she appeared to me not happy. I thought she looked oppressed within, though there is a native cheerfulness about her which I fancy scarce ever deserts her.' That was perceptive, for by now Georgiana was suffering from chronic headaches, was regularly resorting to sleeping draughts and her looks were going. She 'verges fast to a coarseness' noted her former admirer, Horace Walpole.

Above all it was now that she succumbed entirely to the most insidious disease of all – compulsive gambling. Everybody around her gambled; even that tiresome old paragon, her mother, Countess Spencer guiltily admitted her addiction – to which Georgiana answered fatalistically:

> You talk of the bad example you have set me . . . and there I do assure you it is innate, for I remember playing from seven in the morning till eight at night at Lansquenet with old Mrs Newton when I was nine years old and sent to the King's Road for the measles.

One wonders why these eighteenth-century aristocrats gambled so compulsively. Was it to give some meaning to the vast wealth they had never earned? Was it a substitute for action in a rich world otherwise devoid of risk? Or had the whole British ruling class become bored stiff with the Whig stability which guaranteed that, whatever happened elsewhere in society, the nobility would always win?

Sheer boredom undoubtedly played a large part in the Fifth Duke's gambling, but in Georgiana's case it fails to fit the facts. She may have learned to gamble as a child, and later, as *The Sylph* suggests, increased her gambling simply to match and even to spite her husband. But as the acknowledged 'queen' of the most interesting society London has ever known, it is not possible that she was bored.

Her gambling steadily increased once Bess was on the scene. When Georgiana Dorothy was born, Walpole remarked that the Duchess would probably 'stuff her poor babe into her knotting-bag when she wants to play at macao, and forget it'. And the more her gambling grew the more disastrously her losses mounted. Georgiana was clearly one of that breed of self-destructive gamblers who play subconsciously to lose, and her losses were enormous. The pattern always seemed to be the same: a splurge of desperate gambling which would never end until she had lost disastrously; then penitence and several days of misery during which she would make almost any promises to pay off her debts; and when she had the money it would invariably go, not on repayment, but on a further bout of gambling.

The Duke repaid her early debts but soon they had reached the point where she could not confess them to him. The Duke of Bedford discreetly lent her £6,000 on condition that she set aside £300 a year to repay the money. (She did nothing of the kind and he finally waived the debt.) Most of her friends helped out at one time or another, and she often tapped her mother. One confession of her latest debts led Lady Spencer, who was becoming worried for her daughter's health, to write,

For God's sake try to compose yourself. I am terrified lest the perpetual hurry of your spirits, and the medicines you take to obtain a false tranquillity should injure you. . . . Why will you not say fairly: – I have led a wild and scrambling life that disagrees with me. I have lost more money than I can afford. I will turn over a new leaf and lead a quiet sober life from this moment, as I am sure if I do not I shall hurt myself or my child . . .

But a 'new leaf' was impossible by now, and Georgiana's 'wild and scrambling life' started to accelerate – and with it the attendant misery.

It can be no coincidence that this was happening as Bess continued to establish herself as the essential element in the Devonshire House *ménage*. With her abounding health and sense of purpose, she had the strength the others lacked, and she could offer what they needed – love. Through love she had the gouty, often fuddled, Duke totally beneath her thumb, and could persuade him to brazen out the situation as he would have never dared do on his own account. Through love she had Georgiana utterly dependent on her too. But dependence is not necessarily happiness, and Georgiana's actual situation must have been profoundly wretched underneath its surface gaiety.

For she had always to suppress emotions which a wife must inevitably have felt in such a situation. A cold unfeeling woman might have managed it – just –

but Georgiana as we know was 'natural', impetuous and emotional to a degree. And if for a moment she allowed such feelings to emerge, she was in danger, as she knew, of losing everything: husband, children, 'dearest Bess' and the whole world that circled round her. Small wonder that she sought relief in the nightly soporific of the gaming-table, or that her health and looks began to decline.

Bess, on the other hand, was firmly in command by now and practically invulnerable. Old Lady Spencer knew what was going on and loathed her, but she was no real threat. Bess made a token show of placating her; when it failed, she ignored her. Two years later, in 1786, she was once more pregnant by the Duke, and Georgiana significantly was not. Not even Bess could risk having the child in London, but this time there was no question of a back-street birth in Italy. Instead, with Bess' blessing, the Duke sent her with his doctor to Rouen for her lying-in. And there, at last, in May 1787, the Fifth Duke became the father of a son but not, alas, an heir. The child was called Augustus William and with an extra touch of daring the Duke decided he should have the surname Clifford, the title of the famous barony he had inherited from his mother.

The birth was the signal for an ever-mounting round of gambling from Georgiana until, by 1789, her known debts were estimated at £60,000, and the financial muddle steadily increasing. She was borrowing from every imaginable source by now – Louis XVI's former minister of finance, Calonne, the French banker Perregaux, London money-lenders, and the brother of her maid, Anne Scafe. By playing on the snobbery and susceptibility of the banker Thomas Coutts, she even vamped unsecured loans from that most unlikely source. But her gambling still went on, and her losses grew, despite her borrowing. The Duke, of course, could easily have paid, but Georgina had given him her word against further borrowing at interest and dared not tell him she had broken it. She felt immensely guilty for, on top of everything, she now believed, having no real knowledge of the family resources, that she had all but bankrupted the Devonshires. Her only source of consolation lay in Bess, to whom she confessed everything. Bess offered understanding, and promised to use her influence upon the Duke. But nothing happened, and Georgiana was soon pinning all her hopes on one last desperate throw – providing the Duke with his longed-for heir at last.

Ironically Bess' interests were involved in this as well, for should disaster overtake her friend, it would be impossible for Bess to stay on at Devonshire House as the Duke's openly acknowledged mistress. As Georgiana's close friend and companion, Bess' presence in the household was permissible. Without her, according to the standards of her age, it would become impossible. Also the Duke himself, however impatient he was becoming over his wife's gambling and her deceptions over money – and however much he must have preferred Bess's trim figure to Georgiana's increasingly blowsy body – still needed her for that ever-present, all-important purpose of creating the future Sixth Duke of Devonshire. In London, with its distractions and the couple's deteriorating health, this was unlikely to occur. During the first year of their marriage they had enjoyed that healthy holiday at Spa and had returned refreshed and with Georgiana pregnant. Perhaps it would work again.

In June of 1789 – a fateful year in European history – the Devonshires decamped *en masse* from Dover. This time they planned a lengthy visit and headed first for Paris where the Duke and Bess's daughter, Caroline St Jules, now four years old, was living with a family called Nagel. Apart from seeing her – and tactfully and profitably introducing two of Thomas Coutts' daughters to smart French society – Georgiana had long intended to visit Queen Marie Antoinette at Versailles; for the Queen of France was a family friend of the Spencers, and had always taken a great interest in Georgiana as the acknowledged 'queen' of fashionable London.

By a strange quirk of history, the arrival of the Devonshires at Versailles was to offer the hereditary standard-bearer of the English Revolution a chance to witness the dramatic start of its counterpart in France. The Devonshires were actually at the Palace when the populace staged their historic march from Paris and forced themselves past the guards and into the outraged presence of the King; and a few weeks afterwards the ducal pair and Bess were back in Paris as the Revolution gathered strength. With an unrivalled show of English phlegm and insularity, they refused to be concerned.

The court ceremonial at Versailles went on as before, and they seem to have enjoyed their conversations with the royal family. In Paris the mob was tiresome, but it took more than the cat-calls of the common people to distract Georgiana from her pleasure at being back in Paris – besides, as enlightened Whigs, the Devonshires had a natural sympathy for the liberties of the common people, and however charming fat, bald Marie Antoinette might be, the French monarchy could only be improved by a few of those precious principles of 1688. 'I confess I amuse myself,' Georgiana wrote early in July from Paris, 'and have been well the whole time I have been here.' A few days later the Bastille fell.

Back in England Charles James Fox exulted: 'How much the greatest event it is that ever happened in the world, and how much the best!' Georgiana and the Duke probably agreed, but sensibly kept their comments to themselves, and it was only the realistic Bess who foresaw trouble when she saw the arms of noblemen being obliterated from their carriages, and heard the mob threatening to dig the graves of the aristocracy. But the Devonshires had more important matters to attend to and, while the mob was starting to demolish the Bastille, they were on their way to Spa with the Cavendish succession now at stake – and along with this the salvation of Georgiana's debts.

Amazingly they managed it. The Duke and the waters did their work. By the end of August, to everybody's joy, Georgiana was with child; and this time, significantly, Elizabeth was not. With the future of the Dukedom in the balance now, no one could risk any muddles or suspicions over whose child was whose when it was born.

What does seem a little odd is that, with their mission more or less accomplished, the trio did not now return to the comfort and security of England. The answer probably lies in the presence in Paris of Caroline St

Jules; it was inopportune to bring her back with them, but Bess and the Duke were both concerned about her, and wanted to be near her as the Revolution spread. Also Georgiana must have known that in France she was safe from the pressure of her creditors. They were becoming increasingly impatient for their money – particularly Thomas Coutts who was showing all the symptoms of a worried banker with a wildly ill-advised investment.

Georgiana flattered the old usurer quite shamelessly in her answers to his frantic letters. He was her 'second father', she his 'ever affectionate eldest daughter', and she knew exactly how to use promises for the social advancement of his daughters if he would only bear with her. Soon she would give the Duke his heir, and *then* she would be in a position to extract the money that was needed.

She also made the most of the tendency she had always had to miscarry during pregnancy, and used this as an argument to anyone who showed the slightest sign of inquiring about her debts – even the Duke. In the spring of 1790 he had made a brief return to London to attend to his affairs, and must have learned something about the state of his wife's finances, for he wrote to her demanding some sort of explanation. Her reply was masterly:

> Why do you force me, my dear Ca, to an avowal to you which agitates me beyond measure and which is not necessary now. Could I tell you, pay this for me, I owe no more, I should not hestitate to expose myself to your reproof. But as I am still further involved, I dread the opening of an explanation I should not dare encounter in my present situation.

With Georgiana playing up the dangers of any 'agitation' to her unborn child, there could be no question of risking the dangerous crossing back to England. Instead the Devonshire *ménage* installed itself in ever greater state and size in Brussels to await the great event. The Devonshires' two daughters, Georgiana Dorothy and Harriet, arrived with their governess, Miss Trimmer, and a flurry of footmen. Then came Georgiana's sister and brother-in-law, the Duncannons. Doctors and more servants followed, and finally the deeply disapproving Dowager Lady Spencer overcame her feelings against Bess to join the merry throng.

Georgiana's most important hour had almost come, and as a lifelong gambler she must have appreciated the high stakes she was playing for. At thirty-two she knew her looks and health were fading fast, and she was unlikely to get another chance like this. Another daughter or a still-born child would ruin her. She had to give the Duke his heir – or founder. Even Bess's nerve was shaken. 'I can't express to you how my courage fails me as the time draws near,' she admitted. But Georgiana was indomitable – even when a last-minute panic among the Devonshire advisers over the danger of revolution in the Belgian capital made the whole entourage up sticks and trundle back to Paris. 'The news is that Paris and round it is quiet,' wrote Anne Scafe in the journal she was keeping.

Just in time they reached the *hôtel* of their friend, the Marquis de Boulain-villiers, at Passy; and it was there on 21 May 1790, that Georgiana's greatest gamble finally paid off, and she produced the child everyone was waiting for. It was healthy, legitimate, and male. The Fifth Duke had an heir who would one day inherit his possessions and his titles; and the Duchess, counting on his gratitude, had a hope of finally persuading him to pay her debts. As Ann Scafe recorded, as a witness of the birth: 'there never was a more welcome child.'

The only slight blot on the whole successful undertaking was that already there were rumours that the new Lord Hartington was in fact a changeling, and that either Georgiana had feigned the entire pregnancy, or that, having once more given birth to a girl, she had had it switched to a male child conveniently produced by Bess. The strange surroundings of the birth of so great an heir naturally encouraged such suspicions, but there was not the faintest possibility that they were true. This time Bess had emphatically *not* been pregnant by the Duke simultaneously with Georgiana, and there were several well-recorded eye-witness accounts of the actual birth, including one only recently discovered by Brian Masters, in a letter written by Georgiana's doctor, Richard Croft. All agree that Georgiana definitely did produce a boy. But despite this, the rumours would persist for many years, even casting a certain furtive doubt upon the Sixth Duke's right to his inheritance.

Not that this seemed to matter at the time and, in August 1790, Georgiana, Bess and the Duke triumphantly returned to London with their family. 'The family is all arrived safe here,' wrote Anne Scafe at Devonshire House. 'Many hearts are made glad a young heir being brought home. He is three months old – a fine strong healthy child. The Duchess suckles him and is quite well.'

All should have ended happily, but the private troubles of the Devonshires were still far from over. Georgiana's sister, Harriet, was seriously ill; there was further trouble between Bess and old Lady Spencer; and the Duke was not proving as amenable as Thomas Coutts had hoped over repaying his wife's unsecured debts. These worries, coupled with the fact that she had finally done her duty by the Duke by producing an heir, must have led the impulsive Duchess to her greatest blunder yet. Sometime in the spring of 1791 she became pregnant yet again – but not by the Duke. Her lover was the clever, uncomfortably good-looking twenty-seven-year-old Whig politician, Charles Grey. She was seven years his senior; he had long professed his adoration, and for once in her lifetime, Georgiana was emotionally and physically in love.

This probably explains why things became so badly bungled. The cool young Mr Grey, early adoration rapidly forgotten, refused to endanger his political career by becoming too openly involved; Georgiana made no attempt to make the Duke believe the child was his, and very soon the news leaked out. Devonshire House was buzzing with the drama, the Duke inevitably discovered and, his own past behaviour notwithstanding, he was beside himself with honest anger.

Lechers rarely make good cuckolds, and the Duke, in a fit of ill-advised and quite untypical firmness, insisted Georgiana leave her children and depart almost instantly abroad. Here he blundered, for this not only put him in the wrong, but deprived him of the woman he really loved – Bess. She could not stay alone with him without Georgiana as her social pretext, and besides she felt her loyalty go out to her friend in all her troubles. So did the other women in the family, most of whom inevitably closed ranks against the Duke. That October, when Georgiana set off for the South of France, she travelled with a small platoon of supportive females – her mother, her convalescent sister, Harriet Duncannon (soon to be Lady Bessborough when her husband inherited the title) the Duncannon daughter, Caroline Ponsonby, Caroline St Jules – and Bess.

Back in England, the Duke drank more than usual, nursed his considerable sense of grievance, and tried to pluck up courage to insist upon a permanent separation from his erring wife. Their two daughters, Georgiana and Harriet, were devotedly looked after by Miss Trimmer. Charles Grey, embarked upon the political career that would one day lead him to the premiership, wrote very non-commital letters to his distant Duchess.

It was all slightly sad and totally absurd, for the Duke must have known a permanent separation was impossible. Without Georgiana he could not have Bess, and he would inevitably be forced to surrender in the end. But first Georgiana must be made to suffer – and suffer she did with all the strength of her dramatic nature in the gentle surroundings of the South of France. For Georgiana was a great practitioner of pathos, and her letters now are a rich blend of self-pity and remorse; her sentimental masterpiece was the letter penned *in blood* to her infant son, Lord Hartington, in January 1792, on the eve of giving birth. Should she die in childbed, it was her wish he be given it when he was eight. The risk of this was not excessive. She and her entourage had picked the pleasant city of Montpellier for her lying-in. Montpellier was famous for its doctors, and despite her miscarriages, Georgiana had never had any undue complications with her actual confinements. But, dipping her pen in her own life-blood, she wrote:

My Dear Little Boy,

As soon as you are old enough to understand, this letter it will be given to you; it contains the only present I can make you – my blessing, written in my blood. The book that will be also given you is a memorandum of me you must ever keep. Alas, I am gone before you could know me, but I lov'd you, I nurs'd you nine months at my breast. I love you dearly. For my sake observe my last wishes. Be obedient to your dear Papa and Grandmama; consult them and obey them in all things. Be very kind to your sisters. Join with your dear Papa, when you can, in increasing their fortunes, and if you have the misfortune to lose your dear Papa, double your dear sisters fortunes at least. Love always dear Lady Elizabeth and Caroline [St Jules]. Be kind to all your cousins, especially the Ponsonbys. Make piety your chief study, never despise religion, never break your word, never betray a secret, never tell a lie. God bless you, my dear child, oh, how dearly would I wish again to see your beloved face, and to press you to my wretched bosom. God bless you, my dear little boy,

Your poor mother, G. Devonshire.

Shortly afterwards, and with a minimum of trouble, Georgiana was delivered of a daughter, who was given the name Eliza Courtney, (Courtney was a Poyntz family name) and swiftly handed over to a wet-nurse. Grey arranged for the child to be collected, and brought back to England, where she was brought up by his parents as his sister. From then on she effectively disappeared from Georgiana's life and the attentions of the Devonshires.

But the Duke remained implacable, snubbing Thomas Coutts who was still wanting settlement of Georgiana's debts, refusing to write to her, and doing his best to keep her short of money. But he could hardly hope to win. Georgiana missed her daughters – and wrote to them endlessly, expressing her desire to return. The message must have reached the Duke, who was also in contact with Elizabeth. And, in the meantime, everybody made the best of things, as only rich, experienced, titled English travellers could, in those last gentle days before the Revolutionary Terror swept through France, and Napoleon came to change the map of Europe.

It is hard to believe these sentimental exiles suffered overmuch as they dined with the King and Queen of Naples in their enormous palace at Caserta, or discussed antiquities with Gibbon in Lausanne. They botanized and mineralized and saw the sights of Rome and Florence; and by the spring of 1793, it was the Duke, not they, who had evidently had enough. In May he asked them to return.

'God of heaven bless him for his kindness to me . . .' wrote Georgiana to her eldest daughter, 'this cruel absence will be amply made up by the delight of seeing you.' But she was in no great hurry to get back and it was not until mid-September that Georgiana, Bess and the two Carolines reached England. Lady Spencer and her daughter, Harriet, were still enjoying Italy. The Duke had driven down to Dartford in his smart new coach together with Miss Trimmer and all three children. Georgiana Dorothy and Harriet were in raptures to be reunited with their mother. The Duke, despite a bad attack of gout, seemed not displeased, and it was only three-and-a-half-year-old Lord Hartington who gave a slight frost to the occasion. As Georgiana told her mother, 'Hartington is very pretty, but very cruel to me. He will not look at me or speak to me, tho' he kissed me a little at night. He is like the Duke, pretty blue eyes, fine colour, and a very sensible countenance and delightful laugh. . . . The Duke has the gout, but looks pretty well. There was never anything equal to the attention I have met from him – to the generosity and kindness.'

At Devonshire House, the Duke's relief was obvious to all, and the servants were loyally lined up to welcome back their Duchess. The house had been a morgue with her away. Now life could start again.

But although on the surface there was little change, and the bitterness and dramas of the last two years appeared forgotten, the sparkle and wildness of the legendary society which had swirled around Georgiana in her youth were over. Middle-age was creeping up on the adult members of the clan. Everybody seemed a little tired, and that impassioned threesome, which had once seemed so brave and shocking, now apppeared positively cosy as domesticity began to rule the ducal roost. The Duke's eldest daughter, Charlotte Williams, now in her twenties, went off and conveniently married the nephew of the Devonshires' chief agent, Thomas Heaton. Georgiana's wild young niece, Caro Ponsonby, would soon make her own disastrous schoolgirl marriage to Lady Melbourne's son, William Lamb – only to leave him for her 'mad, bad and dangerous to know' poetic lover, Byron. And Devonshire House became the home of a curiously mixed bag of children growing up together under the careful eye of virtuous Miss Trimmer.

Georgiana's daughters – now called 'Little G.' and 'Hary-O' – had inherited much of her vivacity, and inevitably turned against 'Lady Liz', whom they generally despised. Caroline St Jules was supposedly kept ignorant of her true parentage – she was an 'orphan' and the other girls' devoted friend. Pretty young Hartington was spoiled and adored, especially by his sisters. Augustus Clifford was another 'orphan', a tall, strong, healthy boy who would soon be packed off to the Royal Navy as a twelve-year-old midshipman. And, in 1796, when Bess' long-forgotten husband died in Ireland, she was able to insist on being reunited with her teenage sons, Frederick and Augustus Foster. They too joined the Duke's absorbent household for a while, but the girls found them gauche and mocked their Irish accents, and the Duke had to pay for them to go to Oxford. Nevertheless, Bess was pleased to think that they too were now accepted 'as *enfants de famille*'.

As for Georgiana, she should have been able to enjoy her family and friends in middle-aged tranquillity at last. She was still universally admired as the undisputed female leader of society, and was probably the one member of the Devonshire House household everybody loved. But that evil fortune which had accompanied her gambling still pursued her in her life, so that she seems like somebody marked down to end her life in misery. That 'wild and scrambling life' of hers was claiming retribution; there was no escape.

Early in 1795 she was deeply upset to hear that her former lover, Grey, had married her kinswoman, Mary Ponsonby, without a word to her of his intentions. Shortly afterwards she was complaining once again of searing headaches and trouble with her eyes. Her previous eye-trouble had been cured by bathing the eyes in warm milk and vinegar, but now it refused to yield to treatment and steadily grew worse. She had difficulty reading, and by the summer of the following year the inflammation of the left eye had produced a swelling the size of a grapefruit on her face. Ophthalmic surgery in those days was primitive and painful. Blood was drawn off to lessen the inflammation, then leeches were attached to the eyeball. A corneal ulcer had formed and burst, destroying her vision. This was followed by 'a dreadful operation which she bore with great courage' and later she was blistered on the neck and 'causticks' applied behind the ears.

Inevitably Georgiana lost the eye – but worse still was the total loss of beauty. 'The change is painful to see,' wrote Lady Holland. 'Scarcely has she a vestige of those charms which once attracted all hearts. Her figure is corpulent, her complexion coarse, one eye gone, and her neck immense.' Not surprisingly, she virtually retired from society, and started seeking consolation in religion. But God could not assist her with her debts – nor would the Duke – and they went on mounting and plaguing her.

In contrast, Bess, of course, was still in perfect health and made such a pretty widow that the Duke of Richmond actually suggested marriage. She

daintily refused, although it is difficult to believe she was still seriously in love
with 'Canis', who had grown fat, morose and even more lethargic with late
middle-age. But Bess's life was totally involved with the Devonshires; and
with her misfortunes, Georgiana was more dependent on her friend than ever.
This did nothing to prevent Bess enjoying life. In 1802, when peace with
France broke out, she left the Devonshires, and was among the earliest visitors
to Paris – where, despite her professed loyalty to the memory of Marie
Antoinette, she made a great point of seeing Napoleon review his regiments.
'The moment that he came to where I was,' she wrote, 'I only thought of him as
a conqueror amid his troops and forgot the Tyrant.'

But Georgiana missed her badly: 'Do you hear the voice of my heart crying
to you? Do you feel what it is to be separated from you, or do new scenes and
occupations obliterate the image of a poor, dull, useless, insignificant being
like myself?'

'My dearest,' Bess wrote back, 'why are 'oo gloomy? Why are 'oo vexed?'

The answer was the usual one – Georgiana's debts and her now atrocious
health. After months of agony, she passed an enormous gallstone in September 1803. Not long afterwards she went through a so-called 'Final Reckoning'
of everything she owed, and the Duke was horrified by the amount. But,
despite Fox's experienced gambler's advice to her to 'make up the account as
much against yourself as possible', there were sums she felt she could not
admit even to her husband, and she was still gambling and losing. The worry
and remorse pursued her to the end.

War was resumed with France and Fox's lifelong political antagonist, the
Younger Pitt, was firmly in command. Politically the power of the Foxite
Whigs was negligible – so was Georgiana's, who had always been Charles
Fox's staunchest ally. She had long been far more the dedicated Whig than the
Duke who, influenced by Bess, could see the danger of French revolutionary
ideas to the English as well as to the French aristocracy. Accordingly, the
Duke supported Pitt and war with France. Bess, at heart a patriotic Tory, was
even more fervently for Pitt. As she wrote in her diary:

> Perhaps the horrors of the French Revolution which I have seen so much of
> and the persons I love who have suffered in it influences me. The Duchess
> regrets the Duke's voting for the war and is unhappy at his differing from
> Fox, but I feel implicit faith in the Duke's judgement.

The French Revolution and the war with Napoleonic France, had completed
the work begun by George III in destroying the political unity of the great
Whig 'revolutionary' families. When Pitt collapsed and died early in 1806, Fox
succeeded him at last, but the triumph had come too late, although with Lord
Grenville as Prime Minister, Fox at the Foreign Office, Grey at the Admiralty,
and Earl Spencer responsible for Home Affairs, the new ministry 'read like a
dinner-party guest-list for Devonshire House'.

Indeed, to celebrate the great occasion Georgiana forced herself out of
self-imposed obscurity, to give her last Devonshire House supper-party for
the new ministers and forty-six assorted guests. Her brief lover, Charles Grey,

was there. He was now known by the courtesy title of Lord Howick, and this would be the last occasion she would meet him. Fox was dropsical and clearly ailing, and the Duke, who had been offered any post he wanted in this 'Ministry of all the Talents' had – from lethargy or common sense – graciously refused, for this patched-up combination of Georgiana's friends had little hope of lasting.

Nor had she. Despite the spectacles shielded with black crêpe which she had worn to protect her failing eyesight, the strain of the occasion brought on blinding headaches. She was again assailed by the agony which had preceded the gallstone trouble three years earlier, but this time the doctors diagnosed jaundice. Sick, half-blind and in continual pain, Georgiana finally composed herself to meet her end.

Somehow she forced herself to write three last letters. The first was to her son, telling him, 'I live in you again. . . .':

I adore your sisters, but I see in you still more perhaps than even in them what my youth was. God grant that you may have all its fervours and cheerfulness without partaking of many of the follies which mark'd with giddyness my introduction into the world. I was but one year older than you when I launched into the vortex of dissipation – a Duchess and a beauty. . . . But I was giddy and vain. . . . I hope to live to see you not only happy but the cause of happyness to others, expending your princely fortune in doing good and employing the talents and powers of pleasing, with which nature has gifted you, in exalting the name of Cavendish even beyond the honour it has yet ever attain'd. God bless you, Dst Dst Hart.

To her daughter, Georgiana, she expressed 'the most unfeigned repentance for many errors' and after exhorting her to be 'dutiful and affectionate' to the various members of the family, including 'my dear friend Bess,' she concluded, 'Learn to be exact about expence. I beg you, as the best legacy I can leave you never run into debt about the most trifling sum. I have suffered enough from a contrary conduct.'

Her final letter was to Countess Spencer, begging for a bankers' draft for £100 by return of post. She needed it to pay her latest crop of debts. Her ladyship cautiously despatched £20, but before it reached her, and after three days of agony 'more horrible, more killing than human being ever witnessed', Georgiana sank into a coma and on 30 March 1806 expired. The autopsy revealed a severe abscess on the liver, and a week later the whole family assembled in the courtyard of Devonshire House as the coffin was driven past them through the gates on its journey north to Derbyshire. She was interred in the Cavendish family vault at All Saints, Derby.

Sixteen-year-old Hartington watched impassively. The Duke was so moved that he retired to his room and spoke to no one for the remainder of the day. And Bess expressed her feelings to her sailor son, Augustus Clifford: 'She was the charm of my existence, the constant support in all my sorrows . . . our hearts were united in the closest bonds of confidence and love . . . she doubled every joy, lessened every grief.'

With Georgiana gone, the extraordinary social and political influence which had centred around Devonshire House for more than thirty years had vanished too, never to return. Fox died that same autumn – appropriately in the Duke's house at Chiswick – and with him died the political ambitions Georgiana had so fervently believed in.

The Duke was not interested in politics or in society any more. To tell the truth, he was not very interested in anything. 'A sort of unambitious passiveness made him too often silent in general company,' as one observer put it, but he still had Bess to comfort his premature old age, and, the September after Georgiana died, Sheridan is supposed to have been startled at a dinner-party when Lady Elizabeth '*cried* to him and told him she felt it her severe duty to be Duchess of Devonshire.'

Severe or not, she had to wait, but finally, in October 1809, the Duke did marry her – and his children were all too predictably appalled. Even the gentle young Lord Hartington called the new Duchess a 'crocodile', and the rest of the family were less polite. But the Duke himself had only two more years to live. Bess had been his wife in deed if not in name for more than twenty years, and it is hard to believe Georgiana would have minded that her 'brother Canis' had finally made her 'dearest, dearest Bess' an honest Duchess.

11. The Bachelor

The Sixth Duke, William Spencer (1790–1858)

THE Fifth Duke died in August 1811 in much the manner he had lived – quietly, dropsically and very late at night. And, although his passing brought forth a predictable outpouring from his widow – 'I know not what is to accustom me to my misfortune. . . . To belong to such a being was my pride as well as my happiness' – his last years were little more than a depressing postscript to the reign of Georgiana, and it is hard to believe he was seriously mourned.

All eyes were on his successor, his son William Spencer Cavendish, whose twenty-first birthday had been celebrated with quasi-regal lavishness throughout the Devonshire dominions barely two months earlier. But as the richest and most beloved young duke in England he was a distinct conundrum, for no one could know quite what effect his unsettled and erratic childhood would have on him. As the longed-for heir and great white hope of the Devonshires he had been endlessly indulged and spoiled – and frequently neglected – by the family, subjected to blasts of emotional excess from his sick, increasingly unhappy mother, gushed at by his stepmother, offered the consolations of low-church piety by Miss Trimmer, and possessively adored by his older dominating sisters.

Hardly surprisingly, he seemed old beyond his years and grew up a nervous, often solitary child, much given to sulks and tantrums. Byron, who knew him as a boy at Harrow dismissed him for his 'soft, milky disposition', but when, at fifteen, 'Hart' was told his beloved cousin, Caroline Ponsonby, was getting married, he is described as having gone into 'violent hysterics', 'reproached Caro bitterly, saying he looked upon her as his wife', and ended up so ill that the family doctor, Dr Farquhar was summoned to calm him.

But, by the time of his succession, his character had formed – and 'Hart' had turned out rather better than anyone had had the right to hope. He was handsome, tall, intelligent, and had inherited most of his mother's virtues without too many of his father's defects. He possessed great charm and kindness, considerable taste, a sense of fun and a sensible if not excessive sense of duty. He also had full control of the Devonshire fortunes, the entail on the estates having expired when he was twenty-one and not having been redrafted at his father's death. No other Duke of Devonshire started with such high hopes of youthful promise and success from those around him.

Among the first letters he received was one from the Prime Minister, Spencer Perceval.

Mr Perceval presents his compliments to His Grace the Duke of Devonshire, and has the honour to acquaint him that he has this day taken His

Royal Highness the Prince Regent's Pleasure upon the subject of the Lord Lieutenancy of the County of Derby. And Mr. Perceval has it in command from H.R.H. to acquaint His Grace without loss of time of H.R.H.'s pleasure that Your Grace should be appointed to that office 'which', to use H.R.H.'s own words, 'was so long, so worthily, and so respectably held by the Prince's old and ever lamented friend,' the late Duke of Devonshire.

This was in line with the ambitions the family had for him; and his favourite sister, Harriet – soon to become Lady Granville – wrote most earnestly exhorting him to 'be worthy of the race from which you spring and whom you now represent.' She added that he possessed

> . . . so many of the great qualities and requisites to make you distinguished as well as the feelings that make you beloved and amiable, that I have scarcely a fear about you, and yet your youth is so great and your situation so arduous that it is impossible for me . . . to be totally without anxiety. . . . Yours is a situation in which it is difficult to gain tho' possible to lose true greatness.

But what did sister Harriet suggest? He had inherited vast wealth, magnificent possessions, and a position in society second only to the royal family's. What more was this amiable young aristocrat to do to achieve 'true greatness'? What role was waiting for a well-intentioned duke in the early nineteenth century to make him a justified successor to Bess of Hardwick or the great First Duke? The question dogged him for the remainder of his life.

The Sixth Duke certainly started admirably enough by clearing up the emotional and at least some of the financial muddles left behind by his parents. By far the worst of these involved the status and pretensions of his embarrassing stepmother, who could easily become the source of endless trouble. The women in the family were unanimously against her; he himself had little time for her; and he knew quite well that she was out to get all she could for herself and for her children.

It was an awkward situation; because of the way the Fifth Duke died before the details of the inheritance could be rearranged, everything depended on his son's discretion, and Bess had been swift to stake her claims. Her letter has not survived, but she would seem to have been very businesslike for a prostrate widow, and insisted firmly that her husband had intended leaving substantial legacies for herself and Augustus Clifford, and had wanted her to have Chiswick as her dower-house.

This was altogether too much for the new young Duke to take – particularly as he loved the house himself – and, on 13 August 1811, he confided to his grandmother, Lady Spencer, on the subject. He had been down to Chiswick after the gloomy business of visiting Devonshire House to 'examine all my father's clothes, very few of which I shall keep', and he cannot have been best pleased to find the new dowager installed. But he was tactful, not even mentioning her letter, for as he explained,

... after the expectation she has formed, anything that I can say will be a disappointment to her. Her worst adviser could not have made her do a more foolish thing than write as she did. I shall always feel for her what she deserves, but I cannot bear to see art and falsehood employed at such a time.

For Bess was also claiming that her husband intended settling estates worth £3,600 a year on young Augustus. This the Duke also disbelieved, but he felt a responsibility to do 'what I think right to one to whom [my father] gave existence'. A few days later he wrote to Lady Spencer telling her his decision: to give Augustus a life annuity of £2,000, 'a large share' in his will, and he would do even more for him when he married or left the navy. But his half-brother was not to know anything of this, and for the time being was to receive no more than his normal annual allowance, because 'I should think it wrong to throw any temptation in his way that might make him abandon his profession.'

It says much for the new Duke's tact that these arrangements actually delighted Bess. Soon he was telling Lady Spencer how pleased he was with the Duchess 'for seeming so happy and contented with what I have done. She told me last night that she was sure that she would have no more bad nights.' A 'crocodile' no longer, she was by now on affectionate terms with him, and was easily persuaded by the Duke to leave Chiswick for her own establishment in Piccadilly, before she could build herself a house beside the Thames at Richmond. And, thanks to the Duke's generosity, Augustus Clifford would remain a lifelong friend of the younger, infinitely more favoured half-brother he could so easily have hated. After the ructions and scandals which had marred his parents' lives, it was encouraging to find such pacifying gentleness in their successor.

This was soon evident in much else he did. Throughout the greater part of the Fifth Duke's reign, the one indispensable member of the household had been the agent, John Heaton, who with unappreciated skill and loyalty had managed the estates, and supervised the Devonshire finances to the best of his abilities. The Fifth Duke was far too grand and lazy to be bothered with a balance-sheet and passed his life in almost total ignorance of the true state of his affairs. This delightful but dangerous attitude – odd for a descendant of Bess of Hardwick – persisted in his son. When Heaton had dutifully complained to the Fifth Duke, 'My Lord Duke, I am sorry to inform your Grace that Lord Hartington appears disposed to spend a great deal of money', the Duke's reply had been memorably to the point: 'So much the better, Heaton. He will have a great deal to spend.'

The reply was typical, for the Fifth Duke and Georgiana both regarded Heaton as a somewhat meddlesome old bore. For Georgiana he had been 'the Corkscrew', and she had inevitably had several battles with him over the ever-present subject of her debts. The new Duke had not surprisingly picked up his parents' airy attitude to money, but he did take the trouble to meet the 'Corkscrew' during his days in London immediately after his father's death.

In a fascinating letter to Lady Spencer, the young Duke describes how he had spent a boring afternoon with Heaton, doing his best to listen to 'his long-winded histories, but' he adds, 'I must say I am quite delighted with his clearness, exactness and regularity.' The Duke gathered that, largely thanks to Heaton's stewardship, he had a current income of around £70,000 a year. But had he listened more attentively to those 'long-winded histories' he might have understood that the situation was not as rosy as it seemed. His mother's gambling, and his father's fecklessness had left the Devonshire estates encumbered with over half a million pounds of debt. There were also jointures and annuities to pay, which on top of the interest payments on the debts, were absorbing something like sixty per cent of the ducal income.

The poor 'Corkscrew' seems to have done his best to spell this out, but the Duke was no more inclined to listen to Heaton's warnings than his mother had been. He had full control of what seemed to be – and was – a princely fortune, and it would be many years before he fully understood the dangerous legacy of debt he had also inherited.

'Since God hath given us the Papacy,' a Renaissance pope is said to have exclaimed, 'let us enjoy it!' The young Duke's attitude was similar, and he has even been compared with a Renaissance prince in the way he began his dukedom. Unlike his parents, whose lives were ruined from the start by gambling, drink, and social and marital muddles, he was free to make the most of everything he had, and his earliest ambition was to become something his father never was – a great collector and a cultured and discerning amateur of art and life rather on the pattern of his great-grandfather, Lord Burlington.

He particularly loved Chatsworth, and was soon spending lavishly – and not always wisely – in his first eagerness to enhance its splendours. He seems to have been grossly overcharged when he spent over £50,000 on his collection of antique coins, for in 1844, when pressed for money he was fortunate to recoup £7,056 for the entire Devonshire coin collection. A wiser outlay was the money spent in his ambition to make the Chatsworth library one of the greatest in the country.

Soon after his accession he paid £10,000 for the library of Bishop Dampier of Ely, including his rare Greek and Latin volumes, and later made an unsuccessful bid of £20,000 for the library of the bibliophile, Count de MacCarthy. For the next few years the Duke would be a constant purchaser at the important library sales of the day, and his greatest coup was the purchase for £2,000 of the library of Sarah Siddons's actor brother, John Kemble, with its 700 volumes of plays including the first four Shakespeare folios and thirty-nine Shakespeare quartos. His uncle, Lord George Cavendish, also gave him Henry Cavendish's entire library from Soho Square, including its unique collection of scientific books, which he had inherited when the great man died in 1810.

This sort of acquisition must have been pleasing – to a point, but only to a point. Intellectually, he was simply not equipped to be a latter-day Renaissance prince, or even a virtuoso scholar like Lord Burlington. A Lorenzo de' Medici would have enjoyed his classical authors and been fascinated by the scientific works of Henry Cavendish, but the Sixth Duke was assembling his great library as an insatiable collector in much the same spirit as he was amassing thousands of specimens of different marble, without ever being a geologist. His cure for depression was 'booking', which was not reading, but rearranging the books in his library.

Scholarship and coin- and book-collecting were clearly not going to provide that great role everyone expected him to fill and, early in 1813, Lady Spencer had a letter from the Duke at Chatsworth which must have worried her, and which sounds an ominous note for her grandson's future:

> The weather here has been delicious. I shot again today in a lazy manner in the pleasure-ground, and rode on my healthy hills. I am just as I was when you saw me, very well at times, but weak at others, and am obliged to attend greatly to my food as the least indiscretion causes me sickness and giddiness in the head.

Apart from hay-fever, the Sixth Duke's health – and digestion – were in fact admirable, and would see him through the next forty-five years of life. Together with his father he would be the longest reigning Duke of Devonshire (both the Fifth and Sixth Dukes reigned for forty-seven years). But as would so often happen in the years to come, the Duke at twenty-two was already lapsing into hypochondria as an excuse to retire from the world and its expectations, and quietly and lazily enjoy himself – alone.

This almost certainly explains another mystery about the Duke – his much publicized deafness. He supposedly contracted it in youth after the removal of his tonsils and sometimes he did seem particularly hard of hearing – so much so that one writer has described him as being practically 'stone deaf', and another called his deafness 'a private tragedy' which blighted his existence. Tragedy or not, it did not stop him enjoying his private orchestra at Chatsworth, or relishing the music of Rossini – whom he knew – or listening to his pianist perform at Hardwick Hall the night before he died. Nor is there much mention of it in his extensive private diaries, and it is hard not to conclude that the ducal deafness, like his fragile state of health, was often a convenient excuse to retreat into the private life he wanted.

The area where this was most necessary of all was politics. Here, if anywhere as a true-born Cavendish, he should have been aspiring to achieve 'true greatness'. Like it or not, he had inherited the somewhat tattered mantle of the 'Crown Prince of the Whigs', and by inclination he was something of an easy-going Whig himself, believing in such humane principles as religious toleration for the Irish Catholics, popular 'liberty' and a measure of parliamentary reform. But by nature he was not suited to the life of an active politician – particularly one proclaiming principles like these in the reactionary England at the end of the Napoleonic wars – and deafness was an admirable excuse to duck the role in Parliament he never wanted.

Another problem his deafness and hypochondria helped him to evade was over marriage. Here, as with politics, grandeur was very much the order of the day. If he did nothing else, he could at least enhance his line, like all those shrewdly uxorious Cavendishes in the past, with a splendid and impressive match. He may have even tried it – once – and then thought better of it for the future.

According to an anecdote repeated some years after the event by the omniscient Lord Brougham, sometime in 1813 the young Duke was seen publicly flirting at a ball with the Prince Regent's daughter, Princess Charlotte.' Prinny noticed, but allowed the flirtation to continue for a while, actually encouraging the Duke to 'dance and dangle about' his susceptible young daughter. For he was out to teach the Duke a lesson, which he did in no uncertain manner, choosing his moment, then putting on 'his dignified air on which he piques himself and saying, "Your Grace will be pleased to recollect the difference between you and my daughter."'

Brougham was an inveterate old gossip, and not the most reliable of witnesses (despite becoming the most famous Lord Chancellor of his day), but he did know his Regency society, and there was almost certainly an element of truth in what he said. And if the Prince himself was so extraordinarily rude to the son of the man he had recently described as his 'old and ever lamented friend', it can only have confirmed the Duke in another private conclusion he had made. Grand marrying, like high politics, was not for him – or not, at any rate, for several years to come. He was still in his early twenties and enjoying the full freedom of his private life and private pleasures. He had no parents to arrange a 'suitable' marriage for him. Why complicate this most agreeable of lives until absolutely necessary?

Like the Duke's deafness, much has been made of the 'riddle' of his failure or disinclination to get married and dutifully create another Duke of Devonshire, but the answer is fairly obvious if not particularly romantic. His love-life was not blighted by his early disappointment over Caro Ponsonby. Still less, as has been suggested, was his 'deafness' an impediment to honest matrimony. It was simply that with his wealth and new position he was at liberty to enjoy the most sexually sophisticated female company in London or in Paris, just as he could buy the rarest volumes for his library – and, despite considerable excisions and obliterations from his diaries, it is clear that this is what he did.* Regency London was well provided with fashionable courtesans and as yet there were no unreasonable taboos forbidding young men of wealth and rank to enjoy them, provided they were minimally discreet. The example of his parents' marriage can hardly have given the young Duke a particularly elevated idea of holy matrimony, and at this stage of life he remained enviably free from worries over marriage or morality.

What did worry him was still that image of 'true greatness' which he had to find, and suddenly, in 1816, he caught a glimpse of it. After Napoleon's defeat the royal families of Europe reappeared, and among them came the future Tsar Nicholas I, on a much publicized imperial European tour, which inevitably included England. Equally inevitably, he met the Duke of Devonshire, who entertained him at his London house, and something of a

---

*As with many of the Chatsworth papers relating to the intimate lives of Georgiana and the Fifth Duke, the Sixth Duke's copious diaries were carefully and maddeningly censored by an unknown and most efficient hand belonging to someone anxious to preserve the Sixth Duke's reputation. It may have been his half-brother, Augustus Clifford, or even the Duke himself, but thanks to the similarity of the censor's ink to that used by the Duke, not even Scotland Yard's forensic scientists have been able to decipher any of the writing underneath.

friendship started; for the two young men were of an age, and not dissimilar. The Tsarevitch could be most agreeable, and had pretensions to European culture; he was a keen collector, particularly of statuary; he was Anglophile, an enthusiast for spendid buildings, and was anxious to see more of the famous English aristocracy of whom he had heard so much. The Duke invited him to Chatsworth, and the Tsarevitch was most impressed. So was the Duke. At last he was being really useful as he played the host and favoured friend of England's ally and the future ruler of the largest kingdom in the world. It also helped him to see Chatsworth in a different light. It was not just his lazy 'pleasure-ground', but it really was a princely palace fit to arouse the admiration of a future Tsar of Russia. Here, if anywhere, the Duke's potential 'greatness' lay.

But the more Grand Duke Nicholas's visit helped the Duke to appreciate the undoubted splendours of his house, the more it made him also see its defects. Quite simply, it was much too small.

As the author of a guidebook to Derbyshire, published in 1818, noted:

> I once heard an eminent artist remark that the principal fault of Chatsworth was an apparent want of apartments suited for the domestics of so princely a mansion. It is a palace for the eye, where every part seems alike so fitted for the noble owner and his guests only, and on beholding it, the spectator is naturally led to inquire where the servants of such an establishment are to reside.

For, although the First Duke had rebuilt Chatsworth with the express idea of being able to receive a king on terms of appropriate magnificence, much had changed in social and regal expectations since 1700. Guest-lists and retinues were getting longer; food was becoming more complicated and technically demanding to prepare. It was ridiculous to have so many books, and too little space to show them off and house them properly; and the same with the great Devonshire art collection. Most serious of all, the First Duke's Chatsworth still made far too few concessions to the great discovery of the early nineteenth century – comfort.

When 'Hart' had been at Harrow, his mother had been worried that her precious son might be somehow 'led astray' by his friendship with the precocious and spendthrift Bedford heir, Lord Tavistock. As far as one can tell, nothing very dreadful had resulted from his friendship, but now, as the Sixth Duke of Bedford, he was to have an important influence on the Sixth Duke of Devonshire. Bedford, who was also very rich, but not as rich as Devonshire, had been rebuilding and extending his ancestral seat at Woburn Abbey under the direction of a fashionable and versatile architect called Jeffry Wyatt, who had designed a sculpture gallery and a 'Temple of the Muses' in the most refined neo-classical manner.

Devonshire saw the work and fell for it. He met the architect and fell for him as well, for Jeffry Wyatt was a character, a supremely confident, expansive, vulgar man with very grand ideas, and the Duke would always be susceptible to dominating experts. A close friendship started between the Duke and the self-educated architect, and Wyatt agreed to do for Chatsworth what he had done for Woburn – only more so, if the Duke required it. Since the Duke did require it, and on a scale which made even Wyatt pause to think, it was decided they would both go off together gathering inspiration and original antique material from the true fountainhead of Classicism – Italy.

Once again ancient Rome would bring its influence to Derbyshire, for early in 1819 the Duke, with Wyatt to advise him, was busily enjoying the Eternal City, spending several thousand pounds on antique marble columns, – 'at Rome the love of marble possesses one like a new sense', he wrote – visiting the ruins and being particularly impressed by the new apartments being built in the Vatican. Something in the same style, the Duke decided, would do very nicely back at Chatsworth, and Wyatt, with his sketchbook at the ready, saw no reason to disagree. By the time they left Italy, the planned extensions to the house had grown very grand indeed.

But for the Duke, this first trip to Italy had more than just architectural significance, for it gave him a chance to meet a figure from the past. A few years earlier his stepmother had grown tired of London gossip and waterlogged Richmond, and like the indomitable traveller she was, had made her home in Rome and, as the very rich and grand Duchess of Devonshire, she had become something of an institution. Back in England her old enemies still made fun of her, particularly for the way she was said to be turning her well-known energies to digging up the Forum. But, in fact, her excavations were of considerable importance. So was her friendship with the most enlightened Roman of his day, Cardinal Consalvi, and through him she had got to know the great neo-classical sculptor Canova, and important members of the school surrounding him.

It was now that the young Duke's generosity to the former 'crocodile' paid off. He too became a friend, and important patron of the sculptor and, possibly with the Tsarevitch and the Duke of Bedford's interest in statuary in mind, began the collection of neo-classical sculpture which according to a recent critic, 'is without doubt unique in England and would be hard to parallel in Europe'. In fact the Duke had already bought his first example of Canova's work in Paris on the way to Rome – the famous seated portrait of Napoleon's mother, Letitia Buonaparte. (He was later able to check the accuracy of the portrait when he actually met the subject, by then a 'stately' but querulous old lady of eighty who complained 'loud and long about the statue which she says they had no right to sell nor I to buy'.)

During the five months spent in Rome the Duke became enthusiastically involved with Canova and his circle, purchasing and commissioning on a scale which only a duke with £70,000 a year could equal. He bought three important pieces from Canova's pupil, Rudolf Schadow, others from the Englishman John Gibson, and paid 1,000 scudi in advance for another of Canova's followers, the Danish Thorvaldsen, to sculpt the female figure which would be known as 'the Chatsworth Venus'. But it was Canova himself who aroused the Duke's personal enthusiasm and, after persuading him to part with the famous bust of one of his 'ideal women', Petrarch's Laura, he commissioned him to create what would turn out to be the sculptor's final masterpiece and 'the Duke's greatest treasure', his highly polished study of the slumbering Endymion.

The ducal cash certainly played its part in the success of this period in Rome, but credit should also go to the Duke's own sense and taste – and to the extraordinary degree to which he fitted into the society of Rome. The majority of English visitors to Rome were cynically fleeced, and then as cynically despised by the inhabitants, but the Duke took pains to speak Italian, and his stepmother was already popular. He was on terms of close affection with her now, and, according to no less a witness than Stendhal, '*La feue Duchesse de Devonshire et le Duc de Devonshire sont les seuls Anglais à ma connaissance pour lesquels les Romains font exception à la haine profonde qu'ils portent aux Anglais.*'

He loved Rome, which he revisited several times – in 1824 he was at 'Dearest Bess's' deathbed – and the next few years were undoubtedly the happiest of the Sixth Duke's life. Back in England he and Wyatt went ahead with plans that would almost double the existing frontage of Chatsworth, with a whole new wing, complete with tower and neo-classical belvedere, space for a theatre, a picture gallery, and of course an impressive new sculpture gallery. The Duke's auditor, James Abercromby, who would later become Speaker of the House of Commons and the First Baron Dunfermline, remarked like the true Scot he was, 'that he knew the money would be spent, and it was as well to lay it out on something useful.' The work began.

As he watched his house doubling in splendour, like some enormous Roman palace, the Duke must have felt a surge of satisfaction. If he could not actually achieve 'true greatness' for himself, he could at least create the setting for it here in his ancestral home. Both Bess of Hardwick and the First Duke had recreated Chatsworth as an expression of their power and grandeur and the young Duke could be forgiven if he felt that he was doing something rather similar. In a sense he was.

His fame spread once he could use the extended Chatsworth for a round of lavish entertaining. He did the same in London where Devonshire House was once again the scene of the capital's most glittering receptions. The celebrated visitor to Regency England, Prince Pückler-Muskau, now described the Duke as 'a King of fashion and elegance', and wrote admiringly of the Devonshire House concerts and receptions. They were 'very fine entertainments, where only the very first talent to be found in the metropolis is engaged, and where perfect order combined with boundless profusion reigns throughout.'

The Duke's taste for ostentatious splendour was increasing. Unlike most Cavendishes he was personally bored with horse-racing, but put in an appearance at Doncaster Races in a coach-and-six, with twelve outriders gleaming in the Devonshire livery. (Lord Fitzwilliam retaliated the day after with *two* coaches-and-six and sixteen outriders.)

Then, early in 1826, the Duke received word of what would become the proudest moment of his life. His friend Nicholas was now the Tsar of Russia; his coronation would take place in June, and someone had to represent King George IV and the British Government. Who better than the Duke of Devonshire? The minister responsible for relations with Russia was the double-dyed Tory Duke of Wellington, but he raised no objections to the young Whig Duke's appointment as Special Ambassador to Moscow. Devonshire would be expected to make a suitably impressive show, and Wellington wrote the Duke his own instructions, demonstrating that the victor of Waterloo had lost none of his skill in planning a campaign:

> I would recommend that the Horses, carriages, and Servants of the Ambassador to attend the Coronation should be sent from London as early in April as possible.
> The horses ought properly to halt for a week on their landing, and they ought to be a month on their march from St Petersburg to Moscow in order to arrive in condition – They should be able to leave St Petersburg in the beginning of the 3rd week in May – The Ambassador will not, himself, be more than three or four days on his journey.

The Government would provide £20,000, transport for the horses, and a battleship to take the Duke and his considerable retinue across the Baltic, but it was left to the Duke himself to make his own provisions for those little extras which make all the difference at this sort of great occasion. And, never one for doing things by halves, 'the Noble Duke did ample justice to the wealth and dignity of the country he was sent to represent. It is said that the splendour which he thus threw around his mission, cost him a sum little less than £60,000'. He may have read somewhere of the First Duke's diplomatic visit to Hague when he 'outshin'd' all those lesser European princelings with the richness of his state and his possessions, for he more than equalled him in outward pomp and show by grandly transporting much of the ducal household out to Moscow – ceremonial carriage, servants in brand new livery, cooks, wines, horses, paintings of the new Chatsworth as a coronation gift, and the pick of the now legendary Devonshire gold and silver plate.

He arrived in Moscow in early June, all eagerness to meet his friend, the Tsar, and was disappointed to find Nicholas out of Moscow. But on 14 June 1826, the Duke described how the Tsar had finally returned

> . . . and sent for me at once to come *en frac* to the Palais D'Amitchkoff, his beloved residence. I went, was shown into his own sitting-room, and one glance showed that he was unaltered to me. O, may God bless him! To describe his affectionate kindness is more than I can attempt. He showed me my picture hung up, in that, his own room, he talked of old times, gracefully, seriously, sensibly and then in tearing spirits – He said it made him feel a year younger to see me. I stayed with him an hour, and neither of us could mistake the other's happiness.

But this was Russia, and the Tsar, for all his 'tearing spirits', was not quite like other friends. The date for the Coronation was endlessly postponed, and the gentle Duke became impatient. In mid-July he wrote,

> I rode by myself. Hot and very unpleasant weather goes on like scirocco. After dinner I felt tired and had too bad a cold to go out. I begin to worry

myself about Nicholas, whose conduct in neglecting me I think strange and unkind.

But the Duke did his duty, by offering the nobility of Moscow a series of dinners and receptions, and when the Tsar was crowned at last, at the end of August, the reception given by the Ambassador of Britain certainly 'outshined' all others:

> The most magnificent part of the decorations assuredly was the gold and silver plate belonging to His Grace which, for massiveness and beauty, were altogether unrivalled. The Russians were particularly struck with the patrician treasure, as the accumulated wealth of many generations.

The Sixth Duke's Embassy to Moscow was one of the great successes of his life. 'Nothing could be more triumphant' wrote Lord Wharncliffe on his return to England, and a formal treaty of alliance between Britain and Russia followed shortly afterwards. The Duke was quietly upset that his erratic friend, the Tsar, had not yet seen fit to invest him with the Order of St Andrew – he received a diamond-studded snuff-box with a portrait of the Tsar instead – but his own equally erratic monarch, the former Prince Regent, now George IV, more than made up for the Tsar's omission. Early in December the King addressed the Duke as follows:

> My Dear Duke,
> The melancholy event of the death of my lamented friend, the Marquis of Hastings, has occasioned a vacancy in the Order of the Garter. But it is a matter of some consolation to me that I have it in my power to gratify my own feelings in nominating you, my dear young friend (the son of my very dear old friends, the late Duke and Duchess) to fill up the vacancy upon the present occasion.

The King's portly mistress, Lady Conyngham, also wrote to tell the Duke that 'could he have seen the King's delight, it would double the value of the honour.'

Every previous Duke of Devonshire had worn the Garter; now the Sixth Duke had proved himself their equal – in this at least – and other honours followed. Buoyed up by his success in Russia, the Duke was even to participate in active politics, making an effective Lords' speech in favour of emancipation of the Irish Catholics, and working behind the scenes to use his influence, like many a tactful Cavendish before him, to persuade Lord Lansdowne and the moderate Whigs, to support the new Ministry George Canning formed on the death of reactionary Lord Liverpool.

For this he was appropriately rewarded with the traditional Devonshire office of Lord Chamberlain which brought him firmly in the orbit of the Court, and the start of 1827 saw the Duke in frequent, often slightly bored, attendance on the King at Windsor. Past differences forgotten, he did his best to convert the King to a 'moderate' policy in Ireland. He endured the habits of his monarch, 'and the way he makes one eat and drink to keep off old age'. He successfully suggested his friend Wyatt as architect for rebuilding Windsor Castle, (thanks to which Windsor was to be extended almost as drastically as Chatsworth, and Wyatt became Sir Jeffry Wyatville.)* The Duke was assuredly on the path towards 'true greatness' of a sort at last, and had this active life of courtier and politician been able to continue, his subsequent career might have appeared more satisfactory; but as so often in his life, luck was against him.

In August 1827, the Prime Minister was taken ill. It was, the Duke reported to sister Harriet, not particularly serious, but 'his doctors say there is a tendency to obstruction . . . and they say he *must* have quiet.' The Duke invited him to stay at Chiswick, and there, on 8 August, Canning, like Fox before him, died.

The Duke was shaken 'with deep bitter grief for his loss' and his personal reaction was revealing. 'I wrote many letters,' he confided to his diary.

> Over-stretched mind yesterday makes me feel ill. I came to Chiswick in grief and sadness. . . . I try to pray but cannot. I ought to be wretched but have such an elastic disposition and such spirits of frivolity that I cannot feel strongly enough. I have dark forebodings.

For Britain, Canning's death meant three final years of ultra-Tory Government under Wellington; for the Duke of Devonshire, an abrupt retirement back into his increasingly expensive private life, with its uncomfortable mixture of 'frivolity' and 'dark forebodings'. Almost his first act after the shock of Canning's death was to purchase an eleven-foot-high young giraffe, '*pour me distraire*' – he already possessed an elephant – and to supervise her journey from the London docks to Chiswick 'in a great caravan, big enough to hold her and her two cows'. Then it was back to Chatsworth where work on the great extension was proceeding.

The Duke was thirty-seven, often an unsettling time of life for men who see their forties looming with their life's purpose unfulfilled but, unlike lesser mortals, the Sixth Duke had the whole Cavendish inheritance *pour se distraire* – books to be endlessly arranged on the shelves of his new library; more statues to be bought from Italy; his different houses and estates to visit; and 'adorable Chatsworth', which was now the foremost passion in his life.

The extensions were formally complete in 1829. No one could now complain of the inadequate appointments of the 'princely mansion'. It was luxurious and vast, and according to Lord Granville the Duke's celebrations for the completion were on a scale to match – 'the party was immense, forty people sat down to dinner every day, and about 150 servants in the steward's room and the servants' hall.' 'There was about Chatsworth', the neighbouring Duke of Rutland grudgingly admitted, 'a splendour and magnificence to which I neither did nor could aspire.'

And the Duke himself must have appeared the perfect 'princely' host.

---

*According to the Duke, the change of name from Wyatt to Wyatville 'gave him great satisfaction', and the King said, 'Ville or mutton, call yourself what you like.'

According to his second cousin, Greville, during this period he 'lived very much like a Grand Seigneur, hospitable and magnificent.' Greville adds that he was 'very clever and very comical, with a keen sense of humour, frequently very droll with his intimate friends.'

But what of the man behind the 'Grand Seigneur'? Interestingly, Greville also writes, 'at different periods of my life I have lived in great intimacy with him, but he was capricious, so the intervals were long during which we were almost strangers to each other,' and he describes him as at heart 'a disappointed and unhappy man'.

The world-weary disappointment of the discriminating man of wealth and feeling was to become something of a cliché in later nineteenth-century literature, and much of the Bachelor Duke's fascination comes from the way he now emerges as one of the earliest examples of a phenomenon which starts with his own restless contemporary, William Beckford, author of *Vathek* and builder of Fonthill Abbey, and peters out in Scott Fitzgerald's Gatsby. Spanning the uncomfortable period that marks the transformation from the 'frivolity' and hedonism of the Regency to the Victorian pieties that followed, he was very much a creature of his time, and was to find himself increasingly at the mercy of conflicting public aims and personal ambitions.

One sees this particularly in the progress of his love-life from the first years of his dukedom. In 1825 he had endured considerable embarrassment – along with many of the aristocracy, including the Duke of Wellington – when the lively and literate courtesan, Harriette Wilson, published her outrageous 'memoirs'. One of her motives was undoubtedly to blackmail and score off against former clients, and publication provided the celebrated occasion when the Iron Duke told her, 'Publish and be damned!'

It is not known whether she offered the Sixth Duke a similar chance to buy her off. If she did, he certainly refused, and, although the scandal-sheets concentrated on Harriette's revelations of the *vie intime* of Wellington, they could not miss the irreverent slanders she also launched against the unfortunate Sixth Duke, whom she called 'a booby', 'incorrigibly affected and stingy', and added with a cut that must have found its mark, 'if the Town did not talk about Devonshire's pictures, Devonshire's fortune and Devonshire's parties, he would be a blank in the Creation.' 'What right', she concluded, 'had he to visit a woman like me . . . unless he were inclined to treat me with the attention and respect which [I] have been in the habit of receiving from his dearest relations, and everybody else!'

The Duke was decidedly put out by these accusations. In his diary for the last day of 1825, he starts his customary 'List of causes of dissatisfaction during the year' with 'the worry of Harriette Wilson and the licentious personalities of the newspapers,' (which he typically followed with the entry, 'dissatisfaction number 2, a disagreeable scorbutic infection of my head.') But as yet he showed no sense of guilt; still less did he bother to deny having visited a celebrated prostitute. On the other hand the incident did make the Duke more circumspect in his amours, and must have played its part in persuading him, if not that the time had come for marriage – he was still not ready quite for *that* – at least that he should have a regular, domesticated mistress whom he could trust and live with on his own uncomplicated terms. Some time in 1827 he made his choice, and at the beginning of the following year he was to enter in his diary, 'Sick at heart, but Elizabeth did me good and did comfort me.'

The new ducal mistress was Elizabeth Warwick, and thanks to the Duke's discretion – and the conscientious work of the anonymous Chatsworth censor on his diaries and letters – little is known about her. In London she had rooms in Dorset Square, which at that period was frequented by fashionable women of the town,* and it is fairly evident that she was one of them. She was young, the Duke soon found her 'very amiable', and she can have had no objection to being taken into full time protection by a patron as distinguished as His Grace.

He, in turn, grew considerably attached to her, and at the end of February 1828 there is an enigmatic entry in his diary: 'I had an explanation today and a great relief, after anxiety approaching to madness. I drove in a cab all over London . . . with Elizabeth as usual.' Another brief entry, a month later, would seem to provide the answer to the Duke's anxieties. 'Elizabeth, after sad pains, miscarried today. I went to her. She will be in bed for some time.'

For part of that spring and early summer, the Duke was in Paris on his own. Elizabeth, he noted, 'takes London hard in my absence', but on his return from France, she was at Brighton with him, looking 'uncommonly well and fit', and set up in 'a delicious house'. By mid-August, after an entry, 'went to Elizabeth', followed by an entire line inked out, the Duke admits, 'I am grown very fond of her, she has such good sense and tact without being quick.'

A month later, and Miss Warwick was installed as the Duke's *maîtresse en titre*, with her own establishment at 'The Rookery', a small eighteenth-century house belonging to the Duke, at Ashford-in-the-Water conveniently close to Chatsworth. Abercromby, the Duke noted in his diary, was 'sour' and 'quite against Elizabeth inhabiting the Rookery', but this did not prevent his taking sister Harriet there a few weeks later, and 'telling her about Elizabeth'. At the end of 1828, in his diary he heads his list of 'sources of satisfaction' with the brief entry – 'unalloyed happiness with Elizabeth'.

This new period of domesticity undoubtedly appealed to the Duke. 'It is so comfortable to find Elizabeth at home after my outgoings.' 'Elizabeth is perfect – no nonsense and all gentleness and good sense.' But a few weeks later he confesses in his diary, that 'the thoughts of — keep me awake all night. My dear Elizabeth was ill this morning. I am very fond of her which is not inconsistent with thoughts of —.' He also writes, 'my head is full of Fanny/ Jenny —. I can think of nothing else, and but for dear Elizabeth I should marry —.'

Again thanks to the Chatsworth censor we shall never know whom the Duke might have married – or how serious he was – but the general pattern of his love-life does seem fairly clear. Up to this point he had amused himself with 'frivolous' affairs, and now as he started to think of marriage as a possibility, he settled for the undemanding and of course unmarriageable Elizabeth instead.

It was an admirable arrangement for a rich self-indulgent middle-aged

---

* The 1831 census shows an unusually high number of houses in Dorset Square being lived in by women on their own, but by then there is no trace of Elizabeth Warwick among them.

bachelor. By supporting his mistress in considerable comfort in London, Brighton or the Rookery, he could have all the care and domesticity he needed, without any serious interference with his freedom and the settled habits of a lifetime, including his undoubted right to visit 'Fanny/Jenny' when he felt the inclination.

His one doubt must have been over the succession to the Dukedom, and it may have been simply a coincidence that in 1829, the year he set up with the undemanding Miss Warwick, an admirable solution suddenly appeared to this as well. His favourite niece, seventeen-year-old Blanche Howard – daughter of his eldest sister, Georgiana 'Little G', whose husband, George Howard (first known by the courtesy title of Lord Morpeth), had inherited the earldom of Carlisle – was being courted by clever young William Cavendish, eldest grandson of the Duke's rich old uncle Lord George Cavendish (who, in 1831, had been invested with the revived title of Lord Burlington, and who himself was next in line for the Dukedom). In 1829 they married, and a few months later found the Duke drily noting in his diary, 'Blanche fainted at chapel this morning, which means an heir to the family.' She proved him right in the late spring of 1830, by giving birth to a son, who was known as 'Little Cav'. He died in early childhood, but in 1833 Blanche produced a second son – christened Spencer Compton Cavendish after his great-uncle – who would one day become Eighth Duke of Devonshire himself. Blanche was a perfect mother, William an altogether worthy and adoring husband; with such a family of paragons, the somewhat rakish Duke now felt that the succession was in worthier hands than his – and that he was finally relieved of one more tedious obligation.

But before he could retreat completely into that gentle life of *grand seigneur*, which was what he really wanted, there was one duty even he could not evade. The early 1830s were a crucial period for English society, and in particular for the English aristocracy, for it had become obvious at last that the eighteenth-century world of privilege, political corruption and social reaction, which had endured so long, would have to change. The Tories had been in power for fifty years, the country was being swept with rioting, the middle classes were on the warpath for their place in Parliament – and the great question was how gracefully, or violently, the change would come.

George IV died in 1830. Wellington fell from power, and when the Whigs, by allying with the Radicals and middle classes, returned to office, the new Prime Minister was none other than Lord Grey, the father of the Sixth Duke's illegitimate half-sister, Eliza Courtney. One of his first acts was to reappoint Georgiana's son Lord Chamberlain, and with so many other members of the 'great' Whig families in his government as well, it may have seemed as if the palmy days of rule by the old 'Venetian oligarchy' of Whigs had now returned. Many hoped they had, but Grey was for radical reform of the whole parliamentary system, – including the parliamentary influence which families like the House of Cavendish had held since 1688. Where stood the Duke in all of this?

He was not in too much hurry to commit himself. As senior court official, he was responsible for many of the details following the old King's death and the succession of his friend, 'Sailor Bill', King William IV. The Coronation seems to have been a remarkably casual affair – known at the time as the 'Half-Crown-ation' – and an extraordinary muddle. There was no set procession to the Abbey, and Mary Frampton's diary gives an unforgettable picture of the Duke, who was seen 'running halfway up Parliament Street with his coronet on his head, looking for his carriage which could not get near the Abbey, although he was Lord Chamberlain.'

Soon afterwards he was writing in his diary: 'Went to Windsor – saw room where poor George IV died. The floor covered with the stains of his medicines. Ordered them to be planed out – hard.'

When the Duke had had time to think seriously about politics, and when he did publicly commit himself at last – in a speech at Derby in March 1831 – he came out as firmly for Reform as his mother (but probably not his father) would have wished; and also showed remarkable intuition as to where the true interests and future of the English aristocracy lay.

Unlike the majority in the House of Lords, who saw their whole position threatened by Reform, he was entirely behind Lord Grey's proposals which would not only sweep away eighteenth-century parliamentary corruption, but also bring the property-owning lower-middle classes into the electorate. This, said the Duke, would bring Parliament into a 'more intimate alliance with the great body of the people', and a man would henceforth be able to 'feel pride in referring to his electoral franchise, not merely as an instrument of political power, but as the reward of his meritorious exertions and proof of his honest respectability.' Revolutionary words for a Duke in 1831!

But his remarks on the future role of the aristocracy are still more interesting, for he acknowledged the current feeling of resentment being voiced against his class, 'and that the members of the aristocracy have been sometimes considered in an unfavourable light by the people'. Much of this criticism was justified, he felt. The time had come for the aristocracy to 'be relieved from privileges in fact detrimental to all parties. Let them stand on their own merits,' he concluded bravely, 'and I have no fear that the people of England will be unjust to the aristocracy of England, united by mutual kind feelings and good offices.'

The Duke did his best to act by his beliefs. Soon after his speech at Derby, when Grey's proposals for Reform were blocked in Parliament, and the vacillating King looked like refusing him a dissolution to allow a fresh general election, the Duke roused himself, 'went to the Palace early, asked for an audience, and stated my intense conviction that a dissolution alone could save us. The King heard me kindly and very quietly.' The Duke's intervention with 'King Bill' as he called him, helped Grey get the dissolution he required – and a mandate for Reform at the subsequent election; and the Duke was the staunchest of Reformers in the House of Lords, where the majority of peers, unable to see beyond their petty interests, remained petrified at what would happen next.

Thanks largely to this opposition in the Lords, Grey's proposals stalled; popular agitation mounted, Bristol Town Hall was fired by the mob, and the unfortunate King saw himself facing civil war unless he created sufficient fresh Reformist peers to force Grey's proposals through the Lords. But the King was inclined to haver, and the presence of his trusted Chamberlain, with his 'intense conviction' for Reform, was an important factor in making him face reality.

To the last it was touch-and-go and, throughout the spring of 1832, the Duke, with unaccustomed zeal, was tirelessly lobbying at Court. 'Alarming times,' he wrote in his diary for mid-May, 'nothing settled. . . . I came home [from the Lords] quite agitated, and write now in suspense . . .' But finally the King's firm threat to create fresh peers if necessary secured the Bill's sullen passage through the Lords. 'All settled!' wrote the Duke with obvious relief. And by June the Reform Bill was law, the Duke's work done, and the old electoral power of great Whig families like the Cavendishes had gone for good.

With hindsight it is easy to be slightly cynical about the Duke's part in this – just as it is about the 'Great Reform' of 1832 itself.* But he was acting out of genuine belief, and against the apparent interest of the class he represented. He was also acting shrewdly. For, just as Grey's reforms averted dangerous unrest throughout the country, and in fact allowed the aristocracy to retain political leadership through the nineteenth-century with middle-class electoral support, so the Duke's own somewhat sentimental ideas of a loved and 'meritorious' aristocracy would prove a foretaste of the sort of claims upon which much of this upper-class leadership would rest.

But leadership was not for him. He had acted decisively for his beliefs and he had done enough. 'Another long fatiguing bore!' he remarks about yet one more royal dinner he attended, and by the end of 1832 he was at Chatsworth writing in his diary, 'Rain, indolence, rallied. Heard that the King said I never attended him. He is always most kind and praising. What can it mean?'

What it meant was that the Duke had finally retired to enjoy the 'frivolous' life he wanted. The penultimate chapter of his life had started.

'Not till 1832', he stated in the private *Handbook* which he wrote on Chatsworth, 'did I take to caring for my plants in earnest. The old greenhouse was converted into a stove, the greenhouse at the gardens was built, the Arboretum invented and formed. Then started up orchidaceae, and three successive houses were built to receive their increasing numbers.'

Six years earlier, the Duke had been impressed by the personality and obvious intelligence of the twenty-three-year-old gardener in charge of the creepers and new plants at the nearby Royal Horticultural Society's gardens at Chiswick. He was called Joseph Paxton, and despite his youth he was picked by the Duke to be head gardener at Chatsworth. Paxton, described by his biographer as 'a man of daemonic energy' gives a good picture of himself in the account he wrote of his arrival at Chatsworth at 4.30 in the morning from the London coach to Chesterfield.

---

* The Reform Bill of 1832 extended the parliamentary franchise to the new middle classes by giving the vote to 'ten pound householders', and swept away the majority of the 'Rotten Boroughs' on which the control of so much of eighteenth-century politics had rested.

As no person was to be seen at that early hour, I got over the greenhouse gate by the old covered way, explored the pleasure-grounds, and looked round the outside of the house. I then went down to the kitchen-gardens, scaled the outside wall, and saw the whole of the place, set the men to work there at six o'clock; then returned to Chatsworth, and got Thomas Weldon to play me the water-works and afterwards went to breakfast with poor dear Mrs. Gregory and her niece: The latter fell in love with me and I with her, and thus completed my first morning's work at Chatsworth before nine o'clock.

Since this explosive entry on the scene, young Paxton had duly married Mrs Gregory's niece, Sarah, and started on the work which would transform the Chatsworth gardens almost as dramatically as the Duke transformed the house. A Bedfordshire farmer's son, and entirely self-educated, Joseph Paxton would become something of a hero of Victorian society with his construction of the Crystal Palace for the Great Exhibition of 1851 in Hyde Park; and his many-sided genius was to bring him fame as botanist, journalist, engineer-businessman and politician. By 1832, his enthusiasms had already started to infect the Duke.

For, now that Wyatville had gone to Windsor, Paxton could provide the Duke with something in addition to the Chiswick giraffe and Canova's statuary, *pour se distraire*, and add to the beauty and the glory of beloved Chatsworth. Plants have their own insidious fascination, making them as satisfying to collect as books or works of art, and the 1830s were a period of boundless possibilities for the botanical amateur of means. Resourceful botanists were hot-foot in the steps of the British empire-builder; exotic blooms of unimagined shape and size were reported back from far-off shores; and the Duke, with Paxton firing his enthusiasm, found himself longing to possess them.

For a Duke who had imported marble by the ton from Italy, it seemed quite natural to collect the rarest plants on the same princely scale, and he began not merely buying new exotic species, but financing expeditions of botanical discovery to the furthest corners of the globe. No expense was spared. The botanist John Gibson was despatched to the dank forests of Assam to bring back undiscovered orchids for the Duke's collection, along with the spectacularly flowering *Amherstia nobilis*. The Duke was proud to give his name to his own banana, the dwarf *Musa cavendishii*, which, originating in China, and acquired by Paxton, dutifully flourished in his Chatsworth hothouse. Two Chatsworth gardeners, Banks and Wallace, drowned in the perilous Columbia River on an expedition for the Duke, collecting seeds. More happily, in 1849, he was to have his greatest moment of botanical success when he just managed to persuade the recently discovered giant Amazonian water-lily, *Victoria regia*, to flower at Chatsworth before the official specimen bloomed in Kew Gardens.

As the Duke's head-gardener, Paxton was of course the man behind the growing fame of Chatsworth's gardens. In 1832, when fourteen-year-old Princess Victoria paid an official visit to the Duke, Paxton played a large part in the splendour of the great occasion, arranging the fountains, the fireworks, and keeping a hundred gardeners working through the night sweeping the lawns and paths for the Princess the morning after. And besides providing the botanical expertise and inspiration for the Duke's collecting, Paxton showed continual ingenuity in creating the conditions for countless delicate exotic plants to survive and bloom in Derbyshire. But he was also offering the Duke something he had failed to discover in the pleasures of society or love-affairs or politics. The longing for 'true greatness' was behind him, and Chatsworth with its galleries, its new library, its theatre (completed in 1833) and above all the exotic richness of its gardens had become the Duke's own private pleasure-dome, where he could steadily create the idyllic life he wanted.

He still had Elizabeth and saw her when he felt the inclination; he still travelled, entertained, and appeared as much the *grand seigneur* as ever, but only at Chatsworth could he feel at peace. 'My tooth pains me and I have a cold, but my heart is full of joy and gratitude to God for mercy. What happiness I have in seeing Chatsworth!' he wrote in his journal; and the anonymous author of a 'character' published in the *Court Journal* in 1835 described him as 'Nicander, a solitary epicurean', and concluded tellingly, 'He has a thousand pleasures – a thousand gratifications – and a vocation to enjoy them all; – if any created being can afford to dispense with happiness, it is Nicander.'

For the Duke, Paxton increasingly became the magician he relied on for the working of his private paradise. Orchids, streams, fountains, all depended on Paxton's never-failing expertise, and in 1836 work began on the most magical of all his creations for the ducal pleasure – his Great Conservatory, nearly half an acre of steel and glass, its furnace fed by an underground railway, and high enough to house the Sixth Duke's palm-trees and bananas in perfect tropical conditions. Designed by Paxton, in conjunction with the architect, Decimus Burton (who later designed the Palm House in Kew Gardens) Chatsworth's Great Conservatory was a revolutionary building, which started a fashion for conservatories and winter gardens throughout the country. It was also the height of self-indulgence by the Duke, costing over £30,000, and adding to those 'thousand gratifications' he possessed already. The Duke's private 'summary', compiled at the end of 1836, included several items showing that he had certainly enjoyed himself – 'Better health than I ever had', 'Paris in the winter, great enjoyment', and of course, 'Chatsworth – its progress and my happy party there.'

But there were also several ominous items. One of the reasons he had enjoyed himself at Paris had been because 'the exertion there relieve me of the discouraged feeling I had about myself.' He was glad to be able to record – 'attention more turned to religion', and two sources of dissatisfaction were duly noted: 'My unkindness', and 'ineffectual attempts to diminish expenditure'. This last item was more important than it sounds, for a few weeks later the Duke received a startling note from his London lawyer, Benjamin Currey, entitled bleakly, 'Summary of expenditure and income'. For Currey, unlike the Duke, had been doing his arithmetic, which showed that the total Devonshire income between the years 1828 to 1835 had risen to the dizzy average sum of £124,587 a year. But expenditure had mounted still more dizzily – to an average for the same period of £140,925 a year. And old Benjamin was quick to point the moral.

His Grace, like any ordinary overspending mortal, was on the primrose path to ruin, unless he could instantly reduce expenditure by at least a fifth. Failing this, the Duke should 'stop at the earliest practical period, the Chatsworth Buildings, and purchase of furniture, which would meet the difficulty.'

It sounded logical enough, but how could the poor Duke slice expenditure with the foundations for Paxton's Great Conservatory already laid? How could he possibly lop £20,000 a year off what he spent, when every penny went in maintaining his existing style of life? It was most worrying, and in due accordance with one of life's most melancholy laws, the Duke's worries over money led to worries over almost everything else.

One of the first to suffer was Miss Warwick who, after ten years as ducal mistress, had begun to lose her youthful 'amiability' and was troubling his Christian conscience: '29 March 1837. Eliz. came. Melancholy again. I read to her and tried to convince her. . . .' A few days later, and the Duke was 'somewhat better, but still full of aches of body and mind. Alas poor E!'

Then, on 2 May came the inevitable show-down with unhappy E:

> Don Giovanni and then to Elizabeth. When the carriage came for me to go, she worked herself into a dreadful state and was by way of making an attempt to stab herself with the supper knife. I calmed and left her with her maid promising to be calm, but I am disgusted and worn to death.

The time had come for an end to the affair, and the next day, after receiving a letter from Elizabeth, the Duke 'wrote twice and said everything. Dined with the Sutherlands, and there was a party. I was obliged to drink to keep up spirits.'

This was most unlike the Duke, who was not a drinker, and who un-doubtedly felt guilty at his 'unkindness' to Elizabeth. (Suitable financial provision was of course soon made for her through discreet Mr Currey.) But the Duke had other consolations. One was his growing affection for his niece, Blanche, now Lady Burlington and the mother of four children, and he secretly relished the prospect of how much she and her family would enjoy beloved Chatsworth on his death. Another was his ever-faithful gardener: 'Paxton here. O joy of plants!' he wrote. But his greatest comfort was undoubtedly his new found Christian faith which he shared with Blanche: '7 May. Happy thoughts. Church. Reading – walking – prayers at 6 – and Turnham Green.'

Turnham Green was the site of a revivalist chapel, and according to a shocked letter from Paxton to his wife back in Derbyshire, the meetings were held in a schoolroom, with the Duke in the congregation, sitting at a schoolbench 'among all the tag-rag and bob-tail of the place.'

By the summer of 1837, the Duke was in the deepest throes of religious crisis. 'The Duke', wrote Paxton, 'is become a ranting, canting Saint. . . . It is in everybody's mouth here, and all deplore the fall, for I can call it nothing else, of so magnificent a man. Some think it a species of insanity. However I agree with none of them, for I am sure he is well enough in that quarter.' Paxton was right. The Duke, despite Turnham Green, was as sane as ever. The acute stage of his crisis passed, and although evangelical religion played an important part in the remainder of his life, nothing really changed at Chatsworth. Nor did conversion help the Duke achieve that twenty per cent reduction in expenditure suggested by his lawyer, and the following January as the girders of the Great Conservatory began rising in the garden, the Duke was having more trouble with his teeth and, almost as a reflex action, planning yet another change at Chatsworth: 'Settled in mind about West Front Downstairs – library changed – breakfast room to be enlarged with fire opposite the windows.'

He still saw Elizabeth occasionally, but her presence obviously conflicted with the Duke's Christian conscience, and by 1838 she had had enough. 'She behaves very ill and very unkindly,' wrote the Duke, and consoled himself with God and Paxton.

The year had started sombrely enough:

At just past nine the servants were assembled in the anteroom, and the archdeacon read the first two chapters of St. Matthew to us and a prayer for New Year's Day and the Lord's Prayer. Nothing, no nothing ever has made me so happy. A rainy day and threatening sore throat kept me indoors. I read one of Blunt's sermons with Lady Newburgh.

Colds, guilt and endless sermons followed through the spring, but the Duke's happiness in Christ continued. 'I love my uncle more every day,' wrote his pious niece, Georgiana Fullerton. 'There is such a charm about him, a sort of contagious gaiety, and now that all he does is under the influence of religious principle, I esteem him as much as I love him.'

But although the Duke was dutifully attending family prayers each morning, and going at least twice to church each Sunday, his 'contagious gaiety' may have had more to do with a revival of his naturally 'elastic disposition' than to the 'influence of religious principle'. In June came the excitement of the new Queen Victoria's coronation – with the Duke carrying the orb of state as he had for George IV and poor 'King Bill'. In July he was back at 'frivolous' Brighton in the best of spirits, and while there made one of those 'capricious' swift decisions which so puzzled his contemporaries, like Charles Greville, and account for the long intervals when his friends felt they scarcely knew him. Restless as ever, he was off abroad again – first to Paris, then to Switzerland and Italy – and although there were brief afflictions of remorse, 'Lake Lucerne . . . the weather dark and raining . . . my mind harassed by all sorts of wrong thoughts and fancies', he was patently enjoying his escape. For travelling companion, he took the now indispensable Joseph Paxton, just as he had taken Wyatville twenty years before; but Paxton was also something of a *protégé* by now. The childless Duke may well have relished the paternal role with such a talented son as Paxton as he showed him his favourite views of Rome, and helped form his taste and complete his education. At Pisa the Duke had 'liked the camels which my mother used to be fond of going to see'; back at Rome, his beloved Blanche arrived together with her earnest husband and the Sutherlands, and 'despite indifferent weather they saw a lot'. Lord Burlington unfortunately failed to share the Duke's enthusiasm for Rome. 'There was pomp in abundance,' Blanche's husband wrote after visiting St Peter's 'but nothing very striking, the singing very middling – the kneeling to the Pope when he passes or is borne by is very offensive.'

But the Duke was still intent on travelling – Naples, Greece, Constantinople, Malta – and while the faithful Paxton missed his family, the unattached Duke was determinedly enjoying his freedom from the worries and the sense of 'inadequacy' and sin that so afflicted him in England. Although Paxton told his wife that 'the Duke has carried out this journey very economically, at least in comparison with what the expedition cost five years since', he amused himself with a few minor purchases for Chatsworth, including four Egyptian marble pillars for £400; but he was being careful, spending barely £2,000 in five months, compared with the £5,000 he had spent before for the same period.

Careful or not, the Duke's journey could not last for ever. In April 1839 Paxton returned from Malta to his insistent family, together with three dozen carefully boxed orange trees for Chatsworth. 'Paxton going tomorrow; my own wretched unworthiness stares me in the face,' the Duke wrote ominously. And when the Duke followed him to England later in the summer, he did so with considerable foreboding, which not even Chatsworth and the excitement of the almost finished Great Conservatory could dispel. Finance remained a worry which refused to go away. So was his ever-present sense of sin.

> Guilty sinner, guilty sinner,
> Gnash thy teeth and tear thy hair,
> Once in wisdom's path beginner,
> Now the victim of despair,
> Where are those bright resolutions,
> Where thy persevering prayer?
> Banished by thy heart's pollutions,
> Shattered by each breath of air.

The Duke would recite this when he could not sleep, but the words brought little comfort – nor did the role his position still obliged him to act out in society.

'Dined with Queen Victoria, and we had dancing afterwards. She was very civil to me,' he recorded in February 1840. But the Duke was not among the Queen's admirers. 'Perfect she is in grace and manner, but alas, perfectly ugly too. Dull evening, very,' he wrote in his diary, after dining at the Palace after her accession. In youth, the Duke had been a most accomplished dancer, but frivolity was all around him now and dancing, even in the young Queen's presence, might easily contribute to his 'heart's pollutions'. During the troubled early months of 1840, the Duke did his best to pray, and then as usual, found relief in travel. He was soon off abroad again, and, at the beginning of April 1840, he reached Paris. In the old days it had been the scene of all too many of those 'sins' and 'pleasures' which had become such matter for reproach.

The Place Vendôme is lit up with many tallow pots. I think of the Hôtel du Rhin opposite. Be still, old nerves, only now profit, O my soul from all those warnings. I saw the blaze from the back room of my apartment and knelt down and thought of former times and prayed that an impression might be made on me before too late.

It must have been here in Paris that the Duke had had his first attack from that all-devouring sense of sin that had led to his conversion, for on the 13 April he wrote: 'Between churches on the most glorious day I took a walk to the scene of my escape. Boundless gratitude to God – O never may I forget his mercy.' But the Duke's tribulations were only just beginning.

Back in England, the Duke's earnest heir, Lord Burlington had been growing increasingly concerned about the condition of his wife. She was now twenty-eight, the mother of four small children, and like her husband of a serious religious disposition. (One of their favourite pastimes was reading Wesley's sermons together.) But for some time she had been growing increasingly lethargic, and about the time the Duke left for Paris, she was confined to bed at Westhill Park at Wanstead, the house of her sister, now married to the Duke of Sutherland. Dr Lacock and Dr Tupper diagnosed her case as one of 'great nervous debility' and prescribed a heavy sleeping draught containing hemlock. She remained 'languid' in the day, complained of headaches, had a racing pulse, and was unable to read.

By 19 April, Lord Burlington was writing in his diary that 'tho' she had taken no medicine the bowels have been a good deal disturbed and she has been in consequence very languid – more nervous almost than in any preceding day.' Lacock and Tupper now seemed 'anxious' but comforted his lordship with the remark that they saw 'no reason why she should not get over it'. The day after, when Lord Burlington took her for a drive through Wimbledon Park, Blanche was soon 'worse and coughing blood'.

The next few days became a time of torment both for Blanche and for her husband, with the doctors prescribing laudanum, and fever making her frequently delirious. 'Her thoughts were constantly on her children. "My child, my child," were the words she usually uttered,' wrote Lord Burlington. By 28 April, she had lapsed into a coma, and Burlington described how he was summoned in the middle of the night:

> I was awoke by Tupper, standing at the foot of my bed. He said, 'A change has occurred.' I exclaimed, 'Is it hopeless?' He said, 'I fear so.'
>
> I rushed to her room and found my beloved wife gasping for breath, her stomach extremely distended, her eyeballs starting forwards – her pulse had ceased, she was evidently on the brink of death. My darling I believe recognised me. At least her hand turned towards me, and I fancied her look was towards me and that she made an effort to speak. I knelt by her dying bed with her hand in mine, but I know not whether I prayed for her. . . . I did not know the exact moment of her entering eternity, so quietly did that purest of earthly beings pass away.
>
> They left me for a few moments with my best beloved, and Grant to God

that that scene may never pass from my mind, that if I am ever tempted to forget thee, if earthly cares and pleasures are about to engross my thoughts, that chamber of death may present itself to my mind, so that the memory of my Blanche may recall me to purer and holier thoughts. I saw Cavendish and Lou [the two eldest children] – dear little things, they felt more than I could have expected. Both sobbed piteously when they were told they would never see Mamma again on earth, but they talked with great happiness, and I believe quite naturally, of her being now an angel in heaven.

In Paris the first the Duke had heard of Blanche's illness had been a worrying report in *The Times* which had brought him rushing back to England. At Dover he had read another more favourable report, and he did not learn the truth until he reached Westhill, where he was greeted by the grief-stricken Burlington. Burlington himself describes the scene:

We hardly spoke and his look was one of extreme misery and wretchedness. He wished to see her and I went in with him and uncovered her face. We both knelt down and I trust our prayers were heard. She is an immense loss to him – he had talked to her so openly when he first turned his mind to thoughts of religion three years ago, and he could, I know, talk to her more freely than to any other person. George [his brother] dreads what may be the consequence, that he may return to his former ways of life, but I trust to God that he has found such delight in his ways that nothing will ever induce him to step aside from them. Blanche had the fullest affection and interest for him – she always talked of him as an interest close to her heart. She understood him perfectly and made the fullest allowance for all his failings.

George thinks all his alterations and projects at Chatsworth were done very much in the feeling that she would come after him and take pleasure in them.

Blanche's death would haunt the Duke and his successor for the remainder of their lives. Burlington, who survived his wife by more than fifty years, would mourn her till the day he died. For the Sixth Duke it was like the sudden loss of a treasured daughter, and his first reaction was to see her death as retribution for his former unredeemed existence. '4 May. Day of my Blanche's funeral. O unhappy me. . . . An avenging God saw me there. [five words deleted] How dare I complain?'

Instead of complaint to the Almighty, he had a practical proposal for his heir, which had led him to write Lord Burlington a letter on the very eve of the funeral. This personal confession explains more about the Bachelor Duke than any other words he wrote:

Your happy marriage to our lost angel made me contented and satisfied with a fate at which otherwise I should have repined.

Many circumstances combined in my younger days to prevent my marriage – but for ten years of my life I formed a connection which occupied and gave me interest.

When from motives of conscience, I broke that off, my happiness in your union with Blanche, and her attachment to me, one I may say of unusual strength, were sufficient – though at times I felt the pressure of my lonely life.

Now comes my proposal. You *are* my heir. Be as if my son. Get rid of your house in Belgrave Square. Let my houses be your home and the home of your children. They will be as if my grandchildren, only that I should and would not interfere with your direction and management of them. . . .

You and your children would be the consolation and delight of my life, and if that is prolonged, your daughter as she grows up would be the prop of my old age and would recall her mother to me.

Generous though the Duke's proposal was it must have put Lord Burlington in an unenviable position during his period of greatest grief. For Burlington was a kindly Christian who understood the Sixth Duke's feelings for his wife; but he also understood important difficulties the Duke ignored. Despite their shared grief and Christian faith, they had very different characters; his children remained deeply attached to their home at Holker Hall, just as he did to his house in Belgrave Square. Trouble and misunderstandings would inevitably ensue.

The Duke waited anxiously for Lord Burlington's reply. '7 May. No answer from William to my letter,' he noted in his diary. Then on 13 May comes the bleak entry, which the Duke has underlined for emphasis:
'Refusal from William'.

The only person the Duke complained to of his disappointment now was Harriet. 'I think William is not a person quite to understand me or my views,' he put it mildly. 'Another with a different disposition might have gladly accepted.'

Thirty years earlier, Harriet had enjoined her brother to achieve 'true greatness', but that was utterly behind him now along with all his other vanities. He and Harriet were both overwhelmed with Blanche's death, and William's curt refusal seemed to rob life of all semblance of a purpose. He returned to Chatsworth and confided in his diary; 'I am in great depression. The forming of that plan had excited and occupied me, and my return here today with it all overthrown is very trying.'

He might have used a stronger word than 'trying' for the destruction of a life's ambitions, but the word expresses something of the mood of gentle, often self-mocking, resignation in which the Duke was to pass the remainder of his life. Nothing changed dramatically, and ironically what should have been Chatsworth's most light-hearted building – the Great Conservatory – was completed just a few months after Blanche's death in what the Duke referred to as his 'year of greatest sorrow'.

The Duke was proud of his conservatory, which was one of the engineering wonders of the age. It diverted him from dwelling on the past, and it would have been unkind to Paxton to have failed to appreciate it. Indeed, at times it seemed as if Paxton's ingenuity and restless energy were providing the real impetus behind the dukedom now. 'O Paxton, my kind deliverer of all cares! How kind and good are you,' the Duke exclaimed, and the summer after Blanche's death, they were in Ireland together. With Paxton there to egg him on, the Duke was compulsively planning to rebuild and extend Lismore Castle

– which his father never visited – on a suitably ambitious scale; with Chatsworth all but finished, he required something else to occupy his time.

For an unhappy man, haunted with a sense of failure, the Duke was living out his days in style. In 1843, Victoria picked on Chatsworth for a second royal visit with Prince Albert, and the Duke, who was still less enamoured of the Consort than of the Sovereign, was not enthusiastic at the honour. 'The Queen wants to come to Chatsworth. Ah! A deal of trouble, but it's better over, and now is a dull time, not taking a planned bit out of my year.'

For he realized what was expected of him – and Paxton did the rest. Among his other roles, Paxton was an inspired impresario, and having arranged a royal salute from Bess of Hardwick's Tower, his illuminations, with twelve thousand separate lamps, turned the gardens and the Great Conservatory into a place of wonder.

The royal party actually drove into the Great Conservatory in their carriages; and later Paxton had two hundred gardeners slaving through the night to remove the debris in the gardens, an achievement which prompted the Duke of Wellington to tell the Duke: 'I would have liked that man of yours for one of my generals.'

It was a compliment the Duke enjoyed, and it must have made him even more receptive than he might have been to Paxton's next grandiose suggestion for the Chatsworth gardens. In twelve months' time, in April 1844, Tsar Nicholas was due to make a state visit to England; it had been intimated that His Majesty would revisit '*ami Devonshire*' at Chatsworth, and the Duke required something suitable to welcome him. The answer was a fountain – the highest in the world. It could be fed from the waters high up on the moors, and Paxton, whose many-sided nature included a passing interest in hydraulics, was confident of being able to arrange the technicalities. He did, and by the time Tsar Nicholas arrived in England, the 'Emperor Fountain' was all ready with its 267-foot-high jet to welcome him to Derbyshire.

But the 'Emperor Fountain' was rather like the story of the Duke's existence now. Unreliable as ever, the Emperor of All the Russias never came to see it; and, although the Duke was permitted to entertain him splendidly at Chiswick – and finally received the once coveted Order of St Andrew to wear beside his Order of the Garter – it was one more disappointment in another 'trying' year.

For by the spring of 1844 Currey's warnings about money could no longer be ignored, and a few weeks after the Emperor's visit, the Duke was writing,

All my sins and omissions stare me in the face. Anxiety to an anxious nervous disposition like mine is the scourge of life. The imagination works on it, and adds never-ending possibilities to a merely scarcely possible evil.

The 'merely scarcely possible evil', was that the Duke was hideously in debt, and every year the situation was getting worse.

But how to save the dukedom? The Duke, congenitally incapable of facing a balance-sheet, had not the least idea, and, as so often now when at a loss, he turned to Paxton. Paxton swiftly mastered the accounts – as he mastered everything – and was genuinely appalled:

> Although I had heard that Your Grace's debts were large in amount, I was not aware until I saw the balance-sheet, that nearly half your income is absorbed in paying interest thereon.

In fact the debt was approaching £1 million, and the Duke was paying £45,000 a year in interest. Paxton had discovered the truth at last – that the origins of the debt went back to Georgiana's and the Fifth Duke's extravagances. He added, with the benefit of hindsight, that the Duke's advisers *should* have made him pay off all the Devonshire debts when he came into possession, over thirty years before, 'and before a stone was laid at Chatsworth or the smallest outlay made in the way of improvements. This would have saved the debt mounting at compound interest, so that it now stands at around £1 million.'

Paxton was also honest enough to blame himself.

> I have been the cause of your Grace spending a great deal of money; had I been at all aware of your real position, I certainly never should have done so. I *most certainly* regret my responsibility in this respect. The great pleasure I have always had in adding to your enjoyments at this princely seat can be my only excuse.

Remorse apart, what was to be *done?* As Paxton pointed out, it was impractical to think of clearing off the debt out of income. Something would have to go, and after much heartache and discussion Paxton was instrumental in arranging to sell the old Burlington estates of Londesborough and Balderly in Yorkshire, to his friend, George Hudson, the self-made 'Railway King', for a net sum of £690,700.

For the Duke it must have seemed like one more sign of failure. He was the first Duke of Devonshire not to acquire land but to sell it, and as Lord Fitzwilliam soon took pains to point out to him,

> ... the alienation of one of the great masses of your landed property ... cannot fail to make a sensible inroad upon your influence and upon the position you hold in the great national community.

By now the Duke was not too much concerned about his 'influence' and position in 'the great national community', and Paxton sounded a more reassuring note when he said that paying off the debt – or the major part of it – would at least enable 'your Grace to continue to be surrounded with that splendour which is your birthright and which is so magnificently and so generously dispensed to all around you.'

Dispense he did until the end, rebuilding, planting, travelling and entertaining with almost undiminished vigour, for, as Greville wrote about him at his death, activities like these helped 'to fill up the vacuum of his existence'.

The Duke would have agreed, for he had grown lonely and pessimistic with the years. He refused Lord Melbourne's offer of the ancestral Cavendish position of the Lord Lieutenantship of Ireland. The discovery that his valet had been cheating him for years upset him keenly. And in 1848, the 'Year of Revolutions', the English Chartists, with their marches and their threat against the established order, made him feel the precariousness of that common cause he had once believed in between the people and aristocracy: 'The times are fetched up, and *entre nous*, my diary and me, I think there will soon be an end of all distinctions of rank and property in England.'

But that would be a problem for his heirs to face.

The Duke continued to the end to be something of a literary patron and friend of writers. In 1844, the year of the Great Debt, he had taken his mind off his financial troubles by writing his own beguiling guide to Chatsworth – in the form of an extended letter to his sister Harriet. (It was printed privately, and not published until 1982, when substantial extracts were included in *The House* by the present Duchess of Devonshire.)

And early in the same year he recorded in his diary: 'A letter from Leigh Hunt to borrow £200. I never saw him but surrounded by misfortune.' The request was 'very inconvenient' to say the least; but Leigh Hunt, the former Whig essayist and friend of Shelley, who was once imprisoned for a libellous article on the Prince Regent, had a sentimental call upon the Duke. So the Duke invited him to stay at Chatsworth, proposed that he should write a history of the Cavendishes (which came to nothing), and gave him his £200. Knowing Hunt, the Duke wisely paid him the money in instalments.

A less one-sided literary relationship was the friendship between the Duke and Charles Dickens. Here the introduction seems to have come through Paxton, who had met the great novelist in London, and in April 1848 Dickens was writing the Duke a letter of apology for being unable to accept an invitation to Devonshire House. But they met later, and in May 1851 Dickens was actually directing and acting in the gala opening performance of *Not so Bad as we Seem*, a five-act comedy by Bulwer-Lytton on a stage specially constructed by Paxton in Devonshire House. The object was to raise money for indigent authors.

Both Dickens and the Duke set out to make the evening a memorable success. Victoria and Albert came. The Duke's private band performed an overture composed by the Duke's personal musician, Mr Coote, and as well as Dickens himself, the cast included several of his literary and artistic friends – his future biographer, John Forster, the novelist, Wilkie Collins, Mark Lemon, the editor of *Punch*, and the artists Tenniel and Augustus Egg.

Then in October 1851 Dickens was invited up to Chatsworth, and the Duke somewhat diffidently offered Dickens a copy of his own *Handbook* to Chatsworth when he left. Even allowing for a touch of flattery which was called for when writing to a duke, there is no mistaking Dickens's genuine admiration for the book as well as for his host. Reading the guide-book was, he wrote, 'so like going over the house again with you, and hearing you talk about it, that it had a perfect charm for me'. And, thanking the Duke for all his 'kindness and hospitality', he went on to assure him that 'among your "Troops of friends", there cannot be one more obliged to you and attached to you than I am'.

With age, the Duke's charm and gentleness seem to have increased, and the bitterness that he had felt at Lord Burlington's rejection of his offer after

Blanche's death was now forgotten. At Christmas 1852, the Duke, Lord Burlington and all the family were happily reunited with sister Harriet at Castle Howard; and the ageing Duke seemed happy in the presence of the man who would succeed him.

> Dear William and friends and family here. I want to show him my keys and show him how to get at my will but feel slightly shy. . . . Nothing could be kinder or more perfect than he was – and he seems to take pleasure in my liking and approving of his children.

In fact he was anticipating death too soon. The stroke that came a year later failed to kill him but left him an invalid as he struggled on with his round of visiting from one of his great houses to the next. At Lismore, now completed with its great court and impressive new Victorian baronial Hall, designed by Augustus Pugin, he made a great point of entertaining, not only the local gentry, but also the townspeople who, as *The Times* put it, 'had the inexpressible delight of welcoming their beloved Duke, their benefactor and their friend, to his ancestral halls.'

Another 'ancestral hall' he had taken pains refurbishing was Hardwick, which he loved. He was there at the beginning of 1858, and one of the last letters he wrote was to Louisa Cavendish, Blanche's daughter:

> My dearest Lou,
> and perfect darling as you are. It will make me very happy to see you. . . .
> Adieu dearest L. thanks to you also for your kind support of your old,
> Devonshire.

He hoped to see her when he reached Chatsworth at the end of January, but on Sunday the 17th, after supervising the re-hanging of some pictures in Bess of Hardwick's gallery, he 'felt a shivering fit and some of his servants who were with him thought he had a slight seizure', but this did not prevent his coming down for dinner. William, his heir, describes what happened next:

> He ate with some appetite and there does not seem to have been anything to cause disquiet. He remained in the drawing-room till half past ten, listening to Coote playing. The first part of the night he did not sleep well, and was frequently disturbed by the want of retentiveness of the bladder. The man who sat up with him, Marsden, sent to Stukey the valet and asked him whether Dr. Cowdell should be called and was answered yes. Cowdell came but was not alarmed and gave him a composing draught. . . . After Cowdell left him he slept soundly but awoke about six and asked for his repeater. He observed it was after six. Marsden said yes it was a quarter after. He struck the repeater again and said yes a quarter after six. He was then quiet but coughed once or twice. Marsden seems soon to have thought him unusually quiet and after looking at him once or twice ascertained that all was over. He had died in his sleep without pain or struggle.
> I have been into the room where he lies – his countenance is composed and calm and wears what one may call an expression of happiness.

'Such', as the correspondent loyally put it in the *Derby Reporter*, 'was the peaceful end of the noblest, the most princely, and the most beneficent of England's great nobility'.

By no means every one agreed about the 'princely' virtues of the departed Duke, for in contrast with the undisputed worthiness of his successor, he now tended to be regarded as a shade disreputable, a relic from the England of the Regency who had outlived his usefulness. His extravagance and taste were criticized – so were his morals. Worst of all, he was felt to have squandered both his life and fortune in that most unforgiveable of failings for the High Victorians – frivolity. Other fellow aristocrats besides Lord Fitzwilliam felt quite strongly that he had somehow let the upper-class side down through self-indulgent irresponsibility. Henry Leach, the Edwardian biographer of the Eighth Duke of Devonshire was to write the Bachelor Duke off in a single scathing sentence: 'During the long period of his dukedom he achieved little of distinction, save in some eccentricities and in his constant social importance.'

Although the Duke himself might not have disagreed, he appears today a more impressive figure than the nineteenth century gave him credit for. He was certainly of great importance in the history of his family, if only for the way he saw the dukedom through a period of social and political transition with decency and dignity, and played his part in making sure that the untenable political pretensions of his family and class were painlessly abandoned – as he believed they should be.

But his greatest interest lies in the way he offered something in their place. On the one hand he raised the image of the Dukedom to a level of romantic glamour it had never had before. True, he overspent, but what Paxton called 'that princely splendour so magnificently dispensed to all around him' proved an investment for the future of his house and the English aristocracy. As feudalism died, the mid-nineteenth century middle classes found themselves overawed, and largely overwhelmed by the extraordinary illusion of the wealth and grandeur of the aristocracy – and nowhere was this grand illusion more seductive than in the Xanadu-like creations left behind by the Sixth Duke of Devonshire. Forget the Duke they might, but the Victorians could never get over the magnificence of his redoubled Chatsworth, with its fountain and gardens and fabulous conservatory.

At the same time the Duke had done something quite different but equally important. During the discontent that had led up to the parliamentary Reform of 1832, there had been widely-voiced criticism from the middle classes of the arrogance and inefficiency of the aristocracy, who were in danger of becoming a beleaguered caste. This was to change dramatically, and by 1862 the acute French social observer, Taine, could write of England with some surprise as appearing like 'a country dominated by an aristocracy'.

For, as Mark Girouard has pointed out,

During the 1840s the working-class agitation at home and a series of revolutions abroad convinced the upper and the middle classes that they must stick together . . . the social gap between the upper and middle classes narrowed. . . . Finally, the upper classes adjusted their image to make it acceptable to middle-class morality.

None of the upper aristocracy 'adjusted' quite so hard or so sincerely as the Duke. His conversion to evangelical Christianity was sincere; so was his kindness, and the effort that he made to spread the blessings of his state to all around him. The least arrogant of nineteenth-century aristocrats, and an extremely likeable, amusing man, he did his best to make the people – or at any rate the middle classes – and the aristocracy genuinely united by their 'mutual kind feelings and good offices' as he honestly believed they should be.

12. The Rewards of Virtue

The Seventh Duke, William (1808–1891)

The Seventh Duke of Devonshire . . . was, by the consent of his countrymen, one of the finest flowers of the Victorian nobility. . . . None realised so well as he, the significance of the changes which had taken place in national life, and the need for ducal adaptation. In an age of commerce and progress under a settled and satisfactory constitution, more was required of the Duke of Devonshire if he aspired to the respect and renown of his forefathers. There would be no deference from the people without unusual service, whilst mere title only would not serve to save him from consignment to the lumber-room of the peerage, were the effort mediocre. In these critical times, and with no excursion into the fields of statesmanship, he secured his name in a niche of honour and distinction where it will survive during future centuries.

Henry Leach, The Duke of Devonshire, a Personal and Political Biography (1908)

The year the Sixth Duke died, a freak summer storm hit Chatsworth, and hailstones the size of golf-balls smashed 4,000 panes of glass in the Great Conservatory. Under Paxton's supervision, the glass was efficiently and rapidly replaced, but the cost was considerable, and for the Bachelor's successor this dramatic demonstration of divine contumely must have confirmed doubts he had already reached about his spectacular but cumbersome inheritance.

There can be no greater contrast than between the Bachelor Duke and the man who had succeeded him, and nowhere does this show more clearly than in their attitudes to the succession. At twenty-one the Sixth Duke had plunged blithely into enjoying his immense possessions, but at fifty William Cavendish, formerly Lord Burlington and now Seventh Duke of Devonshire, regarded them with grim if dutiful foreboding.

This was partly due to the new Duke's nature. Lacking the Sixth Duke's 'frivolous elasticity of spirits', he had stuck firmly to the resolution made at Blanche's deathbed to remember that 'chamber of death' as a protection against earthly cares and earthly pleasures. Not that he needed too much shielding from pleasure. Never particularly happy since a wretched adolescence when he was bullied cruelly at Eton, even as a young man he had found relief in three activities – hard work, evangelical Christianity and his family.

Instead of simply enjoying the privileges of a nobleman in unreformed Cambridge, he had achieved the laudable distinction of emerging second in the entire University in the rigorously competitive mathematical examinations. 'Placed Second Wrangler and high in the classical tripos at Cambridge', wrote Lord Esher, 'he had never recovered from the shock. Shyness and reserve settled down upon him. His bowed figure tacked into a room like a vessel finding an intricate channel.'

Bowed or not, his married life with the livelier and younger Blanche was by all accounts idyllic. Their shared religious faith had deepened with the death of 'Little Cav', their three-year-old first-born son, in 1833, and, since Blanche's death, her widower had combined a public life of constant usefulness with the private life of a recluse. On the death of his grandfather in 1838, he had already inherited the revived earldom of Burlington together with Compton Place at Eastbourne and 8,000 adjacent Sussex acres, and the splendid Holker Hall in Lancashire, which had even more valuable possessions to the north of Morecambe Bay including Barrow. At Holker, he had jealously guarded his motherless young family, and personally supervised the children's education, imbuing them with his own Christian faith, and always keeping green the sacred memory of the departed angel.

Despite their shared evangelical Christianity and joint worship of the absent Blanche, nothing could have been more different from Lord Burlington's Holker than the world the Sixth Duke had created for himself at Chatsworth, and the Devonshire domains had little in them to appeal to their new possessor. He was not interested in art or orchids. As a serious improving farmer – his herd of Holker shorthorns was already famous – he could hardly fail to regard the cultivation of the Cavendish banana in a £30,000 conservatory as distinctly self-indulgent. And for a man of the Seventh Duke's unshowy nature, the whole quasi-regal panoply of ducal Chatsworth seemed an otiose and ruinous embarrassment.

At first glance one might have thought the new Duke's gloom beside the point – after all, his succession to the Dukedom meant that the not insignificant Burlington inheritance was now united with the accumulated Devonshire possessions. In terms of land and houses and potential wealth he was by far the richest duke in the history of the line. But, as he knew too well, it was not that simple. For unlike the Bachelor Duke, with his calm antipathy to balance-sheets, this former Second Wrangler was perfectly equipped to recognize the financial writing on the wall. There was no fooling *him* and, as he soon discovered,

> The income is large, but by far the greater part of it is absorbed by the payment of interest, annuities, and the expense of Chatsworth, leaving but a comparatively insignificant surplus, and much of this will at present be required for legacy and succession duties. This is a worse condition of matters than I had expected, although from knowing the Duke's ignorance of business, I did not expect to find them very flourishing.

The Burlington inheritance was already carrying a debt of around a quarter of a million – thanks to ambitious purchases of land by the Duke's grandfather; the Devonshire inheritance with *its* accumulated debts took the sum outstanding to well above a million. True, the new Duke could count on gross annual revenue of a staggering £200,000 a year, but the cost of servicing the debts and maintaining the ducal empire was just as staggering. With luck, he might rely on a disposable income of £50,000 a year – which for the Sixth Duke would have been enough to let him leave financial care behind and indulge in another cheerful round of building, entertaining or collecting. But the Seventh Duke's pessimistic nature did not work like that. He anticipated troubles – unforeseen electoral expenses, a rise in interest rates, or a few bad harvests which could soon wipe out his annual surplus. As he gloomily admitted, he felt distinctly 'insecure'.

It was to be this sense of insecurity which would provide the mainspring behind the Seventh Duke's life-work from now until his death in 1891. It would transform the dukedom, give him a constant and extraordinarily ambitious role to play in Victorian society, and bring him his reputation as 'one of the finest flowers of the Victorian nobility'. For with him the dukedom once again assumed its eminent position of leadership and national prestige, but this was to rest on something very different from the previous activities of the Dukes of Devonshire.

In his first flush of melancholy over his new possessions, the Duke's reaction was that the only way to put his house – or rather houses – in order, was to sell and then retrench. Lismore would have to go. It would not be greatly missed, and every part of his possessions would have to feel the pinch. 'I have been very busy looking over the agents' estate accounts which Currey has sent me for inspection. The result shows that great economies are everywhere necessary.'

This was at the beginning of 1859, and having told Currey, somewhat curtly, that there was no call for an auditor – he would do the work himself – he went on to discuss the form these economies would have to take at Chatsworth. His Christian conscience did not apparently conflict with a strictly realistic attitude towards the lower orders. 'I fear the number of people to be dismissed must be very great and that great discontent is inevitable,' he wrote with the sort of calm detachment which would have been inconceivable in his predecessor. And inevitably one of the first to get his marching orders was Paxton. Luckily for Paxton – now Sir Joseph and Liberal M.P. for Coventry – his business interests, and involvement in the new Crystal Palace exhibition site at Sydenham, had long since taken over from his work at Chatsworth as his main activity, but the Seventh Duke saw his presence as a dangerous incitement to fresh extravagance. Paxton understood this perfectly. He could hardly feel particularly at home with the new regime, and his connection with the dukedom fairly amicably ceased.

But the Duke was looking for a fresh adviser for the problems raised by his inheritance, and by a strange coincidence he found one in the successor to the very Duke of Bedford who had made such a deep impression on his own predecessor in his youth. Francis, Seventh Duke of Bedford had succeeded to the Bedford dukedom on the death of the Bachelor's spendthrift schoolfriend, the Sixth Duke of Bedford, in 1839, and had faced a situation similar in many ways to Devonshire's. Finding the Bedford estates in debt and considerable disorder, he had imposed economies, and then applied sound principles of Victorian business and estate management to make them prosper. This had worked spectacularly and Francis Bedford – brother of the future Liberal Prime Minister, Lord John Russell – had become something of a protagonist for the new 'enlightened' Whig aristocracy which was making a determined bid for popular esteem in the mid-nineteenth century. He was, in the words of Professor Spring, a member of that 'formidable generation in the history of the

English landed aristocracy . . . that made a valiant attempt to protract aristocratic leadership into a new and increasingly unaristocratic age.'

But the new Duke of Devonshire asked him for advice, not from such lofty motives but because he saw him as a 'first rate man of business' who had used his business skills to deal with much the same situation he faced himself. Bedford's reply was considerably more hopeful than Devonshire expected. He was against any sale of property, on the grounds that even Lismore could, with proper management, soon be 'turned round' to produce a profit. Properly applied, the proven principles of Victorian capitalism could be the Duke's salvation. Sound investment, modern management, efficiency, economy and a weather eye to profit – the very methods of the rising business classes were the best hope for the landed aristocracy as well – and the final words of Bedford's letter of advice are an interesting mixture of upper-class rhetoric and middle-class hard-headedness:

> The duties and responsibilities of such an estate as yours and mine are very great – we must discharge them as best we can, and make a good amount to look back at the close of life – I am pleased to see you paying so much attention to yours – it will provide a fund of satisfaction to others as well as yourself – and conduce to the well-being of those who live upon them.

Such advice was by no means as revolutionary as it sounded. Bess of Hardwick would have heartily agreed; so would each successful Cavendish until the middle of the eighteenth century, when excessive wealth and political supremacy had begun to make such sentiments superfluous for a self-respecting duke. The Fourth Duke would have been profoundly shocked – and the Fifth Duke as profoundly bored – by the mere idea of it. The Sixth Duke would have found it faintly ridiculous, but the Seventh Duke was totally convinced.

As a young M.P. for Cambridge University, which he had briefly represented as a Reformist Whig in the early 1830s, the future Duke had argued strongly for the Reform Bill on the grounds that the aristocracy in future should rely for their influence, not on their boroughs 'but on their own talents and their means of conferring happiness upon the people'. It was an argument similar to that made by the Sixth Duke at the same time in his speech at Derby; but, whereas the Sixth Duke's idea of 'conferring happiness' lay in the *noblesse oblige* of his personal example and the splendour and lavishness of his entertainments, the Seventh Duke saw the happiness of others in very different terms. The aristocracy needed to be 'useful' if it was going to survive – and what better way of being useful than in making money?

Through thrift, economy and profit, money could be prudently invested to create prosperity and fresh employment. The sacred economic cycle of the times would guarantee that in enriching themselves, the aristocracy would also enrich all classes of society and thus provide a true 'community of interests' to unite the country. It was a beguiling argument – with which the Friedmanite economists of the 1980s would still agree – and the Seventh Duke gives no sign of being worried that, as F. M. L. Thompson put it, 'in turning from pomp and circumstance to investment and income as the bulwarks of status, such aristocrats were already moving towards conceding that it was wealth pure and simple which counted, not birth and tradition.'

The Duke had never been particularly concerned with pomp and circumstance – nor for that matter with birth and tradition. By nature and by habit he was profoundly middle-class himself and even before inheriting the dukedom, he had been paying some attention to the use of modern business methods as a way of paying off his debts.

In 1849 the London, Brighton and South Coast Railway had finally reached his sleepy south coast fishing-village of Eastbourne, and had, as he noted in his diary, 'certainly increased the prospects of the place considerably.' By 1855 he had invested £37,000 in the construction of a sea wall and the sort of well-appointed houses which would lure the wealthy middle classes to the English seaside.

But Eastbourne had its teething troubles, and by the time he inherited the Devonshire possessions, the Seventh Duke's most promising field for investment lay not in promenades and piers, still less in agriculture, but in the village of Barrow almost on his doorstep up at Holker. The largest and richest single deposit of iron ore in Britain had just been discovered at nearby Park Vale, the Furness Railway was built, and Barrow was at the beginning of its transformation from a village of three hundred souls into one of the most thriving industrial centres in the country.

This coincided very neatly with the Duke's succession, so that, just at the point when the Duke of Bedford was advising him to make his great possessions pay, the possibility of doing so was there before him, and the Duke needed little prodding to turn from a Whig grandee into an industrial tycoon. In fact he combined the two to considerable effect. There was no more talk of selling Lismore now; rents and the terms of agricultural tenancies were tightened up in all the ducal lands; the overall deficit began to drop; and the Duke was free to turn his energies and surplus income to the interests that excited him.

As a duke and the greatest local landlord, he was automatically both something of a figurehead and an important beneficiary of the developments at Barrow. Companies were beginning to discover the value of a title on their letterhead and the Duke was Chairman of the Board of all the most important Barrow enterprises – the Furness Railway, the Barrow Docks and Harbour Board, the flourishing new Jute works, and most important of all, the Barrow Haematite Steel Company.

Although the actual development of Barrow was directed by engineers and businessmen like Hannay, Schneider, Ramsden and the Devonshires' legal advisers, the Currey family, the Duke himself was personally and passionately involved. Barrow remained his ducal fief, and its growth into an up-to-date industrial centre appealed to his intelligence and sense of purpose. One is reminded of the determined way the eighteenth-century European enlightened despots encouraged their local industries in the way he now took Barrow under the ducal wing.

As early as March 1859, he was recording in his diary a few of the activities this involved. He had just chaired a directors' meeting of the Furness Railway – which had declared an eight per cent dividend on invested capital – and had conducted his own tour of inspection to see what was going on.

> The restorations of Barrow Pier are in progress and the work so far is admirably executed by the contractor. The traffic returns have lately been very bad on the Furness Railway, and as the expenditure cannot be diminished suddenly, I fear the working expenses are at present very heavy in proportion to receipts. We afterwards went up to see the works on the Coniston Railway. The contractor is getting on well and the work has so far turned out lighter than was expected. I afterwards went over the slate quarries. They are doing pretty well but orders are very slack. The late severe weather has caused some of the pipes supplying the water balance to crack, and the balance cannot consequently be worked.

From now on such entries in the Duke's carefully kept diaries steadily increase as he conscientiously pursued the role of the foremost high Victorian aristocratic industrial entrepreneur, visiting his Park Vale iron-mines, discussing further railway developments, chairing the annual general meetings of his associated companies, and bringing an informed technical intelligence to the development of mines, roads, harbours, factories and furnaces.

Nor were his interests confined to Barrow. Ever since the Fifth Duke built his elegant new crescent and assembly rooms at Buxton, the dukes had been uncomplainingly meeting the expenses of the spa which had never quite fulfilled the Fifth Duke's expectations. According to Buxton's own historian 'the result of the Sixth Duke's generosity was an entire absence of initiative in the village and put a premium on lazy indifference.' The Seventh Duke soon changed all that. His policy was to make the inhabitants of Buxton firmly self-reliant. 'He considered they had been nursed enough' and Buxton began to grow as local worthies were made to take charge of its affairs and its own small industries developed.

More dramatically, Eastbourne was starting to respond to the Duke's initiative. In 1859 his new Eastbourne agent, yet another member of the Devonshires' all-purpose legal family, the Curreys' nephew Henry, had drawn up the first development plan for the Eastbourne of the future which, within twenty years with ducal backing and finance, would grow into the 'Empress of Watering Places', the most resoundingly respectable and carefully laid-out new seaside town in Britain. Here was a new role for the aristocracy to play. At Barrow the Duke was helping to provide mass employment and increasing the industrial potential of the nation, but at Eastbourne he was sharing something of the mantle of the Devonshires' prestige with the status-conscious upper middle classes.

Interestingly, across the Channel, the Duc de Morny was doing something rather similar with the development of Deauville, and in both cases these activities symbolize a new community of interest between an aristocracy inspired by bourgeois aims of 'usefulness' and profit, and a bourgeoisie aspiring to the status of the aristocracy. Through his agent, the Seventh Duke would carefully control the growth and character of Eastbourne, so as to exclude the lower middle classes and the *hoi polloi*. They had Brighton; but, at gentler Eastbourne with its terraces and leafy boulevards, the new backbone of the nation could decorously enjoy the high Victorian summers under the aegis of their ducal patron, who as the major local landlord had ensured that their leases totally ruled out the display of washing in the gardens,* the uncontrolled sale of alcohol, or the faintest hint of industry or commerce in the residential quarters.

For a period, the Duke's control was absolute. His Grace and family would give the town its tone by spending their own summer holidays at Compton Place. He also supplied the earliest essential services – drains, sewerage, waterworks and the new road up to Beachy Head. The Duke had an informed interest in such things. 'I came here yesterday', he records in his diary for May 1867, 'for the formal opening of the main drainage works. All the shops were closed and there was a holiday in honour of the occasion. I had to go in procession with the town band and others to the outfall where the valve was opened and the drain discharged its contents most successfully.' Although through the sale of residential leases Eastbourne was planned to become self-financing, the *Eastbourne Gazette* summed up the ducal role in the memorable phrase: 'the Duke can do without Eastbourne, but Eastbourne can not do without the Duke.'

Still less could the booming industries of Barrow-in-Furness do without him now. By the mid-1860s he was by far the largest local investor, and according to one historian was already 'recognised as the good fairy of Barrow, and that in that district to-day the voices of men and women soften in the spirit of reverence when they utter the name of Devonshire.' But the benefits were by no means one-sided, and by the 1870s it seemed as if the Duke's plans for the redemption of the fortunes of the Devonshires had paid off triumphantly.

Agricultural rents were rising steadily, the proportion of income spent on servicing the ducal debt was already halved, and the Duke's dividend income from the Barrow enterprises had grown prodigiously. The researches of David Cannadine have shown that the Duke's dividend income grew from £14,000 in 1863 to £169,000 in 1874. Barrow had become an extraordinary success, with its steel company and the Furness Railway among the most profitable enterprises in the land.

In 1873, over 80 per cent of all Devonshire investments were concentrated in that town, and some 90 per cent of dividend income came from that source. In that year the Duke probably enjoyed the largest current income of any aristocratic millionaire.

But would success spoil the Duke of Devonshire? Obviously not. His bowed and somewhat melancholy figure seems to have remained as bowed and melancholy as ever. His birthday, 27 April, coincided with the date of Blanche's death, and was a perpetual annual day of mourning. The one indulgence he allowed himself out of his rapidly increasing wealth was to

---

* They still do.

commission the indefatigable Sir George Gilbert Scott to rebuild Edensor Church, chiefly because he was 'anxious to have a new family vault as the old burying-place at All Saints Derby is closed'. With the Seventh Duke, the Devonshires – in common with almost all the late nineteenth-century aristocracy – abruptly ceased their former role as patrons of the arts. This function passed to the middle classes and the *nouveaux riches*. And far from spending now on anything as frivolous as on works of art or anything above his humdrum round of entertaining, every surplus penny of the Cavendishes was frugally ploughed back into the Duke's greatest source of profit and self-satisfaction – the industries of Barrow-in-Furness.

He was not made by nature to be popular, but he was almost universally revered, for just as the eighteenth-century Dukes of Devonshire embodied the ideal of the landed Whig grandees in all their ostentatious splendour, so the Seventh Duke was everything a great Victorian nobleman should be – moral, intelligent, responsible and wise. With his impeccable private life, his sorrow and his sense of service, the Seventh Duke was unassailable; for who but the most hard-boiled cynic or egalitarian could criticize a duke who, with all the Cavendish possessions to enjoy, found his greatest self-indulgence in his Presidency of the Royal Agricultural Society – which he founded – or of the Iron and Steel Institute? And when Prince Albert died in 1861, who was more fitting to succeed him as Chancellor of Cambridge University than the former Second Wrangler, whose whole life exemplified the sense of service and profoundly serious ideals of the Queen's lamented consort? It was as Chancellor that, in 1870, the Duke made his own historic contribution to the future of the University and British science, by spontaneously offering £6,300 to pay for the building and apparatus needed for a laboratory of Experimental Physics.

It was an extraordinarily enlightened piece of aristocratic patronage and in terms of its results was possibly the most important initiative ever made by any Duke of Devonshire. The first Professor of Experimental Physics in the University was the great physicist James Clerk Maxwell, whose work in editing Henry Cavendish's unpublished papers on electricity has been described as 'the finest contribution to the history of science in the English language.' At first, the new building was to be called the 'Devonshire Physical Laboratory', but finally in Henry Cavendish's honour it was entitled simply the Cavendish Laboratory. Since its official opening by the Duke in 1874, the Cavendish has become the most famous physical laboratory in the world, and 'twenty-two Nobel Prize Awards have been made to Cavendish men who accomplished or started their fundamental researches or lines of research, in the Laboratory.'

Apart from such acts of patronage and his work as a great Victorian industrialist – which with the Duke of Wellington now dead had earned him the title of 'The Second Iron Duke' – the Seventh Duke's interests and ambitions were confined, like the true Victorian he was, to the private and religious bosom of his family. Here, for the first time, was a Duke of Devonshire in the role of a stern but devoted paterfamilias, unconcerned with the lure of politics or high society, and living a life of notable simplicity in the middle of his vast possessions.

Although he was devoted to his children, it is hard to know how close he really was to them. At the beginning of the Michaelmas Term of 1851 his eldest son and heir, eighteen-year-old Spencer Compton, Lord Cavendish, was hardly surprisingly accepted by his father's college, Trinity. He was a shy, gangling youth whose inherited portion of Cavendish caution had almost certainly increased with Lord Burlington's refusal to permit him the corrupting fellowship of other members of his age and class at public school; on this his first adventure into the world outside his family he was inevitably accompanied to Cambridge by his celebrated father, who was delighted to find him already allocated rooms on his own former staircase in Trinity Great Court. It was a moving occasion for Lord Burlington, which he duly recorded in his diary before he bade his son goodbye. 'I set off home tomorrow and leave my beloved boy here to battle his way for himself. God grant he may yield to no vicious temptations!'

This was perhaps too much to ask of the Almighty, and Lord Hartington – as he became with his father's accession to the dukedom – would yield languidly to most of the temptations which had traditionally assailed his ancestors, if not his father. A strange combination of reserve and raciness, he might have been a throwback to the youthful world of his great-grandfather, the Fifth Duke, and showed little obvious connection with the high-minded, bourgeois Victorian aspirations the Seventh Duke so earnestly espoused.

Instead, he seemed to share the unwillingness to hurry into marriage which the Sixth Duke had shown at his age, along with the late duke's taste for women of the town. (His affair with Catherine Walters, the notorious Victorian *poule de luxe* who was known by her trade-name 'Skittles', raised many an envious eyebrow in the early sixties.) And his advent into politics – as the twenty-four-year-old Liberal member for his home seat of North Lancashire – showed an even greater lack of the sort of moral fervour which had inspired his father as a young M.P. at the time of the Great Reform Bill.

A bored and boring speaker, he had actually yawned in the middle of his own maiden speech in Parliament, prompting Disraeli to remark prophetically, 'He'll do! To any man who can betray such extreme langour under such circumstances, the highest post in the gift of the Commons should be open.'

Although the Duke was obviously proud of the subsequent political success of his eldest son and stayed on surprisingly good terms with him, he must have turned a blind eye to the private life he led in London. This was not necessary with his other children. Louisa had bravely borne the burden of taking something of her dead mother's place within the family, and the Duke's second son, Lord Frederick Cavendish, was much more like his father than Lord Hartington. A sincere Christian, he had a good deal of his father's moral earnestness. In politics he would be far closer to the almost equally earnest Gladstone than his eldest brother – in the family he was sometimes called 'wicked radical Fred' – and in 1864 he married Gladstone's niece by marriage, Lady Lucy Lyttelton.

She was another determined diarist, and the published journals of this childless, artless, somewhat gushing lady, offer a fascinating picture of the solemn ducal world she entered through her marriage, with its uncanny mixture of extraordinary wealth and holy living. On returning from her honeymoon, she and her husband went to Hardwick Hall. 'Fred and I came here alone, under the ducal circumstances of a special train, twenty-two servants, six horse-boxes and two carriages,' she wrote, and then described how she and Lord Frederick spent their first evening together in the house, reading Bishop Butler on Virtue and John Stuart Mill on Liberty.

Later she was off to Barrow with her husband and his younger brother, Lord Richard:

> . . . saw the new Bessemer process of making steel out of Haematite iron ore: too interesting and wonderful, especially the great blast of air by which the carbon is driven out of the ore, the contact of the two gases making the most tremendous white-hot fire. The hammering delightful too. The town is spreading out and springing up vigorously, and gathers population tolerably fast. The great docks making strides.

Later still she was at Chatsworth when Louisa Cavendish became engaged to the man she married in 1865, Francis Egerton.

> I cried for a long time, thinking of the poor Duke. Take in he has never been separated from Lou except for a day or two at a time since his wife died. . . . If I could only kiss him and call him something it would be a help.

But she never could – any more than she could penetrate the bewhiskered aloofness of her husband's elder brother, Hartington – and she gradually accepted this withdrawn yet regal world of the Victorian Cavendishes.

Meanwhile the Duke appeared to have the God of Business on his side, with his steel company returning dividends in excess of fifteen per cent through to the early seventies, and most of his other enterprises booming. Entries like 'very prosperous' and 'busy and prosperous' appear with monotonous regularity in the Duke's diary. But the world was changing, and the Duke's afflictions in this vale of tears were far from over.

First came a dramatic fall in the demand for steel in the mid-1870s which struck Barrow badly. The Furness Railway was hit; so was the Flax and Jute works and so was Barrow shipbuilding in which the Duke was principal investor. 'It will clearly be necessary for me to find a great deal of money to prevent a smash,' he noted anxiously in 1877.

The Duke and the Duke alone could save these industries which meant so much to him, and despite the alarm and warnings of the Curreys at the re-emergence of the Great Debt of the Devonshires, he did what he gloomily conceived to be his duty, and went on pumping money into Barrow until by the mid-eighties his investments there had topped two million pounds, and 'the resources of the great estates of the House of Devonshire were devoted to shoring up Barrow's crumbling industrial enterprises.'

Nor were the resources from the Devonshire estates all they had been. From the late 1870s bad harvests at home and imports of cheap foodstuffs from abroad had been hitting agriculture too, and even the greatest land-owners had begun to feel the pinch. With income falling, and a fresh round of borrowing essential to enable him to meet his obligations, the Duke began to be despondent. But his tribulations were not exclusively financial, and early in 1882 he received another blow reopening the wounds still tender from the death of Blanche.

The Liberals under Gladstone were in power, having decisively defeated Disraeli's government in 1880, and the Duke's two eldest sons were in the new administration: Hartington, Gladstone's greatest rival for the Liberal leadership, was Secretary for India, and Lord Frederick Cavendish, having once been Gladstone's private parliamentary secretary, was Financial Secretary to the Treasury. One of the government's major headaches was Ireland, with Parnell leading Irish opposition at Westminster, and violence spreading rapidly throughout the country.

At first the British Government tried toughness against the Irish but, in April 1882, Gladstone switched abruptly to conciliation – coercion was to be abandoned, and political suspects freed. As a major absentee Irish landlord, whose estates and rents round Lismore had been badly hit by Fenian agitation, the Duke strongly disagreed. 'Matters are becoming serious and I fear Gladstone is adopting a very rash course of action,' he wrote. Gladstone's Chief Secretary for Ireland, W. E. Forster shared the Duke's views and resigned, at which Gladstone offered Lord Hartington the job.

Hartington was too shrewd a politician, and too cautious a Cavendish, to accept this particular political bed of nails, but his brother, Lord Frederick Cavendish, felt differently. On 3 May, the Duke wrote in his diary:

> I hear from Cav [Lord Hartington] and Freddie that Gladstone is very desirous that F. should accept the post of Irish Secretary, and F. seems to have nearly made his mind up to accept it. I should have been against it if I had known of the proposal before matters had advanced so far.

Next day, Lord Frederick's acceptance of the post became official – producing even gloomier forebodings from the Duke. 'I have great misgivings as to his being sent to a place of such extreme difficulty at the present time.' But the apostle of Bishop Butler and John Stuart Mill was not one to shirk his duty, and on 5 May, together with Earl Spencer, the new Lord Lieutenant of Ireland, the new Irish Secretary boarded the night mail from Euston for Dublin, bearing a 'message of peace' from Mr Gladstone.

There is an eight-day gap now in the Seventh Duke's diary, and the entry for 12 May is written in a quivering hand.

> A most dreadful affliction has befallen me. My dearest Freddie was savagely slaughtered in the Phoenix Park on Saturday evening, a few hours after he had arrived in Dublin to undertake the duties of Irish Secretary. The dreadful intelligence reached me Sunday morning by a telegram from Cavendish to Edward.* He along with Emma arrived in the course of the day, and it has been something of a comfort to hear from him that my dearest boy is not supposed to have suffered much pain. He, along with Mr.

---

* The Duke's youngest son, Lord Edward Cavendish, married Lady Emma Lascelles.

Burke, the under-secretary, were stabbed to death by 4 men in the Phoenix Park, and the wounds were of a kind to be almost instantly fatal. Cav has been most affectionate. . . . We are comforted in some measure by the feeling that Freddie has fallen in the discharge of his duty.

The body arrived on Tuesday morning, and I have had the sad pleasure of seeing again this dear dear face. The expression is most calm – not the slightest trace of suffering. The funeral took place yesterday and the intense feeling excited through the country was manifested by the immense concourse of people who were present. A large number of members of the House of Commons came down from London, and representatives of all the public bodies with which Freddie was connected. The crowds that lined the road through the park were most orderly and well-behaved. The service was read by Edward Talbot, Warden of Keble College. Nothing could have been better or more in harmony with my unutterable grief. Lucy was present and bore up wonderfully.

Next day the Duke added a brief postscript to his account. 'I forgot to mention Mr Gladstone, who arrived for the funeral and who left this morning. He looks ill and shattered. He felt the blow most acutely, having been greatly attached to Freddie.'

Lord Frederick's death was something of a mystery; none of the proscribed Irish organizations ever admitted to it, and although six Irish members of a Fenian gang known as the 'Invincibles' were later to be convicted of the crime, their motives were never properly explained, and it seems almost certain that Lord Frederick had been murdered by mistake. Their target had been under-secretary Burke, and the murderers had not known who Lord Frederick was.

This was no consolation to the Duke in his 'unutterable grief', and during his final years the dukedom seemed to sink into a state of almost chronic gloom and hopelessness. For, along with his private sorrows, the ageing duke was having to accept the fact that much of his life's work had failed as well. Barrow was being hit by a depression which not even the Devonshire millions could stave off; he was personally in debt to the Scottish Widows Insurance Company for £80,000 on the dubious security of his Irish estates, and the days of affluence and dividends were over. 'I am beginning to think large reductions of estate expenditure will soon be necessary as my income is fast falling to a very unpleasant extent,' he wrote.

For the sad truth was that, despite his vaunted business skills, his evangelical ideals, his personal restraint, and his lofty aims of aristocratic leadership in industry, the Seventh Duke had landed his family in a worse financial muddle than all the extravagance and unconcern of his careless predecessor. And the times were changing. By the 1880s much of the earnest fervour of Victorian society had spent itself; a new mood of hedonistic, slightly vulgar raciness had started, and was beginning to infect the upper classes. Respected, worried and revered, the Duke was rapidly becoming an anachronism.

In 1888, he began his birthday entry in his diary:

I am actually 80 years old today and have certainly aged much during the last year. It is difficult to realise the fact that 48 years have passed away since that sad time at Westhill when I lost my beloved Blanche. The time when I shall rejoin her cannot be far distant.

But his days dragged on. With his great political prestige the Duke's heir, Lord Hartington, was now the one adding to the reputation of the family and was Duke of Devonshire in all but name; and in the summer of 1891, the Seventh Duke sustained one final blow on the death of his youngest son, Lord Edward Cavendish. With Hartington unmarried, the heir apparent to the dukedom after him was now Lord Edward's son by his wife, the former Lady Emma Lascelles, young Victor Cavendish.

But the old Duke's worthy and depressing life was almost over. Just before Christmas 1891, at his beloved Holker Hall, he went to join his long dead wife. Not before its time, a new and very different episode in the story of the Dukes of Devonshire had started.

13. The Duke of Omnium

The Eighth Duke, Spencer Compton (1833–1908)

THE new Duke was fifty-eight at his accession. Because of his father's undesired longevity he had had over a quarter of a century in the House of Commons since he first yawned his way through that maiden speech of his, and Disraeli's prophecy about him had all but been fulfilled. He had not quite become Prime Minister, but he had held great offices of state and was already something of a living legend. Affectionately nicknamed 'Harty-Tarty', he would henceforth be known politically as 'the safe Duke' – the man everyone, the Queen included, thought they could trust against tricky Mr Gladstone, the self-denying statesman who was rumoured to have refused the premiership on three separate occasions, the English aristocrat personified, stylish, sage, immensely dignified and rather bored.

No one has ever commented on another fact about him – that the new Eighth Duke was the only Duke of Devonshire ever to have worn a beard. True, the reign of Victoria was a great period for male facial hair, and the new Duke made a handsome figure of a man as he slumbered on the benches of the House of Lords like a recumbent prophet weary from his labours. 'I fell asleep one afternoon,' he recalled, 'and dreamt I was addressing that just assembly, and when someone woke me up I found that my dream was true. I *was* speaking to their Lordships.'

But a beard is one of nature's great disguises, and the Duke was a most elusive human being, whose importance to the House of Cavendish and the English aristocracy, was by no means as simple – or as casual – as it seemed.

Ever since his childhood at Holker, brought up by his prayerful father in the all-seeing presence of his dear departed mother, Lord Hartington had had to hide his nature, and protective camouflage had rapidly become a habit. The truth about him was that, unlike his father, he was in many ways the most traditional of Cavendishes – cautious, pragmatic, addicted to horses, interested in women, a politician to his finger-tips, congenitally anti-clerical, something of a rake, and patently immune to all those middle-class ambitions and concerns that so obsessed his father.

But he had had to be discreet, and the form of his discretion had turned into a sort of act which, as the years went by, had become as much a part of him as his celebrated whiskers. It had made him popular and very famous: it had enabled him to get away with almost everything he wanted out of life; but it has also made it difficult to be certain of the truth about him ever since.

The period of his early manhood came at a time when the upper aristocracy was having to adapt itself against the criticism and challenge of the rising middle classes. One way it did this was exemplified in his father's conscientious life – by trying to adopt the methods and the mores of the aspiring bourgeoisie themselves. But the Seventh Duke, apart from gathering immense and somewhat sanctimonious respect, had ultimately failed. However hard he tried, he had had none of the ruthlessness or hard commercial sense of the true-born businessman; as Bagehot put it, neatly and unanswerably in his *English Constitution*, 'an aristocracy is necessarily inferior in business to the classes nearer business.'

Lord Hartington had no intention of following his father's errors – any more than of copying his self-denying way of life – and as a young man he was shrewd enough to grasp what the people, and particularly the middle-class electorate, wanted from their leaders. There was no future for a pre-Reform Bill authoritative aristocracy clinging to its power by prescriptive right, but there was considerable popular nostalgia for a sort of parody of what people thought of as the old-style English nobleman – easy-going, racy, slightly arrogant, comfortably philistine and something of an ass.

This image had little to do with the earlier Cavendishes, but by nature and physique Lord Hartington was admirably cast for such a role and he had learned to play it to perfection, even acting up his weaknesses to enhance the reassuring myth of an aristocrat who was 'safe' because he was comfortably incompetent and never tried too hard. One sees this with his shooting. At Chatsworth and at Bolton Abbey, the Cavendishes owned some of the best shooting in the country, but far from boasting of the fact, he pretended to be a most indifferent shot.

There is a celebrated anecdote about the day he surprised his friends by killing a high-flying partridge at Creswell Crags with a perfect shot. Everybody cheered, but when the drive was over, Hartington pretended to be puzzled. Mildly aggrieved he asked, 'I wonder why Harry Chaplin and the others cheered when I fired both barrels at a cock pheasant and missed?' Someone answered that he had killed the highest flying partridge of the day.

'Did I?' he replied, 'I didn't even know it was there. However, it's over now, so don't say anything about it, and let me keep my reputation.'

Now nobody kills a high-flying partridge by mistake, not even a Lord Hartington, but as he said, he had to keep his 'reputation' – and his disclaimer worked so well that the spot was instantly nicknamed, 'Hartington's Stand'.

His well-known passion for the turf was similar. He was obviously very fond of racing. As an undergraduate at Trinity, one of those 'vicious temptations' the Seventh Duke had feared so much for him had been the lure of nearby Newmarket; Hartington succumbed and he had been utterly addicted ever since.

In 1877 he was forty-four and leading the Liberal opposition in the Commons, but on his birthday his father was confiding to his diary, 'It seems generally agreed that he has been getting on extremely well as leader of the opposition, but I could wish Cav was not so fond of the turf.' By the 1890s, Lord Salisbury was still moaning quietly about the postponement of important parliamentary business, 'because Devonshire is obliged to go to Newmarket to ascertain whether one quadruped can run a little faster than another.'

As with his shooting, Hartington always managed to appear something of a duffer as a racehorse owner and, although he took great pride reviving the First Duke's pale yellow racing-colours, known as 'The Straw' (which are claimed as the oldest racehorse colours in the world) and even built himself a house at Newmarket, he never won the Derby, the St Leger or the Oaks. But, as he knew quite well, the English never love a lord so much as on a racecourse, and as a steward of the Jockey Club and something of a fixture in the stand at every classic race, his amiable, ill-clad presence was immensely popular.

His dress, incidentally, was another key component of his public image, for here as elsewhere he always made great point of seeming to despise the patrician trappings he so unshakably possessed. He wore the same Court dress for more than thirty years; on one occasion the Prince of Wales had to remind him, somewhat tartly, that he was wearing the Order of the Garter upside down; and in public his inconsequential shabbiness was something of a trademark. It was of course a sign of inverted superiority as well, for, as he must have known, only the heir to a dukedom could have got away at times with dressing so appallingly. No member of the polite middle classes would have dared, and in 1888 the virtuous bookseller and leader of the Conservatives in the House of Commons, Mr W. H. Smith, was profoundly shocked to meet him at, of all places, the ultra-fashionable resort of Aix-les-Bains, 'dressed like a seedy, shady sailor'. But inevitably it was Smith, not Hartington who was discomfited by this. After all, Cavendishes had been coming here to take the waters for over a century, and it would not have occurred to him that anyone would think of criticizing the way he dressed. When Smith calmed down, the two men finally got round to talking politics, and Hartington remarked quite casually that 'it was pleasant in a place like this to have some work to do.'

There is another intriguing fact about the man who became Eighth Duke of Devonshire – almost all the details we possess about his private life are anecdotal, which is a feature of the carefully presented modern public man. With his predecessors there are diaries and private letters full of unguarded revelations and conversations. With him there is almost nothing of the sort. This is partly because most of his purely private papers were destroyed on his death, in accordance with his own very firm instructions. It was also because the aristocracy now faced an avid public audience fed by the popular press and hungry for gossip about their betters. A clever actor, such as Hartington, could play up to this – and did, to considerable effect. But, as he also knew, his really private life had to be protected very carefully indeed. Raciness was one thing, scandal another; and while a vague reputation as a ladies' man enhanced his popularity, much beyond this would have ruined him.

The whole highly moral atmosphere of Holker must have given him a useful training in keeping his behaviour to himself, and although he was famous as something of a womanizer in his day, it is strange how little is really known about his womanizing. Again, what there is is largely anecdotal, like the famous story which went the rounds of how his friend, the Prince of Wales, produced one of his celebrated practical jokes from Hartington's affair with Skittles. Apparently his lordship was making an official tour of Coventry, and the Prince sent an equerry to tell the mayor to make certain Lord Hartington was shown the municipal bowling-alley. This was done and, when a slightly puzzled Hartington inquired why, the mayor is supposed to have replied, 'His Royal Highness asked specially for the inclusion of the alley in the tour in tribute to Your Lordship's love of skittles.'

It was a good story and it may have happened – just – but the point about the anecdote, which was widely circulated, is that it switched attention from Hartington's interest in a famous prostitute into that favourite English diversionary device – a joke. And beyond this it is difficult to find out very much. According to Anita Leslie, Hartington *may* have thought of marrying Miss Walters – which seems most unlikely with a woman Sir William Hardman referred to as 'a whore, sir, much sought after by fast young swells'. It was also rumoured that when the affair was over she received a house in Mayfair, 'carriages, servants and an irrevocable £2,000 a year for life'. This too appears improbable, knowing Hartington's somewhat careful attitude to money. If there ever was such a generous arrangement, all traces of it have long since disappeared from the Chatsworth archives, along with a great deal more concerning the one abiding passion of his life apart from politics – his thirty-year-long love-affair with the former Louise von Alten, wife of the rich and acquiescent Duke of Manchester.

Like Hartington himself, she was a member of the so-called 'Fast Set' which gambled, shot, and generally enjoyed themselves in considerable freedom and privacy round the portly presence of the Prince of Wales. She was admired as a beauty, was an ambitious political presence behind the scenes, and seems to have kept Lord Hartington happy and at least nominally faithful from his early thirties to his death. But although the liaison was fairly common knowledge at the time, Hartington's extraordinary powers of discretion once again prevented gossip ever getting out of hand and resulting in a showdown of the sort that conveniently destroyed his radical Liberal rival, Sir Charles Dilke.

Discretion apart, the stately and presumably satisfactory progress of their long romance is a tribute to the code of highly formalized behaviour now developing among the upper classes of society as they formed ranks against the aspiring middle classes, who were so quick to criticize their betters. The naturalness and carefree indulgence in their feelings with which the *habitués* of Devonshire House had lived their 'wild and scrambling' lives just eighty years before was over. Throughout the seventies and eighties, Lord Hartington was a regular and honoured guest of the Manchesters at their Huntingdonshire house, Kimbolton Castle; his dignified, immensely venerable face peers haughtily from many of the group photographs taken to record these sociable events. Most of the other solemn guests around them, including the melancholy-looking Duke of Manchester himself, must have known about the liaison going on between the mistress of the house and the heir to the Duke of Devonshire; but if passions or jealousies got out of hand in private, no hint seeped out, still less has any evidence survived.

Even in the presence of their friends, the Duchess and Lord Hartington addressed each other by their titles, and Anita Leslie quotes the one recorded occasion when the Duchess actually forgot herself. Louise and Hartington were week-ending with the Duke of Portland at Welbeck, and the Duchess had just finished writing a letter when, to her considerable surprise, the Duke of Portland's mother heard Louise murmur, 'Harty darling, stand me a stamp.'

It is good to know that normal human feelings had their place behind the uncomfortable pomposities of the period, and apart from the light it sheds on Hartington's character – which must have been more devious and complex than it seemed, to have maintained this sort of subterranean affair so long – his relationship with Louise Manchester had an important influence upon the future of the Devonshires. Since she was married, and divorce, even had she and her lover wanted it, would have ruined Hartington politically, he was effectively prevented from fathering a future Duke of Devonshire. In purely practical terms this did not matter, for the succession was assured: Hartington's heir was his younger brother, Lord Edward Cavendish, and after Edward's death in 1891, *his* son, Victor Cavendish.

One wonders whether Hartington ever seriously regretted this. Probably not. Fatherhood has many drawbacks for a busy man, and Hartington of course has left no reference to so delicate and personal a matter. Apart from this, his single state clearly suited him even better than it had his self-indulgent predecessor, the Bachelor Duke. He had Louise when and where he needed her, but was not too cramped by her teutonic presence; he had his bridge, his racing, and all the social life he wanted; he had the use of all the Devonshire houses and their servants even before succeeding to the dukedom; he was, in short, extremely self-sufficient and at liberty to dedicate himself to the most demanding of Victorian upper-class activities – politics.

Here, more than anywhere, one sees how effectively his curiously assembled character could operate; and his long, immensely influential political career forms a key example of how the English aristocracy could effortlessly adapt and extend its power in politics through all the changes leading to a modern popular electorate. According to his secretary, Lord Esher, who had many years to study the man he usually referred to as 'My Chief', Lord Hartington' had entered public life a Whig, and a Whig he was determined to remain.' For him, Whiggism was quite simply 'a creed that registered the experience of the English upper classes during the four or five generations previous to Palmerston's advent to power' – and he never really changed.

As a Whig he had naturally accepted the widening of the electorate, and had taken his place in Parliament as a Palmerstonian liberal, where he rapidly deployed much the same cover-up techniques that he developed in his private life. It took an adroit political actor like Disraeli to spot the significance of that yawn in the middle of young Hartington's maiden speech. For Hartington knew he was no orator, but he had other considerable advantages – not least among them birth and wealth. A hint of patrician arrogance or lordly ambition would have killed his political life stone dead; but a touch of noble lethargy and boredom was profoundly reassuring, and throughout his political career, Lord Hartington would use them as a sort of pick-me-up in any tricky situation.

This pretence of seeming not to care carried him through the not unnatural resentment in the House of Commons when, in 1863 and after six profoundly undistinguished years as a backbencher, he was appointed Under-secretary of State for War by Lord Palmerston, mainly on the strength of being the son and heir of the Duke of Devonshire. Here he displayed an unexpected taste for hard work and considerable common sense which made him a successful minister, and brought him into the Cabinet two years later, at the age of thirty-two, as Secretary for War in Lord John Russell's Liberal Government.

He began to make his name. As the caption to an 'Ape' cartoon remarked about him in the March 1869 edition of the middle-class magazine, *Vanity Fair*: 'His ability and industry would deserve respect even in a man; in a Marquis they command admiration' – for as the readers of *Vanity Fair* would know, marquises were not supposed to be able or industrious. Hartington understood this perfectly – and cashed in on it; for in politics, as in all else that mattered to him, he was a serious, ambitious, clever man doing his best to appear a disinterested, slightly weary amateur, and remaining what Lord Esher said he always was at heart, a traditional Whig 'Chief' determined to enjoy his hereditary place in government.

In 1870, twelve years before Lord Frederick's death, this place appeared assured. Hartington was appointed Gladstone's Chief Secretary for Ireland, and he rapidly confirmed his reputation for steadiness and shrewdness combined with considerable awareness of Ireland's problems. At the same time his popularity was growing with the Liberal party and the public, as he began perfecting his performance as a supremely reliable, no-nonsense politician everyone could trust *because of* his place within the aristocracy.

The political commentator, E. T. Raymond, wrote about him in the nineties,

> The Duke enjoyed public confidence in an extraordinary degree because it was obvious, not only that he was getting nothing, but that it was impossible for him to get anything out of politics. His yawn was in fact his great talisman. Everyone knew that if he consulted his own feelings he would hardly have stirred beyond his park palings.

As Raymond should have known, nothing was further from the truth, but throughout his political career, Lord Hartington took great trouble to create this impression of the honest, somewhat lazy, country-loving nobleman who had wandered reluctantly into politics – hence his celebrated aside when listening to a member of the Lords describing the greatest moment of his life: 'The greatest moment of *my* life' muttered Harty-Tarty, 'was when my pig won first prize at Skipton Fair.'

In fact he was not remotely interested in pigs, and had he been forced to spend too long at Chatsworth, the tedium would have finished him. But, as Stanley Baldwin was to show, pigs and country matters are invaluable props for a politician trying to create a reputation for dependability against a quicker, sharper parliamentary rival – and no one in the House of Commons was sharper or quicker than his leader, William Ewart Gladstone.

Hartington showed extraordinary skill in the way he proceeded to develop his public and political personality as the antithesis to Gladstone's. Where Gladstone was intellectual, he was instinctive; Gladstone was fast and notably erratic, whereas he was slow and totally dependable; Gladstone was brilliant, but Lord Hartington was right. He was also a great aristocrat, which Gladstone was not, and even within the predominantly middle-class Liberal party of the 1870s, Lord Hartington turned this to notable advantage, thanks to the widespread snobbery and deference which still permeated English politics.

For, as T. H. Escott wrote about him in this period, 'his demeanour in the House of Commons would not have been tolerated in anyone but the heir presumptive of a great dukedom', but the members were actually rather proud of his eccentricities, and the way that, when the Speaker rose, two Cavendish grooms in livery instantly rode back to Devonshire House to tell the cook that Hartington would soon be home for dinner.

In 1874, Gladstone blundered by calling a snap election and losing it decisively. He retired in dudgeon from the Liberal parliamentary leadership and, in 1875 in a vote at the Reform Club of the remaining Liberal M.P.s, Hartington was democratically elected leader in the Commons in his place. It was a considerable achievement for a man who was to become a duke. So was the steadiness and skill with which he led the Liberals in opposition and rebuilt the fortunes of the party.

He should have reaped the benefit, and undoubtedly would have done, but for the return of the unpredictable Mr Gladstone from the political wilderness in 1879 to rouse the Liberal conscience through the country with his phenomenal Midlothian Campaign. And when the Liberals were returned to power in the 1880 election, Hartington realized quite well that, whatever his own moral claims to the premiership, Gladstone was still his party's natural and inevitable leader.

Victoria felt otherwise. It was bad enough for her to lose her beloved Disraeli as Prime Minister: it was worse still to have to face ghastly Mr Gladstone for the next seven years. When she asked Disraeli what to do, his advice was clear. Send for Lord Hartington 'in his heart a Conservative, a gentleman, and very straightforward in his conduct'. So Hartington went to Windsor, saw the Queen, was asked to form a Liberal administration – and graciously declined. It must have been a bitter moment for him. For however assiduously he had fostered the impression of never really wanting power, he would have made an excellent Prime Minister, and the role would have been the natural culmination of his whole political career. The Duchess of Manchester urged him to accept, but as he knew quite well, Gladstone would certainly have refused to serve under him, and without Gladstone there, the Liberals would certainly have split between the Whigs and the radicals.

Whatever else he was, Hartington was a realist, and he knew when he was beaten. So did Victoria. Gladstone became Prime Minister; and Lord Hartington, hiding his feelings once again behind his whiskers, went to the races and accepted the Secretaryship for India. Two years later he was back at the War Office, and in 1884 was responsible for sending Gordon to Khartoum.

(He interviewed Gordon just before the hero caught the night-boat to Calais; Gordon remarked afterwards that he would have liked to have given Lord Hartington a Bible.)

One of Disraeli's most famous pieces of political advice was, 'Never complain, never explain', words which Hartington stoically lived up to in the recriminations that followed Gordon's death. In fact, had he had his way, the relieving forces would have been sent to Khartoum earlier and Gordon would never have achieved his famous martyrdom. But he manfully accepted Queen Victoria's cable of rebuke – which he received at Holker, when entertaining Mr Gladstone, whose anti-imperialist policy had been the biggest cause of the delays.

It was Ireland which was finally to cause the historic break between Hartington and Gladstone in 1886, a break which would change the face of British politics for many years to come – and in the process end the traditional adherence of the House of Cavendish to the great Whig cause. Ever since the murder of his brother in Phoenix Park in 1882, Lord Hartington had become increasingly convinced of the need for 'firmness' from Westminster in the face of Irish violence. Gladstone became just as steadily convinced that the answer lay in granting Ireland Home Rule. The Liberals themselves were split, and in May 1886 Hartington led a third of the party into opposition to his leader's Home Rule Bill, ensuring its defeat.

After a meeting of dissenting Liberals at Devonshire House, Lord Hartington accepted the presidency of what was in effect a new political party of Unionist Liberals, pledged to oppose the granting of Home Rule to Ireland. The Liberal government of Gladstone fell and, in the July elections, Lord Hartington and his fellow Unionists, who now included the influential radical imperialist Joseph Chamberlain, helped to ensure a Liberal defeat at the polls.

Power now rested at Westminster between the Conservatives, under Lord Salisbury, and Hartington's 110 Liberal Unionist M.P.s. Salisbury was urging out-and-out coalition and, for the second time in his life, Lord Hartington was offered the position of Prime Minister – and for the second time carefully refused.

This has been cited as proof positive that he really was as lazy and uninterested in power as he appeared; in fact, as a very realistic politician, he knew quite well that his Unionist disciples in the House and in the country were still unprepared for the trauma of all-out collaboration with the Tories. He might have made a different decision later in the year, when Salisbury's fragile government went into sudden parliamentary panic over the abrupt resignation of unpredictable Lord Randolph Churchill. Hartington was Christmassing in Rome, and Salisbury cabled him to return at once to save the government on any terms he wanted.

This was Lord Hartington's third chance of the premiership, and he might finally have taken it, but this time the elements decided otherwise. Storms were sweeping Europe; Hartington's return and cable of reply were both delayed, and when he finally did reach London, Lord Salisbury had managed to resolve the crisis in his absence.

Three bites at the premiership are probably as much as even the most favoured politician can expect within a lifetime, and Lord Hartington had had his quota. He behaved impeccably of course. There were no recriminations, no outward hint of even a moment's disappointment, and his reputation as a worthy politician essentially uninterested in jockeying for power was immeasurably enhanced. It was not true, but it suited him to act as if it were, and Lord Hartington uncomplainingly took his place in history as the best prime minister the nineteenth century never had. He also forms a fascinating subject for the might-have-beens of history. Had he, not Mr Gladstone, led the Liberal government in 1880 – as he had had every right to expect – it is hard to imagine the Liberals splitting in the next decade and thus permitting the interminable Conservative supremacy which, with one short break, was to rule the country and the empire to within nine years of the beginning of the First World War. And had he only had the vision to support Mr Gladstone over Home Rule for Ireland in 1886, a century of strife within that cruel country could almost certainly have been avoided.

As it was, he had proved Disraeli right again. By nature and position in society, Lord Hartington *was* a true Conservative at heart – for traditional Whiggism and the new conservatism had almost totally converged by now. The times had changed since it had suited the interests of the great Whig families to espouse the cause of popular liberty and parliamentary freedom against the encroaching power of the Crown. The ancient battles had been won; reform had come but the aristocracy was still effectively a power in Parliament, the monarchy posed no threat to the great nobility, and Lord Hartington's own brand of Whiggism was really little more than a nostalgic genuflection to the shibboleths and sacred figures of the past.

Beyond this, Whiggism's 'one immutable, unchanging element, the overriding, absolute belief in property' was as unchanging and immutable as ever; and was shared just as fervently by the great land-owners and businessmen and bankers who were the golden backbone of the new conservatism. Whig he may have been by birth, but Lord Hartington had infinitely more in common with a Tory aristocrat like Lord Salisbury than with a middle-class intellectual like Gladstone with his uncomfortable ideals and dangerous tendency for change. By 1891, when Lord Hartington became Eighth Duke of Devonshire, the family had ceased to be a great Whig house, and quietly joined forces with the new conservatism. But the Duke would probably have denied that he had done anything as drastic as changing sides; the sides had simply changed around him leaving him exactly where he always was.

By a curious coincidence, the man he so discreetly cuckolded for over thirty years, the vapid Duke of Manchester, expired within a few weeks of Hartington's becoming Duke of Devonshire; and as Manchester lay dying, Lord Esher had noted that his Duchess, while somewhat concerned about her ailing husband, 'whom she likes despite his slight deserts', was bearing up courageously. Despite her worries, she was managing to 'seem happy. She will now be Duchess of Devonshire! It is certain.'

It was evidently nothing of the sort, for Devonshire was nearing sixty and there was much speculation in Society over whether these two ageing lovers would ever make it to the altar. The years of Louise's legendary beauty were far behind her now. In 1866, Lady Frederick Cavendish had described her as 'too beautiful and winning, with the most perfect manners – high-bred, gentle and intelligent.' Despite this, truth compelled her also to admit that Louise struck her even then as 'somewhat middle-aged', and that was a quarter of a century before. By now the widowed Duchess had aged considerably and put on weight like so many members of her race. The Duke himself was a confirmed old bachelor, and the thought crossed many minds that if he had to marry anyone, he might well pick a younger, more attractive woman and set about fathering a new successor to the dukedom even now.

But yet again to quote Disraeli, the Duke really was 'a gentleman and very straightforward in his conduct'. His heir and nephew, Victor Cavendish, just married to Lady Evelyn Fitzmaurice, Lord Lansdowne's daughter, was all set to produce a family of his own – and Louise Manchester was a most determined woman. E. F. Benson said that 'there was something of the unswerving relentlessness of a steam-roller about her', and when all her friends were out of town in mid-August 1892, in a very private service held at Christ Church Mayfair (and by special licence to avoid the publicity of issuing the banns), she exchanged the title of Manchester for Devonshire; and as something of a tribute to the rare feat of marrying two dukes in succession, Louise would go down in history as the 'Double Duchess'.

Even the well-informed Lord Esher had no idea the wedding had occurred until he read the brief announcement in the next day's *Times*. He collected his winnings from a friend who had bet him it would never happen, and noted in his diary: 'The secret has been well kept. It will make life easier for him. He saw her every day and never took a step without her sanction or advice.'

In fact, Lord Esher, like many of his contemporaries who were secretly amused by the domination of the once rakish Duke by his blowsy Duchess, rather missed the point. Formidable the Duchess may have been, but the Duke was undoubtedly in love with her. In the Chatsworth archives, one or two scribbled notes he wrote her have survived the destruction of his other private papers and reveal that, even after he was married, he remained touchingly besotted. Well into her sixties she is still his 'darling little angel', and when they are parted he misses seeing her 'little face again'. In July 1899, she went off on a short trip to her family in Germany, but they remained devotedly in contact.

My Own Darling, [he wrote from Devonshire House]
I found your telegram this morning and am so glad that you arrived all right and have had fine weather. We had a very nice day yesterday – and I slept a good part of the morning and played bridge this afternoon and 2 rounds of golf in the evening.

Without her, this is how the Duke would almost certainly have spent most of his dukedom; but with Louise firmly on the scene there was no question of the

Devonshires lapsing into drowsy insignificance. For, unlike the Duke, she was remorselessly sociable and energetic, an eager political power-behind-the-scenes, and something of a lion-hunting snob. Most of her friends were titled, Conservative and very rich. She was determined to assert her role as the most important hostess in the land, and as Devonshire House and Chatsworth took on a new lease of social life under her influence, so the whole character of the two great houses changed conclusively.

For over a century and a half the great Whig families – and particularly the Devonshires – whatever else they may have been, had been remarkable for certain qualities: for a level of cosmopolitan culture, for their flair as patrons and their taste in building and collecting, and for political beliefs which had absorbed and sometimes led the most progressive and enlightened thinking of their times. It was a civilized tradition. Even the Seventh Duke, for all his earnest limitations, had done his conscientious best to bring it up to date. With his successor, the tradition ceased.

It was also expiring fast throughout the whole of the late nineteenth-century aristocracy as the last survivors of the older generation Whigs died off to be replaced by an altogether narrower, less educated, and reactionary upper-class society, where skill at bridge was more socially important than a knowledge of the classics. There was more prestige in a well-run and expensive shoot than in adding further paintings to the crowded walls of country houses; it was considered altogether shrewder to collect stocks and shares than Renaissance bronzes or old master drawings; and as for 'modern' painters, the works of the Pre-Raphaelites and the extraordinary French Impressionists could be safely left to the *nouveaux riches* and the middle classes if they were ill-advised enough to buy them. Certainly, none disgraced the walls at Chatsworth.

The Duke himself displayed a gentlemanly ignorance of art, which would have shocked his ancestors but which endeared him to the sort of company he kept. One of the tasks of his Librarian, Mrs Arthur Strong, was apparently to 'tour the principal rooms with the Eighth Duke and his Duchess the day before a house-party began, and tell them a few outstanding facts about their principal possessions.'

Mrs Strong was a distinguished archaeologist who had succeeded her husband, Sandford Arthur Strong, himself a celebrated orientalist whom the Seventh Duke appointed his Librarian in 1885. Two literary ladies, Miss Bradley and Miss Cooper, who wrote under the joint pseudonym of 'Michael Field', left a melancholy picture of Mrs Strong at Chatsworth in 1905, which also conveys something of the atmosphere of the house during the last years of Harty Tarty and Louise, when Their Graces were away.

> Mrs. Strong rang the bell, but no one came. How could anyone come in that mansion of tombs? So she conducted us to the 'grille'. It is the most haunting kind of life to lead for Arthur Strong's wife – dusty, among pictures and old books in black that makes her handsomeness of no avail – she lives like an owl in desolation, but an owl without nerves. Hard and lonely executive and unanswered when she rings – there she is! Even her movements are those of an owl. I saw her little room, a cloth on the table, I

shuddered to think of the meals served in that ducal wilderness where all the bells are unattaining.*

The 1870s and 1880s witnessed a political and social revival of a number of great Tory families like the Cecils, the Derbys and the Churchills; with his Duchess at his side, the Duke of Devonshire could now calmly take his place among them. Thanks in large measure to the influence of the Duke's old friend, the Prince of Wales, the upper reaches of society were simultaneously accepting a new intake of the very rich, and it was this society as well, racy, plutocratic and distinctly philistine, that the Duchess loved.

Above all, she loved her compatriot, the Prince of Wales and all he represented – just as the Prince of Wales loved Chatsworth which was tailor-made to welcome him. No other great house in England was so perfectly adapted for his pleasures. Here, on the princely yet informal scale he relished he could eat, shoot, play his bridge, discreetly enjoy his mistresses and have his jokes applauded by a respectful regiment of friends attended by an army of deferential servants.

The Duchess too was in her element. Her annual Devonshire House ball on the eve of the Derby was soon one of the great fixtures of the London season, and she surpassed herself with the great Devonshire House Fancy-Dress Ball which she threw in 1897 to celebrate Victoria's Diamond Jubilee.

As the event is remembered in Mayfair . . . it was at least one of the most magnificent social functions of the century. It embraced the flower of English society. It comprised hundreds of the most beautiful living pictures that the combined power of money, taste and art could present. It seemed as if all the glories of . . . the French court, and something of the barbarous magnificence of other places and periods had been dragged back from their flight into the ages, and held by some subtle charm in the keeping of the Cavendishes for the six hours of a summer night.

The stout Duchess, resplendently arrayed as 'Zenobia, Queen of Palmyra', must have been a memorable sight welcoming her gilded guests at the top of the great crystal staircase. So must the Duke, obediently beside her, his tapering figure garbed appropriately in black in the character of the Habsburg Holy Roman Emperor, Charles V – and probably longing to be safely back at Newmarket.

For years he had been pretending to be bored; now he had something to be really bored about at last. The act had taken over from the actor as it so often does in life and, as the century drew towards its close, the great ducal yawn seemed to descend on Chatsworth and its doings. It is now that the tales about the Duke's absent-mindedness take on the ring of truth: the way he could not be bothered to select the next day's shooting list at Chatsworth so that guests invited for the shooting would sometimes leave without firing a shot; the way

---

*After the Eighth Duke's death, Mrs Strong exchanged the ducal wilderness of Chatsworth for a life of scholarship in Rome where she became director of the British School and lived on, as a revered foreign resident, until her death in 1943.

he entirely forgot a lunch appointment with the King and had to be summoned by a flustered flunkey from the Turf Club as he was sitting down to eat his soup. 'And whose is Pevensey?' he sleepily inquired when some friends were discussing the great Roman castle on the Sussex coast which the Cavendishes had owned since 1786.

Yet even now, despite his boredom, there was one thing that did engage the Duke's continual interest – money. This was important, and he used his connections in the City to set about solving the ever-present problem of the great Devonshire Debt – and so effectively that he emerges from Dr Cannadine's researches as the unsung and unsuspected saviour of the Cavendish inheritance.

He cut the family losses over Barrow, where his father's investments in steel and jute and shipbuilding had proved a serious liability. He judiciously sold off unwanted land in Ireland and Derbyshire, and Burlington House in Piccadilly, to reduce his mortages. Most important of all, he used this capital from the sale of land for large and usually adroit investment in high-yielding stocks and shares. This was not an entirely new departure for the Cavendishes. Since Bess of Hardwick, the family had usually been ready to invest in industry or profitable speculation, but the traditional ownership of great estates had always been the bedrock of the Devonshire fortunes and their social and political preeminence. Now this was changing fast. Backed by the advice of thrusting, well-informed financiers like the Rothschilds and the Prince of Wales's friend and wizard of late Victorian high finance, Sir Ernest Cassel, the ancient money of the Devonshires was being profitably switched from land into 'a wide range of British, colonial, and U.S. Government bonds and railway shares overseas'.

It was an important move, for, as with a number of rich landed families about this time, it would enable the semi-feudal life-style of the Devonshires to survive when traditional sources of their income – farming, mineral rights and rents – had started to decline. Thanks to the Eighth Duke, the Cavendishes would remain comfortably afloat well into the twentieth century with the lifebelt of the stock exchange around their waist. This change would increasingly affect the character of the dukedom too – a change that mirrored a transformation going on throughout the British upper classes as the ancient aristocracy based on land merged with the new plutocracy based on wealth. Their resources were increasingly the same – invested capital – and the national prestige of an important hereditary nobleman like the Eighth Duke was no longer automatic as it had been with his great Whig predecessors. In his case, it rested largely on his character and his political achievements. He was a celebrity, Trollope's Duke of Omnium incarnate, and part of his achievement rested on the way he instinctively, and cleverly, exploited the sentimental appeal a great title such as his still carried in a country where, as Thackeray put it, 'Lordolatry is part of our creed and where our children are brought up to respect the "Peerage" as the Englishman's second Bible.'

Thanks to this widespread attitude, few felt it strange when in the 1890s this former Liberal and scion of the Whigs took his place in Lord Salisbury's Conservative Cabinet, as the suitably dignified Lord President of the Council, with responsibility for, of all things, education. For the Duke by now was almost universally revered – 'the best excuse that the last half century has produced for the continuance of the peerages', as his biographer, Henry Leach would put it – Chancellor of Cambridge University, like his father before him, Mayor of the south coast Cavendish colony of Eastbourne, where his statue still stands opposite the Grand Hotel and, after the succession of the Prince of Wales in 1901, one of the most regular hosts and closest friends of the King and Queen of England.

The Coronation ceremony in August 1902 almost proved the downfall of the Double Duchess. In her eagerness to reach the ladies' room after the long confinement in the Abbey, she tried to push past the guardsmen in the wake of the royal procession, missed her footing,

and fell headlong down a flight of steps to roll over on her back at the feet of the Chancellor of the Exchequer, who stared paralysed at this heap of velvet and ermine. The Marquis de Soveral swiftly took charge of the situation and had her lifted to her feet, while Margot Asquith nimbly retrieved the coronet which was bouncing along the stalls and placed it back on her head.

But the Duchess soon recovered, and some of her proudest moments were to come as hostess to the King and Queen at her famous house-parties up at Chatsworth every January. One of the many guests was the young Daisy Princess of Pless, who has described the behaviour of the royal party at an amateur production of *Cinderella* in the Bachelor Duke's theatre in January 1904.

At Chatsworth the Sovereigns were simplicity itself. One curtsied when saying good morning and good night, but on no other occasion. For the performance of the play there was just a little ceremony. The King entered first with the Duchess of Devonshire and the Queen with the Duke, and took their places on armchairs in the centre of the first row. The house-party entered in a procession, more or less according to precedence, and seated themselves as they pleased: similar procedure followed the performance. Queen Alexandra always enjoyed Chatsworth enormously, and I have visions of her stealing into the back seats to watch the rehearsals and we humouring her by pretending we did not see her.

Louise had reached an unassailable position in society, and just as King Edward so successfully created a new social and 'ornamental' image for the British monarchy, so the Eighth Duke in old age helped to do much the same for the English aristocracy. Indeed, this would prove to be the Duke's abiding contribution to the future, not only of the House of Cavendish, but of the British upper classes for many years to come. For, with the perfection of that act which he had practised from his earliest days in Parliament, he had become the great exemplar of that role which the Edwardian aristocrat – and would-be aristocrat – would doggedly adopt and imitate in his battle to survive and prosper: the effortless amateur, the titled eccentric who always comes up trumps, the casually garbed gentleman who is so much better dressed than his social inferiors, the effete buffoon who is never quite as stupid as he seems.

But the Duke's chronic boredom grew worse with age, particularly after he resigned from Balfour's government in 1904; despite the efforts of his Duchess, time hung heavy on his hands. Her social energies were undiminished, although E. F. Benson, who saw her now, described her as looking like 'the half-ruinous shell of some castellated keep, with flower-boxes in full bloom on the crumbling sills'.

By 1905 the Duke was suffering from heart disease which made him a semi-invalid, but his wife seemed inextinguishable. In March 1907, the Princess of Pless met her once again at Monte Carlo dining with the Keppels – 'poor old dear, very cheerful and very rouged' – and that winter she insisted on taking her sick husband for a holiday to the warmth of Egypt. The Duke was very ill, and taking strychnine for his heart condition. From the account of one of their companions, this trip must have been a considerable ordeal.

> Louise looks ten years older. . . . What they have all been through during these last five months. It must have been hell! There is only one description possible of Their Graces. It is a d—d cantankerous old couple. Her Grace is very cheery though. She has been into Cairo to have luncheon with Cassel.

This was at Helouan on the Nile in January 1908, and a few weeks later they began the painful journey home. By March 1908 they had reached Cannes, and it was there in a hotel that the Duke expired. His last words were totally in character.

'Well, the game's over and I'm not sorry.'

14. The Reluctant Duke

The Ninth Duke, Victor (1868–1938)

In these democratic days when restlessness and instability are not confined to one class of the community, it is as well, perhaps, that British society is leavened by the sobering influence of a few great historic houses like that of the Cavendishes as a safeguard against the prevailing epidemic of smartness.

From the obituary of the Eighth Duke of Devonshire in The Onlooker, 4 April 1908

GIVEN the choice, few Edwardian gentlemen of right mind and sober judgment would have seriously objected to becoming Duke of Devonshire: ironically, one who did was Harty Tarty's heir, Lord Victor Cavendish. As the childless Duke's eldest nephew, he had lived his adult life knowing he would one day have to shoulder the accumulated honours and responsibilities of the dukedom, and when news came through from Cannes that 'Uncle Cav' was dead, he sadly bowed to the inevitable. He was just forty, and he knew his great inheritance would mark the end of the two things that had made his life particularly agreeable.

The first was the House of Commons. As Mr Victor Cavendish, he had taken his seat there for the family seat, West Derbyshire, as a Liberal Unionist in his early twenties, and along with Brooks's Club, the Commons had been part of his cherished way of life. A shy man and more of a natural Liberal than his uncle, he was not without considerable political ambition. He had served under Balfour as Financial Secretary to the Treasury – a key position for an up-and-coming politician. With Balfour's defeat in 1905, he was back in opposition, but with good prospects of entering the Cabinet in the next Conservative administration. There was only one proviso – that he stayed safely in the House of Commons. By his untimely death it seemed that Uncle Cav had torpedoed his nephew's promising career in active politics, leaving him shipwrecked and a little lonely in the decorative but unexciting landscape of the House of Lords.

This was bad enough for a man of the new Duke's ordered habits. What was even worse was that the dukedom had not only robbed him of a promising political career, but of his home as well. Since a disastrous fire in 1871, Holker Hall had been rebuilt by the Seventh Duke in a style and opulence that give little hint of that mournful man's careful attitude to money or his obsession for his dear departed Blanche. It was very grand and very comfortable, 'a marvellous reflection of its age, with its atmosphere of confidence, spaciousness and prosperity'. Between Lake Windermere and Morecambe Bay it had 20,000 acres of the most idyllic countryside in England. On the almost simultaneous death of the Seventh Duke and his second son, Lord Edward Cavendish in 1891, it had passed to Victor, and hardly surprisingly he and his family had loved it passionately.

But now that he was Duke, it was time for Holker to descend to his younger
brother, Richard. Thanks to the inexorable laws of primogeniture nothing
could be done about it, and there was not a dry eye as the new ducal family
drove off from their beloved Holker for the grim magnificence of Chatsworth.

The new Duke was a very homespun sort of Cavendish, with much of his
uncle's solidity but without any of that unexpected raciness which had made
Harty-Tarty such a fascinating character. There were no Skittles in his
cupboard, no thirty-year affairs with married duchesses for him: nor had he
any of that majestic *hauteur* – what a foreign writer once described as 'His
Grace's you-be-damnedness' – which Harty-Tarty had unmaliciously dispensed towards the world in general.

His niece, Lady Gage, remembers him in his later years as 'looking like a
very old bloodhound, with everything hanging rather loose'; and even as a
relatively young man, Victor's photographs reveal a hint of the faithful, rather
baffled English bloodhound gazing unexcitedly upon the world. The most
striking thing about the diaries he laboriously kept throughout his adult life is
their total lack of imagination, affectation or excess.

This was to be Duke Victor's great advantage in coping with the troubled
times he lived through, for in him the House of Cavendish had achieved
another of those effortless mutations which throughout its history had allowed
it to adapt with such notable success to fresh surroundings. A serpent had
once again taken over from a stag; and just as the British monarchy itself would
soon change its character when that highly moral, somewhat hen-pecked
countryman, King George V, succeeded Harty-Tarty's rakish friend, King
Edward, so the new Duke of Devonshire appeared the epitome of what a
middle-class democracy might well have felt a duke should be – decent, rather
dull, and almost indistinguishable from any other well-to-do Edwardian with
six children and a dominating wife.

The new Duchess Evelyn was an imperious, strong-willed and 'artistic'
woman, who was often compared with her friend, Queen Mary, and the Duke
is said to have adored her. She was the daughter of Henry Petty-Fitzmaurice,
Fifth Marquis of Lansdowne, a former Viceroy of India, Governor-General of
Canada, and Foreign Secretary, who was now Conservative Leader in the
House of Lords. Through his maternal family, the Flahaults, he was descended from Talleyrand, a fact of which the duchess was inordinately proud.

As well as having to leave Holker, the new Duke and Duchess soon found
themselves faced with two urgent problems which afflicted a number of rich
ancient families trying to cope with the transition to the twentieth century –
death duties and drains. Neither would appear desperately serious today for a
man with the resources the new duke commanded, but in 1908 they were very
worrying indeed, confirming the misgivings shared by many members of the
aristocracy about their future.

Ever since the Liberal Chancellor of the Exchequer, Sir William Harcourt,
had destroyed the prime tenet of the Whigs in his 1894 budget, by taxing
property and capital with his graduated, very modest tax on a deceased's
estate, death duties had been seen as the thin end of a devastating wedge which
would ultimately cleave apart the wealth and the privileged position of the

British upper classes. Introduced on estates beginning at £5,000, and rising to a mere eight per cent of an inheritance above £1 million, they had been strenuously opposed by the Conservatives – and inevitably by 'Uncle Cav'* – but as predicted at the time, none of the succeeding Conservative governments had repealed them. For the first time in its history the House of Cavendish had a new enemy to face – the state; and for the first time, part of its patrimony was offered up to appease it.

In a move that demonstrates the changed priorities of the family, it was decided to sacrifice in two areas that would have been unthinkable in the heyday of the Whigs. Chiswick House, now virtually unused and in need of renovation, was sold off to the local council (who, with a touch of probably unconscious humour, decided to use it as a lunatic asylum)† and the Chatsworth Library was scoured for treasures that nobody would miss but that would do well at auction. The Shakespeare folios and quartos were sold, and twenty-five Caxtons, most of them collected by the Sixth Duke, were sent to Sothebys and finally disposed of to the Huntington Library for $750,000. For two generations the Devonshires had ceased to be collectors. Now they had started to shed their treasures; but thanks to these disposals the death duties could be met without resort to further borrowing, extra capital could be profitably invested in the City, and the Chatsworth drainage finally attended to. Ever since the then Prince of Wales had nearly died of typhoid caught from the drains of Londesborough Lodge in 1871, sanitation had been something of a headache for aristocrats with ancient houses, and at Chatsworth it was only one of a number of expenses now required to modernize the house. As might have been expected, the Eighth Duke had lived in splendour and considerable squalor; much of the Chatsworth drainage dated back to the early eighteenth century, and before the new inheritors would consider moving in, an elaborate overhaul was needed which included the installation of full mains drainage. While this was going on, the new Duke and his abundant family took up residence in Hardwick Hall where they spent the autumn and winter by candlelight and oil lamp* before moving back to an electrified and thoroughly hygienic Chatsworth in the spring of 1909. Shortly afterwards, the new Duchess gave birth to her seventh child, her daughter Anne, the first ducal offspring born at Chatsworth since the eighteenth century, an auspicious start for the new Duke's reign.

---

*This produced one of the few recorded witticisms of the Eighth Duke. Sitting next to the Duke at dinner, Lady Harcourt remarked, 'Your Grace, I feel you would like to hang my husband.'

'No madam,' came the grave reply, 'merely suspend him for a period.'

† Chiswick House was purchased by the Middlesex County Council in 1929. After the war it had ceased to be an asylum, and was transferred to the Ministry of Works (now the Department of the Environment), who in 1952 demolished the additions Wyatville had made there for the Sixth Duke, and restored Burlington's villa to something of its early splendour. It is now open to the public.

*There is a fascinating account of this period in the recollections of the Ninth Duke's eldest daughter, Lady Maud Baillie, reproduced in the official guide to Hardwick Hall by Mark Girouard.

With the birth of Lady Anne, there were now seven Cavendish children to inhabit Chatsworth – Edward, Maud, Blanche, Dorothy, Rachel, Charles and Anne herself – and the high politics and somewhat senile splendour of old 'Uncle Cav' were succeeded by a bustling Edwardian family for whom Chatsworth had become a home. Nurseries were created, the Sixth Duke's Blue Drawing-room became a schoolroom, and the older children roller-skated in the Sculpture Gallery. According to Lady Anne,

> We seemed a very close-knit, rather ordinary family, and we were emphatically not brought up to regard ourselves as in any way superior to anybody else. Certainly we were aware that we were the children of a duke; what we were not aware of was that this was in any way exceptional. One result of this was that most of us ended up married to fairly ordinary people, instead of automatically going for the very rich or the very grand.

This was an extraordinary change from the assumptions and attitudes which reigned at Chatsworth up to the death of 'Uncle Cav', and to some extent it mirrored the changes which had been occurring in society and the aristocracy at large as great families like the Devonshires lost their position at the head of a supremely confident, self-perpetuating caste, drawing their income from their vast ancestral lands which had also given them their undisputed status and prestige. The ownership of inherited land had ceased to be a primary source of political power and enormous wealth – votes and investments were what mattered now. Previously there had always been a marked division between the great landed aristocracy and the new plutocracy of the commercially wealthy, but now the lines were rapidly becoming blurred. As Dr Cannadine points out, the Devonshires, with two thirds of their income now coming from investments were increasingly becoming *rentiers*, 'maintaining a life-style that was landed in its mode of *expenditure*, but increasingly plutocratic in the sources of *income*.'

This was to be of much importance for the future, but for the moment the family's great income and resources still permitted the semi-feudal life-style of the past to continue of its own momentum. Chatsworth, though 'modernized', was still run with its hordes of servants much as in the Sixth Duke's time. And in London, according to Lord Esher, Devonshire House remained like some fortress from the past, impervious to change:

> Sombrely ornate, its fine pictures hung but not displayed, [it] had none of the ostentatious glamour of a modern mansion. It framed with singular appropriateness the Cavendish faces of its inmates. The faded damask on the walls, the tarnished gilding, the quiet rooms opening one from another typified the hubristic Whig tradition. The passages and rooms were dimly lighted and there were but few bells. . . . Lady Louisa Egerton used to point out to me the stains on the green silk wall made by the heads of the powdered footmen who in the 'late duke's' time lounged in waiting, and whose yawns of boredom rang through the house.

The family too was always on the move, travelling now in private trains, but otherwise in unassuming grandeur, from one of its great houses to the next as the Cavendishes had done for centuries – Devonshire House for May and June, Bolton Abbey in August, on to Hardwick, then to Chatsworth through to Christmas, and to Lismore for the early spring. (Uncle Cav's favourite house, Compton Place at Eastbourne, tended to be used for ducal children convalescing from infectious illnesses.)

One of the Duke's daughters, Lady Blanche Cobbold, still recalls how

as a family we seemed to be always packing and unpacking as we moved from one house to the next. We thought it all quite normal, but it must have been an extraordinary feat of organization for the servants as each of us children had our ponies who would always travel with us. There were our nannies, nurserymaids and grooms, and for the older children there were the French and German governesses. For us it was all great fun, and it wasn't as unsettling as it might have been as we always had our parents and the same servants with us.

The 'fast' society the Double Duchess had so enjoyed no longer came to Chatsworth, but shy and unassuming though he might appear, the new Duke automatically filled the extremely grand position in society that was expected of a Duke of Devonshire. In his first year as Duke he entertained King Edward for the shooting up at Bolton Abbey just as Uncle Cav had done since the 1890s. (The King as usual topped the table with 570 slaughtered birds in five days' shooting.) King Edward died in 1910, but the following year King George V was there to lead the guns at Bolton Abbey, beating his father's record with a bag of 888.

When the Double Duchess died in 1911, Queen Mary appointed the new Duchess her Mistress of the Robes, and although the new Duke had little of his predecessor's passion for the turf, the Devonshire House dinner on the eve of the Derby continued to be one of the high spots of the London season. Even in 1914, at the end of May the Duke and Duchess entertained over a hundred guests in the presence of the Queen, Count Benckendorff and Arthur Balfour to a dinner that consisted of:

> *Caviar de Sterlet*
> *Tortue claire*
> *Consommé de volaille froid*
> *Filet de turbot à la Matignon*
> *Poularde froide à l'Andalouse*
> *Baron d'agneau aux primeurs*
> *Ortolans rôtis sur canapés*
> *Salade cœurs de laitues*
> *Asperges vertes, sauce Isigny*
> *Pêches à la Windsor*
> *Croustades à l'Ecossaise*

The tables were decorated with pink *malmaisons*, grown early for the occasion and brought specially from Chatsworth. With the carriages, the flunkeys, the great house ablaze with light, and a crowd in Piccadilly watching the arrival of the guests, little had changed since the days when Georgiana and her duke had entertained the future George IV. Then two months later the Great War broke out which seemed to toll the end of a world in which dukes like Devonshire could flourish.

From now on there would be no more special trains for the family and their servants and their ponies, no early carnations grown in the Chatsworth greenhouses, no Derby dinners in the presence of the royal family. The houses were closed up, male servants of military age went off to fight for freedom – as did the new Lord Hartington who contracted dysentery at Gallipoli – but if the Duke himself, now in his early forties, wondered gloomily about his future, he kept his feelings from his diary, where he continued to record the weather and his dutiful attendance at the House of Lords.

Although the dukedom had upset his political career, he had continued as an active politician in the House of Lords, first as Conservative Whip, and later as Civil Lord of the Admiralty in Asquith's first coalition government. His experience of politics and politicians was considerable. In the summer of 1916, as the armies battled on the Somme, the Duke of Devonshire was summoned by his friend, the King, to do his duty for his country. The royal uncle, Queen Victoria's son, the ageing Duke of Connaught, was finishing his term of office as Governor-General of Canada; no member of the royal family was available to take his place and the King suggested Devonshire for this semi-regal role.

The Duke, who was a very modest man, did not appear particularly surprised at being chosen to represent the King in a great dominion in time of war. Ever since the eighteenth century when the Third and Fourth Dukes governed Ireland for the Hanoverians, this sort of task was something the Cavendishes took for granted: his chief concern was, as usual, for his wife, and the King soon set his mind at rest:

> *22 July.* Evie saw the King and Queen yesterday. They were both very nice and kind. They want her to continue to hold the office of Mistress of the Robes. They also said we could use the royal colours on the carriage. That's really a great relief.

But behind the apparent imperturbability, the Duke was secretly delighted that the call had come at last. Here was a chance of the sort of political existence that he loved; he was quietly determined to perform it in considerable style, and, despite the wartime shortages, his departure was reminiscent of the way the Sixth Duke set out on his famous embassy to Moscow ninety years earlier. For not just the Duke and his family, but a good deal of the establishment as well were travelling *en masse* to Canada – china, plate, furniture and pictures, valets, cooks and servants in livery. By the end of October 1916 all were ready for departure and on the 31st the Duke wrote a typically brisk account of his farewell from the Royal Family: 'Weather improved. Busy day. Dentist . . . Luncheon with King and Queen. They were very kind and nice. He gave me the G.C.M.G. Said goodbye.'

Two days later he did permit himself a few words of regret that would prove more prophetic than he knew. 'Sad to think I shall not see Devonshire House again for so long. Said goodbye to Lord Lansdowne. He was really distressed.'

Then came the dangerous wartime voyage to Nova Scotia, and by mid-November the Duke and family were comfortably installed in Rideau Hall, the Governor-General's official residence in Ottawa. The happiest and most successful years of Duke Victor's life had started.

In fact he arrived to face what might have been an awkward situation for the representative of King George V. Conscription had only just been introduced to Canada to something less than universal popularity: in Parliament the opposition were questioning the nature of the link between Canada and 'The Mother Country', and the Duke's arrival was actually greeted by an editorial in the *Toronto Star* urging the outright abolition of his office.

A less experienced man might well have felt distinctly daunted, but the Duke remained as quietly impervious as if still in Derbyshire. Besides, he had grown up with politics and politicians. As a young M.P. himself he had known and observed the greatest politicians of his time in action at Westminster. After Gladstone and 'Uncle Cav' and Salisbury, there was hardly likely to be any politician at Ottawa capable of shocking or surprising – or outwitting – him, and he performed his role as constitutional head of state impeccably throughout what proved to be a turbulent time in the Dominion's politics.

But while he could be politically extremely shrewd, he appeared to everyone exactly what he also was – a courteous and unassuming man with simple habits and the aura of a very grand rich English nobleman. This was the secret of his great success, and paradoxically in democratic Canada, he was more happily a duke than back in Britain.

He was kept busy, for during his time in Ottawa the Governor-General's role had not become the mere figurehead of royalty it became later. The Duke's status was closer to that of the Viceroy of India; he dealt directly with the Prime Minister and leading politicians, and during the period of the war all communications between the Canadian and British Governments passed through his office. He was immensely conscientious, and, despite his work in Ottawa, travelled widely, generally with his family, and as an official historian put it, 'was never happier than when meeting agriculturalists in various parts of the Dominion. The farmers of Canada soon realised that the Governor-General understood their industry, and was one who could talk their language.'

This was a considerable achievement, as the Duke was actually rather bored with farming, but he uncomplainingly laid foundation-stones, planted commemorative saplings, visited steel mills and military hospitals ('mainly mental cases. Very sad, but was told that 50 per cent were completely cured'), and, whether at boy scout rallies, patriotic luncheons or reformatories, was always ready with a few apt words. As the same historian would put it, 'if the Duke's style was dull, he always spoke with point and to the purpose'.

The Devonshires were popular at Rideau Hall, for most Canadians at that period, staunch democrats although they might be, were also flattered and intrigued to have a duke with all the trimmings in their midst. The Chatsworth plate and furniture, the paintings and the Devonshire House footmen lent a touch of grandeur to the official functions. And after the aged Connaughts, the Devonshires were anything but stuffy: five daughters saw to that.

Prohibition, then in force in the Province of Ontario, did not apply to Rideau Hall, and the Duke and his family would be remembered for the best parties and the liveliest dances in Canada. The Duke was particularly careful to avoid any hint of snobbery or condescension in his manner – or from any member of his family – and his youngest daughter once related how as a young girl at a party in Ottawa, she was asked by another small girl who she was:

> 'Anne Cavendish,' I said.
> 'But who *are* you?' she insisted.
> I replied, quite reasonably I thought, that I was the daughter of the Governor-General, but word of this inevitably got back to my parents, and I found myself in dreadful trouble from them both for showing off. I was firmly told that I must *never* boast to anyone like that again.

Apart from such minor irritations, the five years they spent in Canada were an idyllic period for the family. In Ottawa the Duke missed the countryside and built the family a Canadian-style log-house on the shores of the Blue Sea Lake, which he called 'New Lismore'. 'The house is really very nice,' he wrote. 'Did various jobs there. Made hay, cleared bushes, etc.' For his daughters life in Canada was more relaxed than it would have been in England, and early in 1919 the Duke recorded an event in his diary which was to have considerable importance for his third daughter, nineteen-year-old Lady Dorothy, as well as for the future of his family.

'*11 April.* Very wet and muggy. Macmillan arrived. Seems a nice boy.'

Captain Harold Macmillan, whose grandfather, a self-educated crofter's son, had founded the highly successful Victorian publishing house, was recovering from wounds received in France, and had been seconded to the Governor-General as his official A.D.C. in succession to Captain Angus Mackintosh, who had married the Duke's eldest daughter, Lady Maud. The Duke's diary shows how effortlessly the new A.D.C. became accepted by the family.

> *14 April.* Weather improved. Played golf with Macmillan. He plays quite well and is much better than I am. Very jolly out on the course. Lovely evening. Macmillan is certainly a great acquisition.

Lady Dorothy seems to have agreed. 'Macmillan' is soon being referred to as 'Harold' and, in July, the Duke is equably recording: 'Dorothy and Harold got up early to go to Mount Jacques to see the sunrise. Afraid it would not be clear.'

Before long Lady Dorothy followed Lady Maud's example and the crofter's grandson and the Ninth Duke's daughter became engaged. Not all that long before, the idea of such a marriage would have been almost inconceivable, but the rigid attitudes which had made the upper aristocracy something of a separate caste had weakened with the war, and the Duke and Duchess were genuinely delighted at the news. As Harold Macmillan recalls:

The Cavendishes still formed a very closed, tight circle of their own, but they never let me feel the slightest sense of intruding when I married into it. The night before the wedding Lord Lansdowne took me to the Beefsteak Club where we met a number of his friends. They told a lot of what I suppose you'd call smoking-room stories. Didn't upset me in the least after five years in the army, but he seemed rather worried. Next morning I found a letter from him, apologising for the company the night before, and going on to say how very glad and honoured he was to be having a member of such a distinguished publishing family join his own.

The wedding took place in London in 1921 on the Devonshires' return from Canada, and among the bridgroom's guests the upper-middle class Macmillans prominently fielded four of their authors with the O.M.* against the solid ranks of aristocrats behind the bride.

But before this there had been less welcome changes in the air for the Duke to cope with. Late in 1919 the re-election of that fearsome enemy of privilege, Lloyd George, had sent a pessimistic shudder through the ancient and already nervous body of the aristocracy. 'The old order is doomed,' the Duke of Marlborough lamented, referring sadly to 'those fortresses of territorial influence it is proposed to raze in the interests of social equality.' Not long afterwards that wheeler-dealer of the art world, Lord Duveen was able to persuade the immensely rich Duke of Westminster to part with his most famous painting, Gainsborough's *Blue Boy*, to the American H. E. Huntington for £175,000. Duke Victor had little against Lloyd George politically, but 'economy' was in the air, and, in much the same spirit as his fellow-duke, he decided that the time had come for serious retrenchment. Only through sacrifice it seemed could the aristocracy survive, and on 15 October 1920, the Duke made an historic, somewhat melancholy entry in his faithful diary:

> Got a telegram today to say that the formal agreement about the sale of Devonshire House has been signed and so that is the last of the poor old house. Hope we shall not live to regret it.

According to his daughter Lady Blanche, neither he nor any of the family ever seriously missed their huge historic house opposite the Ritz:

> Devonshire House was simply one more house we lived in, but we hadn't really all that much affection for it. It was a marvellous vantage-point for watching royal processions, and it was nice to have a garden and a tennis-court off Piccadilly, but it wasn't really very homey, and none us felt a dreadful sense of loss when it was sold.

As far as one can see, the Duke himself had no particularly pressing need to dispense with a house which had been part of the history of his family since early in the eighteenth century. His investments were perfectly secure, he had saved considerably from the five years spent in Canada and, although the rates

*Kipling, Morley, Hardy and Bryce.

on the three-acre site in Mayfair had been raised to nearly £20,000 a year, he could easily have afforded them had he wanted to.

But the Duke and his Duchess were clearly envisaging hard times ahead when, early in July 1921, their term in Canada expired and 'amid a salute of 19 guns from the Citadel, and the playing of the National Anthem by the band of the Royal Canadian Garrison Artillery, they embarked at Quebec on the Empress of France for their homeward journey.'

The Duke was in sombre mood. 'V. sad to believe that this is my last day in Canada. Wish the time was beginning again.'

But despite the sense of obvious foreboding with which the Ninth Duke and his family sailed home, he was soon reassured to find that nothing appeared to have changed too drastically for dukes in postwar Britain. At Liverpool docks the Rolls was there to meet them. At Buxton he and the Duchess were welcomed by their eldest son, Lord Hartington, somewhat theatrically decked out in the robes and chain of office of Mayor (to which position the heir to the dukedom had just been unanimously elected). And at Chatsworth there was an old-style feudal greeting from the servants, delighted that the house would now be lived in once again:

> Splendid welcome. Very nice. Walked about the gardens which had certainly come on a lot in our absence. Charming letter from the King. . . . After luncheon, Eddy, Charlie and I went up to the shire yard. Horses look well.

It was strange to think of the Devonshires no longer owning Devonshire House; the demolition men would soon be taking over and the property-developers later build a car salesroom and monster office-block on the site of 'the poor old house'. But the Duchess was extremely practical and economical; at her suggestion the family finally moved into a more manageable but still thoroughly appropriate London residence at No. 2 Carlton Gardens off the Mall.

The Rembrandts and Reynoldses from Devonshire House went 'very nicely' on the walls, and some time later Lord Mersey had a conversation with Her Grace which gives an interesting sidelight on the easy-going attitudes of the nineteenth-century Cavendishes, and the far tighter ship the Duchess was intent on running:

> She told me that at the move they found that they had been paying rent for eighty years for a large chandelier at Devonshire House which had been hired for a function in the 1840s – the bill kept coming in. Finally they bought it, having, of course, paid for it over and over again. Two fine Kent tables from Chiswick, which had been sent away for repair, had been forgotten for many years. One had been sold and with difficulty they had just recovered the other.

On his return from Canada, the Duke was actually approached by Lloyd George with an offer of a place in his administration. He was tempted – but refused on the strictly realistic grounds that the Liberals under Lloyd George had no future. He was soon proved right when the Welsh Wizard and his followers were annihilated in the November 1922 election, and by a twist of fate it was this defeat which allowed the Duke to achieve his own completely unexpected niche in the history of his times.

The new Conservative Prime Minister, Bonar Law, had a penchant for the peerage. His Cabinet, with five members of the House of Lords already, was by far the most aristocratic of the period, and he invited the distinguished and popular ex-Governor of his native Canada to join it as Secretary of the Colonies. The Duke was still beset by doubts. He considered himself a Liberal at heart, and was personally wary of Conservatives, but he valued Bonar Law, and the opportunity of power was still immensely tempting. He accepted. Against considerable odds – and despite his dukedom – the ex-Liberal-Unionist M.P. for West Derbyshire had reached the Cabinet at last.

Here he was in his element, dealing with what might have seemed a succession of unrewarding problems, but he was happy to be back in government, and every Monday morning he would catch the 7.30 train from Chesterfield, and spend the week away from Chatsworth working in Westminster. One major issue which he had to deal with was the ever-present Irish problem. Unlike most of his Conservative colleagues in the government, he was in full agreement with the establishment of the Free State of Ireland, and became interminably involved in the discussions on the legal rights of Protestants in Northern Ireland. Barely was this dealt with than in the spring of 1923 another complicated problem landed firmly in his lap – the controversial issue of the status of the Asian minority in Kenya.

Since the beginning of the century, European settlers in Kenya had been enjoying virtually exclusive rights to the prized farming lands of the so-called 'White Highlands' north of Nairobi, but recently well-to-do Asian immigrants had claimed the right as imperial citizens to settle there as well. A number of potentially explosive issues were involved, especially as the Government of India supported the Indian minority. The white settlers were predictably up in arms, and two separate delegations had arrived in London with the Governor, Lord Delamere, to argue the whole thing out before the British Government.

In effect this meant the Duke – and throughout May and June he and his civil servants listened conscientiously to the rival and excited claims of the Asians and the Europeans. Back at Chatsworth at week-ends he was teaching his second son Lord Charles the rudiments of golf. One of his favourite shire mares, Chatsworth Dorothy, was delivered of a still-born foal. Eton were beating Harrow in their match at Lords, but because of a group of settlers in far-off Africa, the Duke of Devonshire for once could not attend.

For as a man who still considered himself a Whig at heart, the Duke's radical conscience was disturbed by what was happening in Kenya. He was surprisingly well-informed on the subject. He had known and admired Lord Francis Scott, one of the pioneer settlers in Kenya, and another settler, Mervyn Ridley, had been his A.D.C. in Canada. From men like these he had heard about the new wave of rich irresponsible European playboy settlers, some of whom would later form the notorious 'Happy-Valley Set' in Kenya. Such people represented exactly the sort of smart, indefensible society of which the Duke had always strongly disapproved; and according to Harold Macmillan, with whom he discussed the issues at the time, 'he thought it intolerable to agree to turning Kenya permanently into a playground for the dregs of the British upper classes'.

The Duke mulled the matter over with his advisers, and insisted on drafting the report himself. Some of the civil servants seemed to think him far too radical in his approach, and he plainly needed to avoid alarming the Conservative members of the Cabinet. But the Duke had a lifetime's experience of politics and how to get results. His report on the Kenya problem safely passed through Cabinet, and on 23 July 1923 the Duke rose in the House of Lords to present his judgment on the whole affair. In his diary he described what happened in his inimitable manner:

> Got my speech ready for the Lords debate. On the whole I felt it went alright, but Birkenhead had got my brief and queered my pitch. Don't feel I said anything that mattered. Cabinet accepted Kenya proposals. Great relief if we can have no more Kenya for the present.

It sounded something of an anti-climax, and there was nothing particularly startling in the main Government proposals – which more or less confirmed the Europeans' *status quo* in the Kenya highlands for the time being, and kept the Asians firmly in their place. But tucked away within the pages of this Conservative Government's White Paper, was one paragraph of radical Whig doctrine which the Duke himself had written as an unambiguous pointer to the future.

> Kenya is an African territory, and His Majesty's Government think it necessary definitely to record their considered opinion that the interests of the African natives must be paramount, and that if, and when, those interests and the interests of the immigrant races should conflict, the former should prevail. . . . In the administration of Kenya, His Majesty's Government regard themselves as exercising a trust on behalf of the African population, and they are unable to delegate or share this trust, the object of which may be defined as the protection and advancement of the native races.

When the Duke wrote in his diary about not having 'said anything that mattered', he was being far too modest, for that single paragraph in the innocuous-seeming report on the Asian minority in Kenya would have a more long-lasting impact than any other act of Bonar Law's short-lived administration. In time, it would be known as the 'Devonshire Declaration' and be seen as a solemn pledge by a British Government to the cause of ultimate Kenyan self-determination. In years to come this Declaration became something of a pledge to the end of White supremacy in Kenya and throughout Black Africa, and assured this least revolutionary of noblemen his place in history for his apparent advocacy, not just of Kenyan independence, but of the peaceful transformation of the British Commonwealth.

This was ironic, for the Duke, despite his Whig inheritance, was a dedicated

Empire man at heart. When the ailing Bonar Law left politics at the end of 1923, the Duke followed him, and took on the responsibility of organizing that resounding showpiece for the British Empire, the 1924 Wembley Imperial Exhibition. It was a complex task which he dealt with in his usual dogged, highly conscientious manner. When it was finished, Stanley Baldwin was back in power, and the Duke was hoping for a summons to return to his former place in the Cabinet. It never came, and according to Harold Macmillan, 'It broke his heart.' Doing his best to hide his disappointment, he took his family to Southern Ireland in the spring of 1925 for a look at Lismore and a few weeks' fishing.

The castle was uninhabitable. It had escaped the fate of Lord Lansdowne's house Derreen which had been burned down by Irish 'Irregulars' during the Civil War that followed Irish independence, but it had been occupied by both sides in the fighting, and the family had to stay in the village at the 'Devonshire Arms'.

One of Lismore's oldest inhabitants, Clodagh Anson, a spry octogenarian who has lived in the district all her life, remembers the occasion well:

> On Easter Saturday the Duke and Duchess and the family had gone off walking through the woods, as they often did, and when they got towards our house they'd all sing out 'We want *tea*!' I used to do my best to oblige, but the maid we had in those days could only make potato cakes which we ate with thick local butter and treacle. The Duke loved them. They were terribly indigestible of course, but on this occasion I remember how he went on eating them. He had three dishes of potato cakes and I've always hoped they weren't what caused the trouble.

The Duke's diary for the next day, Easter Sunday, starts off with the customary weather report. 'Lovely day, but there was heavy rain in the night. . . . Went down to the bridge to fish before breakfast.' He must have written this soon afterwards, for the entry is concluded in a different, all but illegible scrawl: 'Collapsed in a foolish and uncomfortable way after breakfast. Sort of fainting fit. Got two nurses and doctors and went to bed.'

His daughter, Anne, who was present at the time, remembered the incident as something more dramatic:

> I heard the butler shouting that my father had fallen down and hurt himself, and suddenly all hell broke loose. My brother Charlie and I were hustled off to church to get us out of the way, and it was only later that I learned that my father had had a stroke.

Six weeks later he was sufficiently recovered to recommence his diary, with a single sentence: 'Pretty dreary way of spending a holiday.' From now on the Duke's existence was to prove a 'pretty dreary way of spending' the remainder of his life.

With the Duke's gradual recovery, the most disturbing effect of his illness seemed to be a complete reversal of his personality. Previously the most patient and polite of men, he became profoundly irritable and unpredictable; the devoted husband was transformed into a man who could not bear his wife; the loving father started to dislike his children. Like something in a gothic nightmare, the Duke became an increasingly miserable old monster, and the family was left to cope as best they could.

It would have been a tragedy in any family; for the Devonshires the Duke's situation produced countless complications and embarrassments. One of the difficulties was that the Duke was neither mad nor seriously impaired; as one of the Chatsworth servants put it, he was 'afflicted' – but he was still the Duke of Devonshire, and most of the functions that had always centred round him had to continue. It is extraordinary how many of them did.

This was largely the achievement of the Duchess. The English upper classes are remarkably resilient. Often insensitive and intolerant of weaknesses in others, they can be at their most impressive in this sort of human crisis, particularly when they have a role that tradition and society prescribe for them to play. The Duchess had, and she acted on it now with grim determination.

'An unpleasant woman, accustomed to authority', is how her brother-in-law the Duke of St Albans described her, when jokingly warning the present Duchess against following in 'Grannie Duchess's' footsteps. But unpleasant or not, it was Evelyn Devonshire who kept the dukedom more or less intact despite her husband's stroke. A lesser woman might have been defeated. But at Chatsworth her chilly, strong-willed presence actually enhanced the authoritarian regime which still survived from the nineteenth century. She was intensely mean, particularly with servants; this was not attractive, but it earned Her Grace a sort of grim respect. No Chatsworth employee from this period forgets the Duchess's response in 1931 when Ramsay MacDonald increased income tax to five shillings in the pound – widespread dismissals and abolition of the beer-money which the remaining servants had enjoyed from time immemorial. At the time she was paying her housemaids £22 a year – £6 a year more than they had earned in 1860 – and the beer-money came to an extra 2s. 6d a week.

Some of her economies were actually quite funny – like her sudden eagerness for nettle soup. She had first tasted this in Ireland, liked it, and since nettles could be had for nothing, soon established nettle soup as a regular fixture on the Chatsworth menu. Some time later, when inspecting the Chatsworth gardens she noticed a large expanse of nettles being cultivated under glass. Puzzled, she asked the head gardener for an explanation. 'But Your Grace,' he replied, '*those* are the nettles for Your Grace's soup.'

Despite such occasional setbacks, she was an energetic lady who was convinced that she invariably knew best. When Laguerre's frescoes in the Great Hall were being restored, she ordered the restorer to give Hercules a less pugilistic nose – which promptly and prudently he did. She had a passion for discovering dry rot in old houses; she could smell it out in the most unlikely places with unerring accuracy. She had her own store of Chatsworth timber, specially cut and seasoned under her personal supervision for restorations in the house; and when Paxton's conservatory had become so ruined from neglect during the First World War that it would have been expensive to restore and heat yet difficult to dismantle, her advice was simple – dynamite. Paxton had done his work so well that it took several blasts to level it. Remarkably, there were no casualties from flying glass, and the Duchess was soon hard at work with her gardeners planting roses on the site of one of the most original buildings of the nineteenth century.

There is a theory, subscribed to by the present Duke, that the Duchess was actually jealous of the Bachelor Duke and did her best to obliterate his memory. A great devotee of cream distemper, she had one of Pugin's spectacular ceilings at Lismore painted over, replanted much of Paxton's Chatsworth garden with rhododendrons and bamboo, and Wyatville's tower and belvedere might well have followed the Great Conservatory but for the expense.

For, like dry rot, expense had rapidly become something of an obsession with the Duchess. The Duke, as befits an easy-going aristocrat, had never possessed much money-sense, and after his illness the Duchess took power of attorney. Her presence was a guarantee that the Cavendishes would never founder through extravagance while she was there to check through the accounts. In conjunction with the Curreys – still the trusted family lawyers – she also found a solution to the most worrying of all the financial horrors bedevilling the future of the dukedom and the Cavendish inheritance – death duties.

These had been rising steadily from the gentle days of Sir William Harcourt's famous eight per cent, and it was clear that, whatever the complexion of the government in power, the state from now on would be a constant threat to the landed aristocracy. The Duke's stroke had been a close run thing for the House of Cavendish, for had he expired that Easter Sunday morning, almost half the Cavendish capital and property, including the art collection, might well have vanished with him. It was a timely warning which the Duchess and the lawyers could not possibly ignore.

With a little legal and financial ingenuity, death duties could still be minimized or totally avoided. Until now the reigning Duke of Devonshire had always enjoyed full possession of the family properties and fortune. Early in 1926 this ended. An unlimited liability company was formed with the title of the Chatsworth Estates Company, which purchased all the family estates in exchange for an issue of shares. Most of these shares were then assigned to the Duke's heir, Edward Lord Hartington, and provided the Duke himself re-mained alive for the three-year 'quarantine period' somewhat sportingly laid down by law, they would not be liable to death duties when his son succeeded him. The Duke's health became a matter of considerable importance to his family.

He was indulged. Everyone around him, family and friends included, did their best to overlook his outbursts of impotent bad temper as he laid about him with his walking-stick; as the present Duchess puts it, 'People learned to be nimble in his presence.' The only person who could really cope with him was the head Chatsworth gamekeeper, a towering Scot called John Maclauch-lan. An imperious presence on his own account, Maclauchlan became the

Duke's most trusted companion, with a chauffeur of his own and the additional position of Chatsworth farm manager. His overbearing manner, which was used without particular regard for rank or wealth – the Duke's included – was inevitably resented by the majority of Chatsworth servants, who nicknamed him 'The Duke of Derbyshire' or, less politely, 'The Little Duke'. But Maclauchlan kept the Duke as happy now as anybody could, driving with him every day around the estates, managing the shire horses, and even minimizing the considerable risks to life and limb when the Duke went shooting.

Thanks very largely to Maclauchlan's pacifying influence on the Duke, the Duchess was able to maintain appearances at Chatsworth much as in the past. Distinguished guests, the Royal Family included, continued to be entertained in considerable splendour at Chatsworth and at Bolton Abbey for the shooting; and at Christmas the whole clan of Cavendishes, children and grandchildren and servants, would assemble for several weeks for a gathering which Harold Macmillan once described as 'almost as remote from present-day England as the descriptions of Count Rostov's family in *War and Peace*.'

The Chatsworth Christmas was the great occasion of the year, and is almost universally looked back to with nostalgia, especially by old Chatsworth servants from the period, despite the prodigies of extra work it meant for them. Sally Barnes, a retired Chatsworth housemaid and widow of one the family chauffeurs, is quite unsentimental over the hardship of the old regime that continued at Chatsworth almost up until the war:

> Winter was always the hardest time for us, what with the guests for the shooting and then the Christmas parties. During those eight weeks or so, we'd get up at five, clean out the grates and burnish them till they were like silver, then dust and clean the carpets before we had our breakfast in the servants' hall. Then we'd take hot water up to the bedrooms for our ladies, and at nine o'clock we'd collect the calling trays from the kitchen and take them up as well. After that we'd make the beds, change the linen, tidy, dust and do whatever our ladies wanted. We had a rest-time in the early afternoon, but it was back on duty for us before tea, sewing for the Duchess, then tidying the drawing-room, plumping up the cushions and emptying waste-paper baskets. Then it was time to help our ladies wash and dress for dinner, and we'd have to wait till dinner was over to take round the last hot water before the ladies went to bed. You didn't have much time to think how tired you were.

Despite this, Mrs Barnes insists that there was nothing like a Chatsworth Christmas in the bad old days.

> That was really something, I can tell you, particularly the Christmas party for the staff. The family and the gentry all came of course, and we could invite two guests as well. There must have been three hundred of us there. Mrs. Tanner the cook used to do the food wonderfully, and the dancing went on till three or four in the morning.

The servants received their Christmas presents, which were still dispensed much as they must have been by Bess of Hardwick. According to Gladys Grafton, another of Chatsworth's now retired housemaids,

> The men got a piece of beef and a loaf of bread for Christmas which was given out in the big shed by the wood yard. They used to call it 'Beef and Bread Day'. And the maids would have a choice of stockings, gloves or an umbrella. One year I caused no end of trouble by asking for a woollen vest.

But for the indoor staff at Chatsworth, the great excitement was the arrival of the Duke's children, and their spouses, the grandchildren and friends, so that the house was fully lived in for these few brief Christmas weeks.

> These days it's hard to explain to anyone how satisfying it was for us, [says Maud Shimwell, Mrs. Tanner's daughter and herself a former cook at Chatsworth]. It was just lovely hearing voices once again in all the bedrooms and children playing in the corridors. It was like one big family coming home again. We all felt part of it and loved it.

This sense of loyalty and close involvement with the family goes a long way to explaining how this large, semi-feudal household managed to survive like a relic from the past, despite the hardship and the meagre wages. Large-scale local unemployment also played its part – particularly for male servants and estate-workers with dependent families. Gladys Grafton's husband, Jesse, went to work at Chatsworth straight from school, and was earning 32s. 9d a week when they married in 1935.

> I felt that I was lucky. There wasn't much work about – only farm labouring if you could find it, or work in the quarries, where you got no pay if it was wet. At least the pay was regular at Chatsworth, although they probably paid less than any other big family in Derbyshire, and they worked you hard. I paid 2s. 6d. a week for our cottage with heat and light on top. Life was work and bed and not much else.

Mrs Grafton nods, but is quick to add:

> But they've always been a good family to us. My Duchess now – that's what I call Grannie Duchess, Duchess Evie – she was Queen Mary's type, very regal, wouldn't speak to you unless she wanted something, and I can't say she ever thanked you either. But when my daughter was born she came and saw me in the hospital and brought me some roses from the garden and some Chatsworth peaches. I've not forgotten.

This sort of *noblesse oblige* from members of the family was particularly appreciated by the Chatsworth servants, in part for the prestige that it conferred in a way that higher-paying, less hard-working posts with *nouveaux riches* families never could.

'Like it or not, there was something to be said for working in a ducal family,' says one retired housemaid, describing how just before his stroke the Duke had passed her in the Mall and raised his hat to her. 'Always a perfect gentleman, the Duke, and he'd always stop the Rolls and offer you a lift if he passed you on the road near Chatsworth.'

Mrs Shimwell tells of how, when she was still a girl at a south-coast boarding-school and due to travel back to Chatsworth for her Christmas holidays, arrangements were made by the Duchess for 'young Maudie' to meet Lady Anne and the Duchess's ladies' maid Miss Webb, under the clock at St Pancras, and travel up to Chesterfield, then on to Chatsworth in the car together. On leaving school Maudie started work beneath her mother as a vegetable-maid – 'and very hard it was,' she adds. 'If anything she worked me harder than the others just because I was her daughter.'

In her day Mrs Tanner was a famous cook, of the sort that could flourish only in a household like the pre-war Devonshires. Her father had been butler to Dean Liddell at Christ Church Oxford – where she remembered the Dean's daughter, Alice Liddell, who was the original of Lewis Carroll's 'Alice' – and as first kitchen-maid to Lord and Lady Savile she had originally had lessons from the great Escoffier at the Hôtel Cecil. Later as the Saviles' cook in the South of France, she had had further lessons, paid for by Lord Savile, in the kitchens of the Hôtel de Paris at Monte Carlo, so that by the time she came to Chatsworth in 1924, at £14 a month, she already had a considerable reputation, and for an English cook an unusual knowledge of Continental *haute cuisine*.

In her way, Mrs Tanner was a star. 'She had a marvellous palate,' says her daughter, 'was a total perfectionist, and so artistic in the presentation of her dishes that it often seemed a sin to put a knife into them.' She planned all the Chatsworth menus personally, even for the most important banquet, and in her the Duchess seems to have met her match. 'All she did was sometimes cross something off one of my mother's menus and say, "No, not *that* for His Grace. It won't agree with him."'

But the strain and responsibility must have been enormous, and Mrs Tanner, artist though she was, was never very easy on those around her. Her marriage was unhappy, and she was regularly surrounded by weeping and departing kitchen-maids. In her own way she was every bit as autocratic as the Duchess, and the discipline at Chatsworth was extremely strict. Mrs Tanner's counterpart below stairs, the housekeeper Mrs Woolman, was another martinet. Dress and deportment for the staff were rigidly prescribed. Church was compulsory on Sunday mornings, and when young Gladys Grafton arrived one Sunday in a discreetly flowered dress, Mrs Woolman was indignant. 'A suitable dress for the river, Gladys, but *never* for church at Chatsworth.'

The discipline extended to a total ban on fraternizing between laundry-maids and kitchen-maids and housemaids, even off duty, and the only time they could meet officially was at the Christmas party. 'I want you all to be good workmates, but not good friends,' said the dreaded Mrs Woolman, and as far as 'the gentry' were concerned, the servants were supposed to be invisible. 'You soon got used to doing your work quietly, and if we heard Duchess Evie coming we'd just vanish. More so if it was the Duke', says Mrs Barnes. 'You could always hear *him* coming from the way he used to growl and puff. But once I was on the landing when he came out of the bath, stark naked. I did my best to hide, but I don't think he even noticed I was there.'

In her novel *The Edwardians*, Vita Sackville-West described the owners of her fictional ducal mansion, 'Chevron' as in effect the prisoners of the enormous house, the true custodians being the upper servants whose lives were dedicated to the effortless continuation of the whole extraordinary establishment, with its intricate below-stairs snobberies, its lavishness, its deferential discipline and countless traditional activities, all carefully pre-scribed by age-old practice, which still formed the pattern for the servants' lives.

> The house was really as self-contained as a little town; the carpenter's shop, the painter's shop, the forge, the sawmill, the hot-houses, were there to provide whatever might be needed at a moment's notice.

This was very much the case at pre-war Chatsworth too, which had become as ritualized and self-contained as a medieval monastery surviving in an alien world.* Just as monastery existed to serve God, so Chatsworth still existed for the greater glory of the House of Cavendish, but its true guardians were the servants who kept it functioning and knew it better than any member of the family except the Duchess, who has been described as 'something of a curator herself'.

Francis Thompson, the librarian and historian of Chatsworth, was the unfailing repository of the history of the family and the one person in the house with a true appreciation of its great artistic treasures. (The Duchess's interest in the Chatsworth drawings was largely confined to having them taken from their cabinets once a year 'for an airing'.) Maclauchlan ruled the surrounding moors and woods and farmlands. The head gardener, Mr Weston, kept the Chatsworth gardens the show-place they had always been, and care for the fabric of the house was the life-work of Maud Shimwell's husband, William, the Comptroller of the Household.

The son of a Chatsworth gamekeeper, who started work at 'The House' in 1908 as a twelve-year-old bell-boy, Willie Shimwell was a good example of the sort of many-sided talent which a great house like Chatsworth could still produce. He accompanied the Duke to Canada, and became his Secretary, before his appointment as Comptroller at the age of twenty-six. As such he was responsible for almost everything that moved – or failed to – both at Chatsworth and at Carlton Gardens, and he rapidly became the supreme factotum who could turn his hand to anything, from supervising the installa-tion of a boiler or the repair of a fountain in the garden to the organization of a royal visit. He was a proud man and before his death he admitted that he had come to regard Chatsworth 'almost as my own. I knew every inch of it, and by the time I left there wasn't a door that squeaked, or a chimney that smoked or a window that wouldn't open.'

---

* For a fuller and fascinating account of the functioning of pre-war Chatsworth see *The House, a Portrait of Chatsworth* by the Duchess of Devonshire.

The sad old Duke had no such interest in his great possessions, and once he had survived long enough to release the family from the three-year threat of death duties, his work was done and he lived on, a cantankerous recluse whose presence guaranteed that nothing would really change until his death. His heir, Edward Cavendish, Lord Hartington, had married Lady Mary Cecil, daughter of the Marquis of Salisbury, in 1917, and since 1923 had followed his father as Conservative M.P. for the traditional Cavendish seat, West Derbyshire. He had four children – William, born in 1917, Andrew, Elizabeth and Anne – but after his father's stroke the two men had little real contact, and the Hartingtons had their own establishment at Churchdale Hall at Ashford-in-the-Water five miles from Chatsworth. It was here that their children grew up, and it was only the very youngest of the Cavendishes who could still appeal to the 'afflicted' Duke.

Adults tended to enrage him, but he was the gentlest of men with babies. His granddaughter, Lady Elizabeth, still remembers him as 'kind and rather touching. He was marvellous with small children. Perhaps they were all he felt he could relate to. I've never forgotten the care he used to take to peel me a grape.'

Her sister, Lady Anne, has similar memories of him:

As children we were always fascinated by the way he used to put his false teeth in a glass of water which we could see through his study window up at Bolton Abbey. Rather endearing. To encourage us to be brave on horseback he'd pay us five shillings if we fell off and then remounted. As you can imagine we fell off a lot.

On the other hand his grandson, Andrew, was soon too old for such indulgent grandpaternal treatment, and his boyhood memories of Chatsworth are of occasional appalling luncheon parties with his elder brother, William, his parents and his grandparents, where no one spoke directly to anybody else. The Duchess's secretary, Miss Saunders, was always present to alleviate the atmosphere and 'translate' between the Duke and other members of his family.

The Duke was apparently upset by the way his grandsons seemed to show more resemblance to the Cecils than the Cavendishes; and they had little contact with the alarming old gentleman. One Christmas at Chatsworth, Andrew was summoned into his grandfather's presence to receive a tip. The Duke was in his study; Andrew entered, but the Duke said nothing. Silence reigned for several minutes at the end of which the Duke produced two pounds, silently gave them to his grandson who just as silently departed.

During the Duke's last years, people remember him occasionally riding a docile old grey pony with Maclauchlan always by his side, or sitting in an armchair with a black spaniel at his feet watching Derbyshire play cricket. On one of these occasions a Derbyshire batsman hit a six which smashed a window in the Ducal Rolls. The Duke sent the man ten pounds and his congratulations.

His shire horses delighted him until the end, and one of his last pleasures was to see a Chatsworth shire foal take first prize at the 1937 Bakewell Show.

But by then he had little other contact with the world outside, and his brief entries in his diaries show an old man's mounting loneliness and gloom. The last entry is for 30 April 1938. 'Nice day. Very wretched. More gout in the foot. Things get worse and worse.'

A week later he was dead, and with him the old regime at Chatsworth really died as well. With a new Duke and a new war looming, nothing would ever be the same again.

15. Death and Taxes

The Tenth Duke, Edward (1895–1950)
The Eleventh Duke, Andrew (1920–   )

He was a gnarled man with dark grey eyes and a moustache and one shoulder slightly higher than the other. With his paper collars and patched tweed jacket he might have been a very old-fashioned railway porter, but he was really what the French would call, *un numéro*, a genuine original in an entirely unshowoffy way, and I always thought he looked more like a Frenchman than an Englishman. He was one of the most tolerant men I've ever met, although he disliked nuns and was wary of clergymen and probably preferred plants and animals to people. He was wonderful with his hands, and used to do carpentry in the drawing-room. He made his own fishing-tackle and when he was doing this the whole house reeked of varnish. He spoke perfect French, was an accomplished botanical painter, and I've never known anyone quite like him.

THIS is how his daughter, Lady Anne Tree, describes the man who, in 1938 at the age of forty-three, succeeded his long moribund father as Tenth Duke of Devonshire.

The arrival of this sort of *numéro* upon the scene seemed to guarantee that the spell that had kept the dukedom anchored so firmly to the past was broken. Chatsworth's presiding spirit, 'Grannie Duchess', swathed in her dowagerdom, departed. One of the unremarked advantages possessed by families like the Cavendishes is that there is usually a house somewhere for members of the family who might otherwise become a problem. For the Dowager Duchess the obvious residence was Hardwick Hall, and it was here she found the perfect setting for her powerful old age, as Bess of Hardwick did before her. Like Bess she was an expert and remorseless needlewoman, and at Hardwick there was work to keep her more than busy, repairing and restoring the remarkable collection of tapestries and hangings which had been preserved across the centuries. In time she was to bring several experts from the Royal College of Needlework up from London to help her in the task, and one of them was so impressed with what she had already done that she told her, 'Frankly, you're wasted as a Duchess.' Grannie Duchess recounted this to all her friends, as one of the greatest compliments ever paid her.

Meanwhile, at Chatsworth her successors had begun to realize the scale of the task before them. The new Duchess had made Churchdale Hall a home that all the family adored; in contrast Chatsworth seemed a mausoleum haunted with often painful memories. It also appeared horribly uncomfortable. Despite the plumbing done in 1908, there was a dearth of bathrooms, and the new Duchess had not forgotten the occasion early in the 1930s when she and her husband had been allocated one of the state bedrooms for their Christmas visit and woke to find the water in their wash-stand basin frozen solid. Nor had she forgotten how the cold had often ruined Mrs Tanner's famous dishes during their long and tedious processions from the kitchens to the dining-room. Clearly there was work to do before the family could bow to duty and finally take up residence at Chatsworth. But according to Chips Channon, Eddie Devonshire 'hated being a Duke and was really a bit bored by all his possessions and palaces', and he was certainly in no hurry to leave Churchdale before he had to. Apart from plants and carpentry, the great passion of his life was politics, and it was this that took his time and his attention.

After his death, *The Times* – in a curious obituary which reveals a lot about the changing attitude to dukes in English politics – would praise him for the 'selfless' way in which, 'having had every temptation to a life of ease and no material advantages to gain' he had nevertheless 'devoted himself to the toil and stress of public service' out of what it called, 'his sheer sense of duty'.

This would certainly have struck the Duke as a two-edged compliment, for far from being a wealthy, titled amateur indulging in politics as he might have taken up good works among the poor, he was, for all his occasional eccentricities, a dedicated politician through and through. The whole tradition of the Cavendishes remained passionately political, the habit of many generations had driven him instinctively towards the House of Commons in his twenties, and between the wars there was still considerable mileage for an aspiring young politician in being a duke's eldest son.

Certainly, at constituency level local loyalty towards the Cavendishes, which had so regularly returned his father to Westminster as a Liberal Unionist in the 1890s, did the same for Lord Hartington in the 1920s and 1930s, and he had proved as dedicated a politician as his father. The Cavendish type had changed again to suit the times. In contrast to his father's down-to-earth stolidity, he was a subtle, somewhat diffident man of considerable charm and perfect manners. He was amusing and urbane, he was popular with other members of the House, and he was politically ambitious.

Following his father's interest in the Empire, he had been appointed Under-Secretary of State for Dominion Affairs by Stanley Baldwin in his 'National Government' in 1936. As such he had travelled widely through the Dominions, proved himself an effective junior minister, and had kept his place in Neville Chamberlain's government after succeeding to the dukedom. Early in 1939, with the Chatsworth renovations barely started, he and the Duchess left for an extended official tour of South Africa which enhanced his political reputation. The dukedom now seemed set, not merely for a change, but for a positive revival under its new incumbent.

For the new Duchess too was very different from her formidable, tight-fisted predecessor. The least forbidding of aristocrats, she had inherited her share of the Cecil love of talk and openness to fresh ideas, and in time it seemed she would inevitably help to bring, not just the dukedom, but Chatsworth and the Cavendish possessions into the twentieth century at last.

Thanks to the deft arrangement of the Chatsworth Estates Company in 1926, the new Duke and Duchess had the resources this required, for the inheritance had been scarcely singed by the death duties of £379,000 on the Ninth Duke's demise. These were met fairly painlessly, and there had been no need for sales of land or property or works of art: the current decline in rents and agriculture, which had hit so many landed families during the 1930s, had been more than cushioned by the Cavendish investment income, now well in excess of £100,000 a year; and the Duke himself had a keen financial brain and a passion for the Stock Exchange. Few noblemen seemed better placed, or suited, to protect the fortunes of their families than Edward Cavendish, Tenth Duke of Devonshire.

During his absence in South Africa, work began at Chatsworth on two of the Duke's personal pet projects to improve the amenities of the house – a large passenger lift in the north-west corner and plans for a patent small electric railway to propel at speed the steaming dishes from the ground-floor kitchens to the first-floor dining-room a furlong away. And that summer, after the Duke and Duchess's return, Chatsworth and its gardens were suddenly *en fête* to celebrate the majority of their son and heir, William, the new Lord Hartington. A quarter of a century before, the last Devonshire House Derby dinner marked the ending of an era on the eve of war. Now, in the sunlight of that perfect August, the family was once more tempting fate with a show of splendour in those last few days of peace. This was the first twenty-first birthday celebrated at Chatsworth by the family since the Bachelor Duke's majority in 1811, and there were separate parties for the tenantry and servants, as well as for local dignitaries and family and friends from London. With over 3,000 guests to greet, by the second day the Duchess's arm was already in a sling. The fountains played, there were fireworks in the evening and for a moment it might suddenly have seemed as if the gloom of the last Duke's final years had gone for good.

A few weeks later, Germany invaded Poland, and on 4 September, the day after war broke out, Harold Nicolson recorded in his diary:

> I dine at the Beefsteak. Devonshire is there and is as sane and as amusing as ever. I must say, I do admire a man like that, who must realize that all his grandeur is gone for ever, not showing the slightest sign of gloom or apprehension.

As Nicolson should have known, 'grandeur' was the last thing the Duke would miss, and according to his daughter, Anne, the family reaction was, 'Hooray! Now we can all stop bothering about Chatsworth, and simply stay at Church-dale.' And at Chatsworth, work on the Duke's new lift and patent electric railway ceased, treasures were crated, pictures taken from the walls, and the Duke, shrewdly realizing that even schoolgirls were less destructive tenants for a stately home than troops, leased the house to a girls' boarding-school for 'The Duration'.

The ancestral splendours of the Cavendishes were forgotten in a world of hockey-sticks and gym-slips. Lord Andrew Cavendish followed his brother Hartington into the Coldstream Guards. Most of the old Chatsworth servants were dispersed – into the Forces too, or to 'Work of National Importance' – and as the war continued it must have seemed increasingly unlikely that the great old house could ever be restored to even a shadow of its former glory.

Only at Lismore Castle, in what was now the neutral state of Southern Ireland, could something like the old life of the Cavendishes flourish after a fashion. The castle was now the property of the Ninth Duke's second son, Lord Charles Cavendish, having been passed on to him some years before his father's death. Lord Charles, who as a second son was one of the casualties of primogeniture, had long been something of a problem to his family. As a Cambridge undergraduate he had fallen on his head while riding in a point-to-point, but refused to go to bed. Shortly afterwards he fell off again in another point-to-point and although he did recover he was never known to refuse a drink for the remainder of his life. He was amusing and immensely popular, but employment was a problem. Being interested in finance, he was sent to work with Pierpont Morgan in New York, during the hard-drinking days of Prohibition, and his fate was sealed.

Morgan, who christened him 'Lord Useless', became so exasperated with him that he fired him; and shortly afterwards, the two men found themselves on the same transatlantic liner, as Lord Charles sailed back to England. Lord Charles, a cheery soul, got his revenge on his bad-tempered ex-employer by inciting fellow-passengers to make ghostly noises outside the financier's cabin every night. Thereafter, Pierpont Morgan always crossed the Atlantic in his private yacht, and Lord Charles made his home at Lismore.

An authentic P. G. Wodehouse aristocrat, he even continued the old tradition of the Edwardian nobility of finding their wives in the theatre by marrying Fred Astaire's sister, Adele Astaire, the star of musical comedies such as *Lady Be Good* and *Funny Face*. He met her at the races and used to claim that he never actually remembered proposing to her. 'Just think of it happening to *me*. A thing like that after a night like that!' he used to say.

But, despite the strain put on the marriage by the demon drink, Adele proved a loyal wife, a popular hostess at Lismore and a dignified Lady Charles Cavendish. There were no surviving children, but she loved the castle, where she installed a swimming-pool, lived in considerable style and kept herself young with Gayelord Hauser exercises. After her husband's death, in 1944, she was to marry a New York stockbroker and, as Mrs Kingman Douglass finally settled in California; but, thanks to her nephew's generosity, she continued to spend part of every summer at Lismore Castle almost until her death in 1980, just as she had when she was Lady Charles Cavendish.

As for the Duke, he retained his position in the government after Churchill succeeded Neville Chamberlain in 1940, and, when the Carlton Gardens house was gutted by German incendiary bombs, stayed on in London in a suite in the Mayfair Hotel. Whenever possible, he and the Duchess would get back to Churchdale, where his children sometimes saw him gardening at night by torchlight. (His sister, Lady Dorothy Macmillan, another manic gardener, used a lighted miner's helmet for the same purpose.)

Totally uninterested in pomp and ceremony, he refused Churchill's offer of the Viceroyalty of India. Preferring to remain in active politics in London, he moved on to become Under-Secretary of State for India and Burma in 1942. One of the few practical advantages he gained from his dukedom now was that, as President of the Zoological Society, he got in free to the London Zoo on

Sunday mornings. Sometimes as a great treat he would take his daughters when they were in London, and they always made a beeline for his favourite animal – the wart-hog.

The one member of the family who was making an outstanding political reputation in the war was his brother-in-law, Harold Macmillan, who, as the British Government's Minister Resident for the Mediterranean, based first in Algiers, then in Italy, was Churchill's direct political representative in the wake of the Allied victories in North Africa, Greece and Southern Italy. The Duke's two sons played an active part throughout this fighting, with Lieutenant Lord Andrew Cavendish winning the M.C. for gallantry when leading his platoon in battle south of Florence. In April 1941, aged twenty-one, he had married Deborah Freeman-Mitford, daughter of the Second Baron Redesdale, the original of that amiable monster, 'Uncle Matt', in his daughter Nancy Mitford's best-known novel, *The Pursuit of Love*, thus linking the Cavendishes with one of the most original and genuinely eccentric families in England.*

Deborah – 'Debo' as everybody called her – was also twenty-one, extraordinarily pretty with her forget-me-not blue Mitford eyes, and as the baby of the family curiously uncontroversial – like her only brother, Tom Mitford, who was to die of wounds received fighting in Burma in 1945. She still had a schoolgirl passion for hens and horses, was resolutely anti-intellectual, and according to a famous passage in *The Pursuit of Love*, had made it clear while in the nursery that whereas most girls dream of marrying that 'Mr Right', she had her sights set firmly on 'The Duke of Right'. In fact this was one of Nancy's jokes: Debo somewhat wearily denies ever saying any such thing.

As the Tenth Duke's second son, Andrew Cavendish's chances of the dukedom were extremely slim, and the idea of one day succeeding his father would have shocked him deeply. At twenty-two, with more than his fair share of the Cavendish reserve, he had only just overcome a childhood stammer and planned to become a publisher when the war was over. Throughout his life he had been largely overshadowed by his more extrovert and glamorous elder brother, William, who had automatically received the adulation and attention of the favoured heir on whom the family's hopes for the future rested. Andrew was usually ignored – and was rather grateful for the fact. Somewhat surprisingly the two brothers were fond of one another.

William's own marriage had been long delayed by unusual circumstances. Just before the war he had fallen in love with Kathleen Kennedy, the daughter of the celebrated anti-British American Ambassador to London, Joseph Kennedy. She was exuberant, fascinating and rich, and the Cavendishes – the young ones in particular – soon fell for her as well. But she was a Catholic, and

---

*Nancy: born 1904, author of *The Pursuit of Love, Love in a Cold Climate, The Sun King*, etc., married the Hon. Peter Rodd, died 1973. Pamela: born 1907, married Wing-Commander Derek Jackson, O.B.E., D.F.C., A.F.C., D.SC., F.R.S. Thomas David: born 1909, barrister, Major Queen's Westminster Regiment, died of wounds in Burma, March 1945. Diana: born 1910, married the Hon. Bryan Guinness (now Second Baron Moyne), divorced 1934, married Sir Oswald Mosley 1936. Unity Valkyrie: born 1914, died 1948. Jessica Lucy: born 1917, author of *The American Way of Death, Hons and Rebels*, etc., married 1937 Esmond Romilly (killed in action 1940), married Robert Treuhaft 1943. Deborah: born 1920, married Lord Andrew Cavendish 1941.

for the Cavendishes the idea of Catholic offspring one day succeeding to a dukedom which was founded on the Protestant succession, was profoundly worrying.

For Ambassador Kennedy, the prospect of his daughter marrying both a Protestant and an Englishman was even worse. (The fact that he was also in direct line for a dukedom was neither here nor there.) Because of such obstacles, marriage had seemed impossible, but the romance continued. Kathleen had remained in England, working for the American Red Cross and, early in 1944, she was in London when Lord Hartington was recalled to Derbyshire to perform his mandatory political role.

In 1938, when his father succeeded to the dukedom, the local constituency, West Derbyshire, had obediently returned yet another member of the family – Colonel Henry Hunloke, who had married the Ninth Duke's daughter, Anne. The Colonel was now anxious to retire from politics, causing a by-election and, since the family had held the seat almost uninterruptedly since 1885, Lord Hartington was dutifully offered the Conservative nomination like his father and grandfather before him. As a serving officer, he was barred from fighting an election, but the War Office – with what some saw as excessive haste – transferred him to the Reserve, granted him leave for the period of the election, and the battle for West Derbyshire began.

It was to prove unexpectedly bitter. William was personally popular in the constituency, and possessed the cachet, which his Independent Socialist opponent lacked, of being a young serving soldier during time of war. But for the Cavendishes – as well as for the wartime government – it was ominous that none of this appeared to count as it undoubtedly would have done in years gone by. William stood foursquare as a 'patriotic' candidate, claiming his election as a vote of confidence in Winston Churchill's government and the war against the common enemy. On the other hand his socialist opponent, a local alderman called Charlie White, skilfully turned the issue into an attack on what he saw as the 'feudal' influence of families like the Cavendishes and upper-class 'dictatorship' in politics. The by-election became rapidly transformed into a test of the government's popularity and the old social order against the new; and Churchill himself possibly made things worse with a public broadside in his grandest manner:

10, Downing Street.

My Dear Hartington,

I see that they are attacking you because your family has been identified for about 300 years with the Parliamentary representation of West Derbyshire. It ought, on the contrary, to be a matter of pride to the constituency to have such long traditions of constancy and fidelity through so many changing scenes and circumstances. Moreover, it is a historical fact that your family and the people of West Derby have acted together on every great occasion in this long period of history on the side of the people's rights and progress.

But history was changing. Old ties of deference and loyalty to the Cavendishes were loosening – just how dramatically was shown when the vote was counted and Alderman Charlie White defeated William Marquess of Hartington by a majority of 4,561.

It was a bitter moment, and for the Cavendishes a sombre warning of what they might expect when the war was over. The gallant Marquess made the best of things. 'It has been a fierce fight. Now I am going out to fight for you at the front,' he told his loyal supporters from the Matlock Town Hall balcony after the declaration of the poll. And a few days later he was with his unit training for the D-Day landings.

But before he went to France he had one final piece of business to attend to. Despite the opposition of her father, Kathleen Kennedy was now prepared to change her religion as the price of marrying the man she loved, and in May the two were married in a civil ceremony at Chelsea Register Office. The Kennedy parents were not present at this pagan and bureaucratic rite, but the marriage register was signed by the Duke and by Kathleen's brother, Lieutenant Joseph Kennedy. Soon afterwards the bridegroom left to fight in France.

In retrospect, an air of impending tragedy surrounds the whole event. A few weeks later young Joseph Kennedy, the favourite of the Gods and of the Kennedys, was killed in action. Then, in September, William himself was killed by a German sniper just across the Belgian frontier from France. Like many Guards officers, he had been wearing pale corduroy trousers with his battledress, marking him out as a target from his men. Andrew Cavendish found himself heir to the family possessions and his father's dukedom.

Everyone, not least Andrew, was profoundly shocked by the unexpected, almost accidental nature of William's death. Kathleen was in America when it happened, trying to console her parents after Joseph's death and there was just a chance that she was pregnant. Had she been and had the child been born a boy, the Kennedys would have added the dukedom of Devonshire as well as the United States Presidency to its accumulated honours. When it was clear that she was not, the Cavendishes were able to make plans to face the future. No one was very optimistic about what would happen when the war was over.

William's death had been a bitter blow. 'For my parents', says Elizabeth Cavendish, 'a light went out when Billy died', and for the Duke in particular the loss of the beloved heir was certainly the greatest disappointment of his life. He bore it stoically, but it might be said he never properly recovered. For Andrew too there seemed little matter for rejoicing in the fact that he was now directly in succession for the dukedom. 'It was honestly the last thing I wanted, and I rather dreaded what would happen.' For he knew quite well that his hopes of a private independent life were over; like it or not, he would finally be saddled with the postwar problems of the dukedom instead of being able to enjoy the leisurely existence of a gentlemanly publisher. By now he had a family – a daughter, Emma, born in 1943; and his infant son, Peregrine, born a fortnight before his brother's marriage, now became the heir with the title of Lord Burlington.

In 1945, with the ending of the war, and the landslide election of a Labour Government, it seemed as if the days of dukes might well be numbered anyhow. Certainly the world of deferential, underpaid domestic labour which had enabled pre-war Chatsworth to survive so long had gone for good, and when the last schoolgirl had departed, and an attempt was made to put the treasures and the pictures back in place, the Duke himself had no intention of returning. He and the Duchess were comfortable at Churchdale, and could not contemplate the major renovations and repairs required to make Chatsworth even habitable. Compton Place, at Eastbourne, was a happier, more manageable house, and they went there for their holidays. Chatsworth reopened to the public but it rarely saw its Duke.

His Grace's main concern by now was to protect as much as possible of the Cavendish inheritance for his successors in what he felt was bound to be a hostile world, and it was to this that he applied all his financial ingenuity. With the death of his brother, Charles, in April 1944, Lismore had passed to his own second son, Lord Andrew, and early in 1946 the Duke had totally reorganized the Chatsworth Estates Company which had remained unchanged since 1926. Under new government legislation shares in a private company controlled by an individual would no longer receive the 45 per cent relief from death duties previously accorded to agricultural land. To make his heir eligible for this valuable benefit, the Duke in March 1946 transferred the £2,225,000-worth of shares he owned in the Chatsworth Estates Company to a new discretionary trust, the Chatsworth Settlement, of which his wife, the Duchess, and the Duke of Buccleuch were joint trustees.

But because the Duke was relatively young, and there were financial advantages in keeping the shares temporarily in the Estates Company, the transfer was kept in escrow. It was stipulated that it was to be signed by the trustees if the Duke's life was thought to be 'in special danger' – making it legally binding at his death. After 1946, the Duke was fond of saying that all he actually possessed were the extremely ancient clothes he stood up in.

Now that he was legally if ludicrously a pauper, the wealth of the Devonshires seemed as safe as the expertise of lawyers and accountants could make it, and like his father twenty years before, the Duke's most important role was simply to survive throughout the following crucial three years of financial 'quarantine'. This hardly seemed too much to ask, for the Duke was only fifty-one, and unlike his father during a similar period, he was in perfect health. Even the surprise decision of the Chancellor of the Exchequer, Stafford Cripps, to extend the period of 'quarantine' from three years to five in his 1946 Budget, just a few days after the creation of the Chatsworth Settlement, should not have been a source of real worry.

But the Duke was soon receiving painful intimations of mortality – particularly in the spring of 1948 when his daughter-in-law, Kathleen Lady Hartington, perished in an air-crash in the south of France and all the memories of William's death were cruelly revived. According to Andrew, his attitude towards the dukedom, despite his elaborate tax precautions, was that it would be *après moi le déluge* and as the five years dragged towards their close he was increasingly aware of just how many months he had to live to free the House of Cavendish from the shadow of the tax man. (To make things that much worse, the Government increased the top rate of death duties to a swingeing 80 per cent in 1948.)

The Duke almost made it. In November 1950, and with only fourteen weeks to go, he and the Duchess went to Compton Place for a few days' holiday. As usual he was soon immersed in gardening and decided to take down a smallish oak behind the house. As with Gladstone, felling trees was an activity the Duke particularly enjoyed, but the effort overstrained his heart; two hours later he was dead of a massive heart attack and, with his tree, the Duke finally brought down the fortunes of the Devonshires as well. The defences so elaborately raised by the Duke and his lawyers to protect the centuries' old Cavendish inheritance against the tax-man had collapsed by fourteen weeks. 'Eddie dead at 55!' wrote a shocked Chips Channon when he heard the news. 'Is it the end of Chatsworth and of Hardwick? What dread score has Destiny to pay off against the Devonshires?'

The new Duke must have asked himself much the same questions when he heard the news. His father's death was so completely unexpected that he was on a business visit to Australia when it happened, and as he took the first flight home he was distinctly stunned by the prospect of what lay in store.

At first he could only guess at how much the family would lose, but one thing was all too clear – the House of Cavendish had just sustained by far the greatest single blow during the four centuries of its existence. Everything the family possessed – investments, houses, land and the library and art collection – stood to be mulcted by four-fifths. A total break-up of the Devonshire possessions seemed inevitable, with the traditional role and character of the dukedom disappearing in the process. Interviewed soon afterwards, the new Duchess wearily admitted that 'everything did seem the most appalling mess'.

The full extent of the mess became clear only when the valuers and Inland Revenue officials had done their sums and the Devonshire indebtedness was revealed in its bleak simplicity. The total agreed value of the assets of the Chatsworth Estates Company belonging to the trustees at the Tenth Duke's death stood at £5.9 million. The duty owing to the Treasury was £4.72 million, and since this amount was payable at once, interest on the debt was ticking up at eight per cent – £1000 a day – from the hour the Tenth Duke died. No other duke in the history of the family had had to face quite such a crisis as the one that greeted the Eleventh Duke from the moment of his accession.

He seemed to have one obvious way out of all his difficulties – simply cut his losses, sell up everything as soon as possible, pay what was owing to the Treasury, and begin his dukedom unencumbered with the albatross of Cavendish possessions round his neck. He would still be very rich. Lismore Castle was not subject to British death duties and, freed from the worry and expense of attempting to maintain houses like Chatsworth and Hardwick, he and the Duchess could enjoy a most enviable existence. Few of those who had known Andrew in the past can have doubted this was precisely what he would do; and up at Chatsworth, Francis Thompson, the Librarian, began making contingency plans to preserve the house by turning it into a centre of the arts attached to Manchester University.

Since leaving the army, Andrew Cavendish had been an urban, unrepent-antly pleasure-loving man who still jokingly remarks that of all his predecessors, he used to feel he had most in common with Georgiana's husband, the Fifth Duke. As a young man he loved gambling and racehorses almost as much as he was bored by those staple pastimes of the recent dukes, farming and shooting. (When asked why, as the owner of some of the finest shooting in the country, he never fired a shot himself, his reply was simple – 'The truth is I'm just not very good at it.') His memories of Chatsworth were deeply unnostalgic, and it was hard to see what satisfaction such a character would find in an expensive, complicated battle to retain it.

But, as so often in the past, the act of succeeding to the dukedom brought out unexpected qualities in the Duke, and, instead of following the predictable and profitable line of least resistance, he began to be obsessively concerned with preserving what could still be salvaged from the fiscal wreckage.

He was soon left in little doubt of the difficulties this involved. The tax-man was already clamouring for payment of the £4.72 million in cash, and, unlike the days when the English had regarded their aristocracy as part of the natural scheme of things, there was little public sympathy by now for a wealthy dukedom whose tax avoidance scheme had unexpectedly misfired.

The Cavendish possessions too were an extraordinary jumble of fortuitously inherited estates, which no one since Paxton had seriously attempted to assess. Some, like the Eastbourne ground-rents and the Derbyshire mineral rights were highly profitable. But although the Cavendishes owned *in toto* something over 120,000 acres at the Tenth Duke's death (a combined area slightly larger than the Isle of Wight), the actual income this great area produced was surprisingly small. Much was moorland, used primarily for shooting, and the greater part of the agricultural land was let to tenant farmers with an average annual rent of less than one per cent of the estimated total value of the land. Chatsworth and Hardwick Hall, despite their paying visitors, and the treasures they contained, were run at a substantial loss.

The Duke's first task was clearly to devise a strategy of what possessions could be painlessly dispensed with and which were essential to retain if the dukedom was to have a viable future. His Chatsworth agent, Hugo Read, started a business-like assessment of the various estates in preparation for what the press was already calling 'the sale of the century'. At Chatsworth too the Duke began the painful process of trying to decide how he could possibly retain a meaningful part of the historic Devonshire collections for the future, while surrendering four-fifths of their value to the government.

The Duke's battle with the tax-man was to last fifteen years, before all the legal disputes had been decided and the last debts paid – and throughout it all he showed the stubbornness and skill of the early Cavendishes as he struggled to retain what he believed vital to the family inheritance.

Having swiftly sold off properties in Buxton to pay the first instalment on the debt, the best hope for some mitigation of the total sum lay in obtaining the 45 per cent 'relief' on death duty payable on agricultural land, which his father had prepared for in the transfer he had made in 1946. But the suddenness of the Tenth Duke's death had upset even these arrangements. Since he had died before anyone had time to realize his life was actually in danger, neither of the trustees of the Chatsworth Settlement had been able to sign the all-important deed of transfer – which was still in escrow with the lawyers. It was actually signed four days after the Duke was buried, and the tax-man questioned its validity.

With so much at stake, this was challenged by the trustees – in an expensive High Court action which dragged on for two years before being lost. Another complicated legal action followed – over the actual valuation of the Devonshire estates. This too was lost. The full amount of £4.72 million owing was confirmed, and Andrew and his advisers now had to decide what had to go.

A large agricultural estate in Scotland went, together with extensive property in England, which included lands on the Derbyshire High Peak first acquired by Bess of Hardwick. But although the rising cost of land brought prices considerably above the valuations made at the moment of the Tenth Duke's death, this was to some extent offset by Andrew's insistence that some of the smaller tenants were to be allowed to buy their properties at under the current market value.

These sales were still insufficient to meet the debt in full, and Andrew had to make the decision on the next and biggest portion of the Cavendish inheritance to sacrifice. This was in June 1954. It was a decision only he could take, and he remembers making up his mind while sitting in a train at Bedford Station on the way to London.

'It was then and there I realised that Hardwick Hall would have to go. I made my mind up while the train was waiting at the platform, and although it was horrible to think of getting rid of Bess of Hardwick's house, it proved the best decision of my life.'

For by sacrificing Hardwick, there was still a chance of holding on to Chatsworth, and from now on this became his chief concern. This involved him in continuing negotiations with the Inland Revenue over the next three years, and in August 1957 a settlement was finally announced. In the largest single deal ever struck between a private family and the Treasury over death duties, Cavendish possessions valued at something over £1,200,000 were accepted by the government as the next instalment on the money that was owing.

Hardwick Hall, together with its park and art collection passed to the nation – and the government, having agreed to pay for extensive renovations that were needed, transferred the property directly to the National Trust. At the same time the Treasury accepted eight of the greatest works of art in the Chatsworth collection, which according to the valuers formed the requisite four-fifths of the value of the whole collection. These included the priceless fifth-century Greek bronze head of Apollo, the exquisite Memling triptych, the tenth-century Winchester Benedictional of St Aethelwold, Rembrandt's *Philosopher*, and the Second Duke's proudest acquisition, Claude Lorrain's *Liber Veritatis*.

This was by no means the end of the great Devonshire death duty drama, which dragged on for ten more weary years, enriching lawyers and accountants in the process, and providing Andrew with a never-ending source of *Angst*. Not until 1967 were the accounts complete: the Devonshires had paid off the £4.72 million in full, Hardwick had gone, Compton Place in Eastbourne had become a girls' school, and the family's total acreage had shrunk from the 120,000 acres they had owned in 1950 to the 72,000 which they own today.

But according to Hugo Read, these sacrifices produced unexpected benefits:

It made us look far more closely at what we owned, and although a lot of valuable land was lost, the sales also enabled us to shed a number of marginally profitable estates. Before the Tenth Duke's death, the family's attitude to its land was that they owned it largely for reasons of tradition. This changed. For ease of management, the four separate agents who had run the Derbyshire estates, were reduced to a centralized central unit after 1955. This was based at Chatsworth, and we ran it as a modern, profit-conscious operation as it had to be. There is no question but that, thanks to this slimming down process, we became far more efficient than we had ever been before.

This was only the beginning of the revolution Andrew himself began at Chatsworth where some decision needed to be made about the future. Now that the Chatsworth death duties had been paid and the sacrificial treasures had been crated and despatched to appropriate national museums, the great uninhabited house was still much as it had been when Duke Victor died in 1938. Professor Mario Praz, the anglophile Italian connoisseur and historian of the Romantic Movement, made a pilgrimage to the house about this time to see the Canova statuary, and describes himself 'struck by a feeling of extreme melancholy for things vanished and remote', as, desperate to find a lavatory, the poor man scurried through 'the enormous rooms and corridors and galleries', shivering with cold and unable to find physical relief or the famous bust of Petrarch's *Laura* he had come specially to see.

This was no way to run a stately home which was going to depend increasingly on the admission fees of visitors for its support, and once again it was the astute Mr Read who hit on a solution that was to transform the whole character of Chatsworth. When he had worked as agent at Hardwick he had been impressed by the interest 'Grannie Duchess' had inspired among the visitors. Passionately interested in the house herself, the old termagant had proved an excellent curator, and it was a considerable tourist attraction that the house was lived in by an authentic duchess. Surely, said Mr Read, what had worked so well at Hardwick, could be more successful still at Chatsworth.

The Duke, for once displaying a touch of the Cavendish caution, had his doubts. He and his family by now were living in Edensor House, an elegant but modest eighteenth-century house near the gates of Chatsworth, where a third child, Sophia, was born in 1957. In London they had bought a small house in Chesterfield Street which, although in Mayfair, was a far cry from the great old Devonshire House with its gardens and tennis-courts opposite the Ritz. Still occupied with finding the remaining million or so owing to the Treasury, Andrew was not inclined to take on the additional expense and endless trouble which he knew would be involved in setting up home again in Chatsworth. The Duchess disagreed.

She still loved her hens and horses and, unlike her husband, actually enjoyed taking on the sort of problems that a house like Chatsworth represented. She was also totally convinced by silver-tongued Mr Read, and as Andrew says, 'because I was more in awe of my wife than my accountant', he finally agreed as well. The Great Return had started.

No one – not even Debo, who as a Mitford did not really understand the meaning of the Cavendish motto, 'Safe with Caution' – had realized what lay ahead in the battle to bring Chatsworth back to life. The fabric of the house with its ancient stonework, its 175 separate rooms and its 1.3 acres of roofing, had suffered from what she describes as the ravages of 'woodworm, death-watch beetle, fire, water, snow, frost, wind and sun', in the twenty years since Duke Victor died. It had twenty-one kitchens, but all of them were obsolete. So was the central-heating. As Professor Praz discovered, the sanitary arrangements left much to be desired. There was still a dearth of bathrooms, the Tenth Duke's patent railway to the dining-room was not considered feasible, and all too many of the private rooms had suffered from the scourge of Grannie Duchess's distemper.

But as the work of rehabilitation started, Debo found that she possessed two great advantages. The first lay in the knowledge and enthusiasm of a nucleus of the remaining Chatsworth work-force, in particular that of the clever old Comptroller, Willie Shimwell, and his deputy Dennis Fisher, who in the war had reached the rank of major in the Royal Marines. Under their direction, much of the building work, carpentry and decorating could be undertaken by existing Chatsworth staff who took a close and intelligent personal interest in the work. The other bonus she discovered was that Chatsworth was an enormous squirrels' nest where, for years, little had been thrown away. Hidden in stable-blocks and distant attics was an antique-dealer's dream – whole rooms stacked high with long-discarded sofas, marble tables, chests-of-drawers, elaborately canopied eighteenth-century beds, magnificent arm-chairs in need of covering, and every imaginable object needed to refurnish the private section of the house in style.

The real problem was to rationalize the house rather as Andrew and Hugo Read had begun to rationalize the Devonshire estates, and this was to be Debo's particular achievement. Pre-war Chatsworth could function only with its regiment of servants, many of whom had disappeared never to return. But the sort of self-perpetuating despotism of domestic labour which had reigned so long at Chatsworth, had been highly inefficient. Its unlamented passing in the social earthquake of the Second World War had nevertheless posed owners of enormous houses with difficulties of commensurate proportions if they wished to live in them.

Debo's solution was intensely practical. She was lucky to be able to call on sufficient resources to modernize the private section of the house completely, and up-to-date heating, bathrooms, plumbing, private telephones would make Chatsworth something it had never been before – extremely comfort-able. It also began to be efficient, operating on a fraction of the work-force needed in the past. A single brand-new modern kitchen was created below the dining-room and, instead of using an electric railway, food was put in a simple service lift, and brought in to the dining-room through a hidden doorway sliced through the knee-caps of Lely's full-length portrait of the long-suffering Cromwellian General Monck.

By 1959 the work was far enough advanced to allow the Devonshires to move into Chatsworth as a family, and from now on the enrichment and improvement of the house and its estates and gardens became Andrew and Debo's joint life-work. The house became more continuously occupied than ever in its history, and the complementary interests of its Duke and Duchess served to make the whole enterprise an extraordinary success after so many years of tragedy and setback. Debo could finally indulge her unsated interest in animals by taking on the tenancy of the now enlarged Chatsworth home farm (which Andrew made a point of never visiting) and becoming an internationally renowned breeder of Shetland and Haflinger ponies, as well as of several inevitable exotic breeds of chickens. Andrew was a compulsive purchaser of books, both for his private pleasure and for the Chatsworth library which he has steadily enhanced with rare eighteenth- and nineteenth-century illustrated volumes.

Debo's business instincts soon led her to reorganize the whole system for the Chatsworth visitors – whose numbers steadily increased – establishing a Chatsworth shop, and later on a farm shop where she could profitably market a whole range of products from her farm. Andrew on the other hand revived an interest that had lain dormant among the Cavendishes since the death of the Bachelor Duke almost a century before. Starting on a fairly modest scale he began collecting pictures, and, apart from commissioning an important series of portraits of himself and his family by Lucien Freud, his purchases have included works by English painters as diverse as Samuel Palmer, Gertler, Carrington and Augustus John. He persuaded the aged Epstein to execute a portrait bust of the two-year-old Sophia Cavendish, and was an enthusiastic patron of the young and then virtually unknown sculptress, Angela Conner, whose bronzes of Harold Macmillan – and of a host of Devonshire cronies – have brought a new interest to the house, and helped establish her considerable reputation.

One of the enthusiasms Andrew and Debo share is for gardening. Andrew, although not in the same league of botanical expertise as his father, is a dedicated amateur, and during his dukedom Chatsworth's gardens have begun to flourish on a scale unknown since the golden days of Paxton. Nothing could bring back the exploded splendours of his Great Conservatory, but the Bachelor Duke would certainly enjoy the smaller but technologically improved new greenhouse which was built in 1970 (to designs by George Pearce), with its three separate climates. In the tropical part, the *Victoria regia* water-lily blooms again in Derbyshire, and the Bachelor Duke's banana fruits dutifully for his successor.

Throughout the work of restoration and enrichment which has gone on at Chatsworth, Andrew has firmly set himself against the sort of gimmicks and crowd-inducing novelties which have brought the tourists by the coachload to other famous houses. At Chatsworth they have not been necessary. The house has steadily responded to his stewardship, and, as Hugo Read predicted, the visitors appreciate its value as a living, lived-in house, with so much of its treasure and its history still miraculously intact.

To achieve this it was necessary to change the social structure of the house, and here again Andrew's influence has been of great importance. Clearly there was not the faintest chance of reviving the regimented pre-war life of below-stairs Chatsworth, even had he wished to. But the resurrected Chatsworth, for all its labour-saving gadgets and machinery, still had its workshops, offices, estate departments, gardens, farms and woodlands as well as the actual house to staff. Altogether the whole complex needed over two hundred people to function as it should, and whatever sentimental kudos there may once have been in 'working for a ducal family', this was no longer a particular attraction in itself.

Andrew appreciated this and, in marked contrast with his predecessors, set out from the start to be a model employer, and as well as paying the competitive wages that he had to, he took the initiative to create a genuine community on the estate for all the Chatsworth staff – a modernized clubhouse with its bar and billiard-room, a superb village hall, an indoor swimming-pool, a golf-course and an extension to the village school. He and Debo paid particular attention to modernizing the estate housing they provide, and have gradually established their own private welfare state in miniature, through which at present more than eighty-six retired Chatsworth staff – and Chatsworth widows – are guaranteed their pensions and their house or flat on the estate for life.

The result has been a not unnatural sense of loyalty and involvement with 'The House' which has formed the basis of the revival which has been going on at Chatsworth. Throughout their history the Cavendishes have always managed to survive through a combination of the serpent and the stag – the wealth and splendour always flexibly adapting when it had to with the times. This happened in the English Civil War, in the 'Glorious Revolution', in the early eighteenth century, and again with the financial changes under Harty-Tarty. But Andrew, the Eleventh Duke, is among the most intriguing of these Cavendish survivors and adaptors. For, under this deceptively hesitant and modest man, the family decline was halted and a new sort of modern dukedom constructed on the wreckage left behind him by his father.

The return to Chatsworth coincided with a burst of Devonshire vitality which might have been an echo from the past. Chatsworth was once again the centre of an elaborate social life, with writers like Evelyn Waugh, John Betjeman and Patrick Leigh-Fermor invited along with politicians and livelier members of the aristocracy. The traditional peripatetic life continued with the seasons, as the family and servants travelled in style to Bolton Abbey for the August shooting, and to Lismore for the salmon fishing in the spring. Andrew was described by Anthony Sampson in his *Anatomy of Britain* as 'quite witty' and 'irreverent', and 'about as near as one can get to the debonair young dukes of novelists'.

His luck had turned, even on the turf. The keenest racing Duke since Harty Tarty, his earlier efforts as an owner had been undistinguished, but in 1965 he bought a mare, Park Top, for a mere 500 guineas. Between 1967 and 1970

Park Top was to earn £136,922 in prize money,* and proved herself one of the greatest horses of her time, 'the best of her sex I've ever ridden' in the judgment of her jockey, Lester Piggott.

But as so often in the past it was politics which still provided the prevailing interest of the family, and it is of some significance that the year the Devonshires moved back to Chatsworth coincided with the appointment of 'Uncle' Harold Macmillan as Conservative Prime Minister in the aftermath of Suez. Like all his family, Andrew is a strongly political animal. As Lord Hartington, he had unsuccessfully contested what was by then the local Labour stronghold of Chesterfield in 1945 and 1950, and although regarding himself as 'far more Whig than Tory', had sat as a Conservative in the House of Lords.

Ever since marrying Lady Dorothy, there had always been a strong dose of Chatsworth in Harold Macmillan's make-up too. Along with his concern for the sufferings of the unemployed in his pre-war constituency at Stockton, went a romantic hankering for great Whig houses with their grouse moors and libraries and black-and-white marble floors. One of his private political heroes was Harty-Tarty – particularly as portrayed by Trollope in the Duke of Omnium. And when Harold Macmillan gained the premiership which had eluded Harty-Tarty on those celebrated three occasions, it must have given him particular satisfaction to appoint his nephew, the Duke of Devonshire, as his Minister of State for Commonwealth Relations – a similar post to that held by the Ninth and Tenth Dukes of Devonshire before him.

This brought forth inevitable accusations of nepotism (literally the undue favouring of nephews) from the Loyal Opposition. Political journalists began referring to the so-called 'Cavendish Connection' as they counted the aristocrats related to the Prime Minister by marriage who joined the Duke in office. These included Lord Lansdowne at the Foreign Office, David Ormsby-Gore (now Lord Harlech), Ambassador to Washington, and Julian Amery, Secretary of State for Air. The outcry was a touch exaggerated, and much of the indignation came from middle-class Conservative M.P.s jealously concerned at what they felt to be a recrudescence of the old Whig 'government by connection'. 'There has been nothing like it in England since the days of the eighteenth-century Duke of Newcastle', wrote one of them.

Such hyperbole was silly, but the incident did serve to show that the power of the Devonshires in politics was not completely spent. As a minister, the Duke was particularly successful in his dealings with Commonwealth politicians in their transition to independence. (Kenyatta, for instance, was delighted to be lunched with *both* his wives by the grandson of the Duke he knew as the author of the now famous Devonshire Declaration.) And during Macmillan's premiership the most important Cavendish Connection was one that the critics missed – the close family ties between 'Uncle Harold' Macmillan, and the brother of the former Kathleen Lady Hartington, John F. Kennedy.

---

*Trained by Bernard Van Cutsem, Park Top won the Ribblesdale Stakes, the Coronation Cup, the King George VI and Queen Elizabeth Stakes and the Hardwicke Stakes. The Duke has told her story in his book, *Park Top, a Romance of the Turf.*

The 1960s were an optimistic period for both Chatsworth and the House of Cavendish. Andrew's ministerial career ended in 1963 and, whatever the truth about the 'Cavendish Connection', that vanished too with the Labour victory of 1964.* But during the rest of the decade, Chatsworth was flourishing as never in its history, for it was both the centre of the family and increasingly a national institution, attracting nearly half a million visitors a year and firmly established as one of the great tourist sights of Britain. In 1967 Andrew's son, Peregrine Lord Hartington, married Amanda Heywood-Lonsdale; with the birth of a son, William Lord Burlington, two years later, the succession and the future of the dukedom seemed assured.

But even now, Andrew knew that appearances were deceptive. The house, for all its popularity, was running at a steady loss – which could be met only by selling off a further slice of property each year. And, although he had carried the dukedom safely through the greatest disaster in its history, this was no guarantee that his own son could avoid selling up when he succeeded to the title.

By 1975 this threat became something of a certainty with yet another change in the fiscal law of property, and the replacement of the old estate duties by a new Capital Transfer Tax with a periodic charge to be levied every tenth year at thirty per cent of the full rate payable on the market value of all assets held in discretionary settlements.

The state was closing in. There seemed no way now for the lawyers and accountants to protect Chatsworth and its treasures for the future. At first Andrew accepted the hopelessness of the position, knowing that nothing could stop Chatsworth ultimately following Chiswick and Devonshire House and Hardwick Hall. But he also found a certain sympathy from politicians among all the major parties who agreed that Chatsworth was unique. All too many great houses had been lost, and their possessions scattered, many of them ending up abroad. There was a widespread feeling – both with the general public and in the so-called 'Heritage Lobby' – that somehow Chatsworth had to be retained intact and its character preserved. Andrew could argue too that he and his family had proved themselves efficient custodians and good employers who made no demands upon the state, and that whatever else his uses in the modern world, a duke surviving in his own ancestral home was an undoubted attraction for the tourists and the visitors. The alternative, which Andrew refused to countenance, would have been to make the house over to the National Trust, but the fact was that the Devonshires themselves were among Chatsworth's most important fixtures. Judged by what had happened at Hardwick since it was given to the Trust, a resident duke was worth a minimum of 50,000 visitors a year.

It was facts like these – and the widespread outcry following the sale and break-up of the Rothschild collection at Mentmore – that had offered Andrew a solution. Instead of sitting back and sadly watching mounting expenses and

* Since then Andrew's 'Whiggish' tendencies have been increasingly apparent. He resigned the presidency of his local Conservative association over a luncheon invitation to Enoch Powell; he has become a strong advocate of radically reforming the House of Lords; and in March 1982 he became the first – and so far only – duke to join the Social Democrats.

the Transfer Tax bring the sale of Chatsworth ever nearer, why not set up a private 'National Trust' of his own, which could legally assume ownership of the house and at the same time guarantee that Chatsworth retained its dukes as well as its library and gardens and artistic treasures in perpetuity?

It was an idea that took considerable working out. In law there was no provision or precedent for such a course, and it took Andrew and his lawyer, Tim Burrows (the present head of Currey and Co.), four years of careful lobbying and negotiation before the details of his plan were accepted by the Treasury. In essence it involved the creation of an independent charitable trust 'for the long-term preservation of Chatsworth and its essential contents for the public benefit'. The house and the contents in the public rooms, together with the park and gardens, would be offered to the trust on a ninety-nine-year lease with a rental of £1 a year. In return the Duke and his successors would remain sub-tenants of the existing private part of the house, for which they would pay a full market rent, to be reviewed every five years.

To strengthen his argument, Andrew was insistent that the scheme was not to cost the taxpayer a penny. The Chatsworth House Trust – as the new lessee of Chatsworth would be called – was to be adequately endowed to run the part of the house open to the public as it operates at present, and to provide the nucleus for this endowment fund, the Chatsworth collection made another sacrifice. In April 1981 at Christie's, one of its most valuable remaining paintings – Poussin's *Holy Family* – was auctioned for £1,650,000. This was followed by sales of certain rare books from the library so that finally, with an additional contribution from the family, the Chatsworth House Trust could be endowed with £2½ million. The Trust itself was legally established earlier in the year, making Chatsworth seem secure against its ultimate potential enemy – the tax-man.

In an uncertain world, no one can be sure about the future of the House of Cavendish and its possessions. Dukes have become a rare and possibly endangered species and, although the succession to the Devonshire dukedom seems assured, there is no certainty about the long-term tenure of Lismore and Bolton Abbey. But Chatsworth was built by Bess of Hardwick in an even more uncertain world. For more than four centuries it has survived as the bedrock of the family. The First Duke of Devonshire rebuilt it; the Second Duke filled it with artistic treasures; the Sixth Duke enlarged and adorned it; and the Tenth Duke neglected it. Under the Eleventh Duke and his Duchess, Chatsworth has been retained, renewed, revived, and thanks to them the great dynastic dream of Bess of Hardwick seems set to survive into another century.

Sources

ABBREVIATIONS

Bickley: Francis Bickley, *The Cavendish Family*
DNB: *Dictionary of National Biography*
DP: Devonshire Papers at Chatsworth
HMC: Historical Manuscripts Commission
PRO: Public Record Office

Chapter 2: The Third Wiffe

5 *domynical Letter B*: Derbyshire Archaeological Society Journal, 1907
6 Zouches: *DNB*
7 *the Chronical Distemper*: Margaret Cavendish, Duchess of Newcastle, *The Life of the thrice Noble ... William Cavendish* (1667)
8 *a man called Gernon*: Bickley, 2
9 *for Anne Boleyn*: Henry Morley, introduction to George Cavendish, *The Life of Cardinal Wolsey*, 5
9 *and profitable reverence*: G. M. Young, *Last Essays, 142*
9 *Saynt Sepulcres in Canterbury*: *DP* 1.0
10 *a wise woman*: DP 1.1
10 *the forsaid priory*: ibid
10 *to their house*: DP 1.3
10 *orgy of loot*: Hilaire Belloc, *Characters of the Reformation*, 90
10 *and honest man*: DP 1.2
11 *Letter then G*: Derbyshire Archaeological Society Journal, 1907
11 *a blue livery*: Durant, *Bess of Hardwick*, quoting Bess's account books in the Folger Library
12 purchase of Chatsworth: Bickley, 23
13 *nedefoulle and nesesary*: quoted in Joseph Hunter, *Hallamshire*, 107
14 *unto her majesty*: PRO E101/424/10
15 *our greate Misserie*: Derbyshire Archaeological Society Journal, 1907
16 *untyll we mete*: Hunter, 108

Chapter 3: Mistress of Hardwick

17 of the monarch's: Hunter, 78
18 linking of stepchildren in marriage: Lawrence Stone: *The Crisis of the Aristocracy*, 604
18 Cavendish-Talbot marriage contract: *DP* drawer 278.1

19 *be from you*: Hunter, 112
20 details of Shrewsbury's business: Stone, 343
20 Bess's agreement with Shrewsbury: Durant, 77, quoting *DP*, cupboard 1, shelf 3.
22 William Cavendish's fight with Shrewsbury: Durant, 121
23 *can do it*: Longleat MSS, Talbot letters, vii f267
23 *this burdensome charge*: *HMC* (Rut) v.1, 170
23 *folks without number*: Hunter, 73
25 *industry or agriculture*: Christopher Hill, *Century of Change*, 15
26 *for the gutters*: Durant and Riden (eds), *The Building of Hardwick Hall*
28 Arbella Stuart: David Durant, *Arbella Stuart*

Chapter 4: The Foundations of the House

30 *they grow contemptible*: quoted by Stone, 164
31 *belief in property*: Lewis Namier, *England During the American Revolution*
31 *Henry Cavendish*: Bickley, 36–9
32 *Cheap in England*: Stone
33 *nearly fifteen years*: Stone, 372
33 William Cavendish's accounts: *DP* account books 1620–1, second cupboard.
34 *worse by £100,000*: John Nichols, *Progresses . . . of James I*, ii 194
34 *his political prospects*: Stone, 194
35 Bess's library: Mark Girouard, *Life in the English Country House*, 165
35 *facetiousness and good-nature*: John Aubrey, *Brief Lives*
36 Hobbes and the Second Earl: Noel Malcolm, *Historical Journal*, 24.2 (1981), 297–321
36 *than a subject's*: Thomas Pomfret, *The Life of Christian, late Countess Dowager of Devonshire*, 25
37 *impaired his fortune*: Joseph Grove, *Lives of all the Earls and Dukes of Devonshire*, 2
37 *in good living*: Pomfret, 28
37 *constituting her inheritance*: J. L. Sanford and M. Townsend, *The Great Governing Families of England*, i 147
38 *of a woman*, Pomfret, 28
38 Charles Cavendish and Descartes: C. V. Wedgwood, *The King's Peace*, 69
38 *bred a gentleman*: Margaret Cavendish, Duchess of Newcastle, *The Life of . . . William Cavendish*
39 Newcastle's Court: Geoffrey Trease, *Portrait of a Cavalier*
40 *a loyal subject*: Eliot Warburton, *Life of Prince Rupert*, ii 468
42 *thoroughly awake yet*: Margaret Cavendish
43 *of the learned*: Virginia Woolf, *The Common Reader*, i 98

Chapter 5: The Patron of Our Liberty

45 *with equivalent status*: introduction to Lord Montagu of Beaulieu, *More Equal than Others*

45 *of his tradesmen*: Gilbert Burnet, *History of My Own Time*, i 350
45 *withal exasperating man*: Thompson, xxii
46 *wholesale mutual slaughter*: Stone, 242
48 *said to him*: John Evelyn, *Diaries*, ed. Bray, ii 237
50 *Earl of Devonshire*: *DP*, First Duke's collection, 18.01
50 *in after ages*: A. Collins, *Memoirs of the House of Cavendish* (1741)
50 *decaying and weak*: quoted by Thompson, 33
51 *of his country*: Grove, 193
52 *then in agitation*: W. Pegge, *The Revolution House* (Nottingham 1788)
53 *and fig-tree*: Grove, 202
53 *any other palace*: White Kennet, *Sermon at the Funeral of the Duke of
    Devonshire*, 170
54 *Crown to confer*: Lord Macaulay, *The History of England*, iv 509
54 *a deceitful court*: Bickley, 174
54 *however, were overcome*: Macaulay, iv 509
55 *as suddenly demolished*: James Lees-Milne, *Country Life*, 18 April 1968
55 *of his ideas*: Thompson, 51
56 *Mrs. Hacket*: Edward Croft-Murray, *Decorative Painting in England*, i 59
57 *as of right*: J. H. Plumb, *Men and Places*, 103
57 *Quatorze in 1683*: James Lees-Milne, *Country Life*, 2 May 1968
57 portable commodes on wheels: Lewis Mumford, *The Culture of Cities*,
    440
57 *were of marble*: Mark Girouard, *Life in the English Country House*, 254
58 *in their company*: Joseph Williamson, *Essay on the Character of the Duchess
    Dowager of Devonshire* (1710)
58 *had four months*: Ms note in British Library copy of *Hazards of Deathbed
    Repentance* (1710)
58 *of her marriage*: First Duke's will, *DP* 18.14
59 *subject can attain*: Christopher Hobhouse, *The Shell Guide to Derbyshire*.
59 *say too much: The Court in Tears* (1707)

Chapter 6: The Great Collector

61 *Party in England*: Burnet
61 *again in him*: Bickley, 187
62 *possessed great charm*: J. H. Plumb, *Sir Robert Walpole*, i 100
62 *to his dignity*: Burnet, ii 553
63 York Building Waterworks: Plumb *Walpole*, i 7
63 *and profound inertia*: J. H. Plumb, *The Growth of Political Stability in
    England, 1675–1725*, xviii
65 a certain philistinism: Lord David Cecil, *The Young Melbourne*, 8
66 *all are there*: A. E. Popham, introduction to first catalogue, Chatsworth
    Old Master Drawings Exhibition, 1949

Chapter 7: A Man of His Word

67 *negligent of dress*: James, Second Earl Waldegrave, *Memoirs*, 26

67 *point of honour*: James Boswell: *The Life of Samuel Johnson*, iii 167
67 *habit of caution*: Horace Walpole, *Memoirs of the Reign of King George II*, i
     195
68 *had been thought*: Walpole, *George II*, i 196
69 *aides-de-camp already*: quoted by Bickley, 191
69 *be done soon*: DP 3D 186.0
69 *dish of roast*: Walpole, *Letters*, iii 101
71 *the child died*: Elizabeth Duchess of Devonshire, *Anecdotes* (1822)
71 *cameos and brilliants*: DP 3D 260.418
71 assigned Burlington Gardens: DP unsorted documents, box 112
72 *as your happyness*: DP 3D 344.0
72 *have for you*: DP 3D 260.77A
73 *[deal] upon it*: DP 3D 344.1
74 *affectionate K Devonshire*: DP 3D 344.2
74 *for at present*: DP 3D 348.0
75 *his new alliance*: DP 3D 203.4
75 *that is impossible*: DP 3D 344.3
75 *or Lady Hartington*: Walpole, *Letters*, ii 389
77 *house is beautiful*: Walpole, *Letters*, iv 423–4
77 *danced with us*: Walpole, *Letters*, iv 422

Chapter 8: Crown Prince of the Whigs

78 *in eighteenth-century England*: J. H. Plumb, *Men and Places*, 99
78 *the bon ton*: David Garrick, *Letters*, ed. Little and Kahrl, 347
78 *to the company*: quoted by Girouard, 190
79 *have no money*: Garrick, *Letters*, i 419
80 *a suave Viceroy*: Bickley, 213
80 *seats in parliament*: Lewis Namier, *England in the Age of the American
     Revolution*, 206
82 *Duke of Devonshire*: Bickley, 219
82 *no day light*: Namier, 292
82 *are not so*: Namier, 295
83 *key and disgust*: Walpole, *Letters*, 272
83 *into no engagements*: DP 4D 260.387
83 *as you can*: DP 4D 640.2
84 *day to Chatsworth*: DP 4D 182.292
84 *en voila!* Walpole, *Letters*, V 271
85 *in the Administration*: DP 4D
85 *and one side*: Charles Greville, *Memoirs*, ed. Strachey and Fulford, ii 441
85 *such a phantom*: Walpole, *Letters*, iv 126

Chapter 9: The Genius of Clapham

86 *passion against prudence*: DP 5D 669.0
87 *Brother, I did*: Bickley, 199

88 *benefit of mankind*: J. G. Crowther, *Scientists of the Industrial Revolution*, 272
89 *of the atmosphere*: Crowther, 297
90 *so utterly barren*: Bickley, 207
90 *of reciprocal proportions*: Crowther, 214–15
90 *dream of regretting*: T. H. White, *The Once and Future King*

Chapter 10: 'Racky', 'Canis' and 'Mrs Rat'

91 *at this period*: G. M. Trevelyan, *English Social History*
91 *his distinguishing characteristic*: Sir Nathaniel Wraxall, *Memoirs*, iii 342
92 *sense, but spring*: Joseph Farington, *Diary*, ii 212
94 *you like it*: *DP* 5D 682.0
94 *auprès de lui*: *DP* 5D 682.1
95 *her a phenomenon*: Walpole, *Letters*, ix 161
95 *martyrdom for her*: Garrick, *Letters*, 1035
95 *a little patience*: *Georgiana, Duchess of Devonshire*, ed. Bessborough, 26
96 *in the sun*: Harold Nicolson, *Good Behaviour*, 204
96 *much of her*: Brian Masters, *Georgiana*, 34
96 *much and nastily*: *DP* 5D
97 *shifting silken colour*: Lord David Cecil, *The Young Melbourne*, 58
98 *and sorrow also*: Greville, *Memoirs*, v 308
99 *is purely speculative*: *The Sylph*, i 33
99 *of the catalogue*: *The Sylph*, i 133
101 *to my heart*: *DP* 5D 507.1
102 Buxton and Bath: Robert Grundy Heape, *Buxton under the Dukes of Devonshire*, 27
102 *brother and sister*: *DP* 5D 594
103 *here, Mrs. Bess*: *DP* 5D 683
103 *mind being seen*: *DP* 5D 684
103 *of your face*: *DP* 5D 566
104 *ever deserts her*: *Diary and Letters of Madame D'Arblay* ed. Barrett, iii 369
104 *to a coarseness*: Walpole, *Letters*, xii 454
104 *for the measles*: Bessborough, 71
105 Duke of Bedford's loan: Georgiana Blakiston, *Woburn and the Russells*
105 *or my child*: Bessborough, 97
107 *have been here*: *DP* 5D 961.1
107 *much the best*: Christopher Hobhouse, *Fox* 223
108 *my present situation*: *DP* 5D 1052.1
109 *it is quiet*: Ann Scafe's journal, *DP* 5D 1054.1
110 *mother, G. Devonshire*: *DP*, 5D 1117
111 *of seeing you*: Castle Howard papers
112 *her neck immense*: *Lady Holland's Journal*, ed. Lord Ilchester, i 244
113 *forgot the Tyrant*: Bessborough, 277
113 *being like myself*: DP 5D 1677.1
113 *for Devonshire House*: Masters, 265
114 *Dst Dst Hart*: DP 5D 1873

114 *a contrary conduct*: Castle Howard Papers
114 *lessened every grief*: Vere Foster, *The Two Duchesses*
115 *Duchess of Devonshire*: Thomas Creevey, *The Creevey Papers*, ed. Maxwell, i, 84

Chapter 11: The Bachelor

116 *soft milky disposition*: Byron, *In My Hot Youth*, Letters and Journals, i 5
117 *Duke of Devonshire*: DP 6D 11
117 *lose true greatness*: DP 6D 13
118 *such a time*: DP 6D 16
118 *abandon his profession*: DP 6D 18
118 *deal to spend*: Handbook to Chatsworth, 133
120 *in the head*: DP 6D 85
121 *and dangle about*: Creevey, i 183
122 *are to reside*: E. Rhodes, *Peak Scenery*, 165
123 *parallel in Europe*: John Kenworthy-Browne, 'A Ducal Patron of Sculptors', *Apollo*, October 1972
124 *portent aux Anglais*: Stendhal, *Journaux* (Pléiade ed.) 1215
124 *on something useful*: Augustus Clifford, *Sketch of the Sixth Duke*, 8
124 *profusion reigns throughout*: *A Regency Visitor*, Letters of Prince Pückler-Muskau, ed. E. M. Butler, 180
125 *on his journey*: DP 6D 1289
125 *less than £60,000*: Clifford, 26
125 *the other's happiness*: DP 6D 767.450
126 *strange and unkind*: DP 6D 767.450
126 *the present occasion*: DP 6D 1345
126 *off old age*: DP 6D 767.451
127 *have dark forebodings*: DP 6D 767.451
127 *her two cows*: DP 6D 1535
127 *what you like*: Handbook to Chatsworth
128 *hospitable and magnificent*: Greville, *Memoirs*, vii 332
128 *and everybody else*: Harriette Wilson, *Memoirs of Herself and Others*, 273
128 *of my head*: DP 6D, Sixth Duke's diary, 31 December 1825
129 *did comfort me*: DP 6D, Sixth Duke's diary, 20 February 1828
129 *for some time*: DP 6D, Sixth Duke's diary, 27 April 1828
129 *I should marry*: DP 6D, Sixth Duke's diary, 27 January 1829
131 *was Lord Chamberlain*: *The Journal of Mary Frampton*, 405
131 *his honest respectability*: DP 6D 767.455
131 *and very quietly*: DP 6D, Sixth Duke's diary, 21 April 1831
132 *their increasing numbers*: Handbook of Chatsworth
133 *before nine o'clock*: Handbook of Chatsworth
134 *in seeing Chatsworth*: DP 6D, Sixth Duke's diary, 16 August 1829
134 *it is Nicander*: quoted in Clifford
134 *expenditure and income*: DP 6D 767.895
136 *in that quarter*: quoted in Violet Markham, *Paxton and the Bachelor Duke*, 82

136 *I love him*: quoted in Markham, 82
137 *is very offensive*: *DP* 7D, Seventh Duke's diary, 24 December 1838
137 *five years since*: quoted in Markham, 104
137 *breath of air*: *DP* 6D, Sixth Duke's diary, 23 February 1840
139 *angel in heaven*: *DP* 7D, Seventh Duke's diary, 28 April 1840
140 *mother to me*: *DP* 6D, Second Series, 1.0
141 *of my year*: quoted in Markham, 148
141 *scarcely possible evil*: quoted in Markham, 157
142 *my only excuse*: *DP* 6D, Second Series, 231
142 *great national community*: quoted in Stone, 264
143 *property in England*: *DP* 6D, Sixth Duke's diary, 13 April 1848
143 *surrounded by misfortune*: *DP* 6D, Sixth Duke's diary, 8 January 1844
144 *his ancestral halls*: *The Times*, 6 September 1855
144 *your old Devonshire*: *DP* 6D, Second Series, 1.102
144 *expression of happiness*: *DP* 7D, Seventh Duke's diary, 18 January 1838
145 *constant social importance*: Leach, 12
145 *by an aristocracy*: Hippolyte Taine, *Notes on England*, ed. Hyams, 13
145 *to middle-class morality*: Girouard, 270

Chapter 12: The Rewards of Virtue

147 *an intricate channel*: Lord Esher, *Cloud-Capp'd Towers*, 97
148 *them very flourishing*: *DP*, 7D, Seventh Duke's diary, 26 January 1858
149 *are everywhere necessary*: *DP* 7D, Seventh Duke's diary, 16 February 1859
150 *increasingly unaristocratic age:* David Spring, *English Landowners and Nineteenth-Century Industrialism*, 20
150 *upon the people*: Bickley, 278
151 *birth and tradition*: F. M. L. Thompson, *English Landed Society*, 191
152 *consequently be worked*: *DP* 7D, Seventh Duke's diary, 7 March 1859
152 *on lazy indifference*: Heape, 87
152 Seventh Duke and Eastbourne: David Cannadine, *Lords and Landlords*
153 *name of Devonshire*: Henry Leach, *The Duke of Devonshire*, 26
153 *any aristocratic millionaire*: David Cannadine, *Agricultural History Review* (1977), 84
154 *Derby is closed*: *DP* 7D Seventh Duke's diary, 4 April 1861
154 *in the Laboratory*: J. G. Crowther, *The Cavendish Laboratory*
155 *no vicious temptations*: *DP* 7D Seventh Duke's diary, 17 October 1851
156 *and two carriages*: Lady Frederick Cavendish, *Diaries* i 243
156 *crumbling industrial enterprises*: Pollard, *Barrow in Furness and the Seventh Duke of Devonshire*, 217
157 *course of action*: *DP* 7D, Seventh Duke's diary, 2 May 1882

Chapter 13: The Duke of Omnium

161 *classes nearer business*: Walter Bagehot, *The English Constitution*, 107
161 *keep my reputation*: J. Ruffer, *The Big Shots*, 64

161 *faster than another*: quoted in Kenneth Rose, *The Later Cecils*, 55
162 *seedy, shady sailor*: Bernard Holland, *The Life of Spencer Compton, Eighth Duke of Devonshire*, 234
163 *fast young swells*: Anita Leslie, *Edwardians in Love*, 77
164 *me a stamp*: Leslie, 82
164 *advent to power*: Esher, *Cloud Capp'd Towers*, 98
165 *his park palings*: E. T. Raymond, *Portraits of the Nineties*, 90
166 *a great dukedom*: T. H. Escott, *The Personal Faces of the Period*, 45
168 *It is certain*: Esher, *Letters and Journals*, 155
169 *gentle and intelligent*: Lady Frederick Cavendish, ii 21
169 *steam-roller about her*: E. F. Benson, *As We Were*, 174
169 *in the evening*: DP 8D uncatalogued
170 *their principal possessions*: Thompson, *Chatsworth*, 159
171 *bells are unattaining*: B. L. Add. Mss. 46794 f100v
171 *a summer night*: Leach, 318
172 *whose is Pevensey*: Benson, 176
172 *Englishman's second bible*: W. M. Thackeray, *The Book of Snobs*, 11
173 *of the peerages*: Leach, 3
173 *on her head*: Leslie, 220
173 *not see her: Daisy Princess of Pless* by Herself, 102
174 *the crumbling sills*: Benson, 176
174 *and very rouged*: Pless, 127
174 *luncheon with Cassel*: DP 8D uncatalogued letter, 24 January 1908

Chapter 14: The Reluctant Duke

Private information from: Lady Elizabeth Cavendish, Lady Blanche
Cobbold, The Dowager Lady Gage, Harold Macmillan, Lady Anne
Montagu, Clodagh Anson, Sally Barnes, Gladys Grafton, Jesse Grafton,
Maud Shimwell, William Shimwell

178 *sources of income*: Cannadine, 90
178 *through the house*: Esher, *Cloud-Capp'd Towers*, 93
179 570 slaughtered birds: DP game book 1808–1912
179 *Croustades à l'Ecossaire*: DP 9D
180 *a great relief*: DP 9D Ninth Duke's diary, 22 July 1916
180 *said goodbye*: DP 9D Ninth Duke's diary, 31 October 1916
181 talk their language: J. Cowan, *Canada's Governors-General*, 115
183 *of social equality*: quoted in Thompson, *English Landed Society*
184 *recovered the other*: Lord Mersey, *A Picture of Life*, 339
186 *for the present*: DP 9D Ninth Duke's diary, 24 July 1923
186 *the native races: Indians in Kenya*, H.M.S.O. (1923), 10
190 *War and Peace*: Harold Macmillan, *Winds of Change*, 189
193 *a moment's notice*: V. Sackville-West, *The Edwardians*, 25

Chapter 15: Death and Taxes

Private information from Tim Burrows, The Duke of Devonshire, The Duchess of Devonshire, Hugo Read, Lady Anne Tree.

197 *possessions and palaces*: Sir Henry Channon, *Chips, The Diaries of Sir Henry Channon*, 346
197 *sense of duty*: *The Times*, 27 November 1950
198 *gloom or apprehension*: Harold Nicolson, *Diaries and Letters, 1930–1939*, 418
201 *rights and progress*: *The Times*, 11 February 1944
204 *dead at 55*: Channon, 450
204 *most appalling mess*: Daily Sketch, 11 June 1954
206 High Court actions: *The Times* (Law Report), 22 July 1965
207 *corridors and galleries*: Mario Praz, *The House of Life*, 84
208 *wind and sun*: The Duchess of Devonshire, *The House*, 83
210 *dukes of novelists*: Anthony Sampson, *The Anatomy of Britain*, 211
211 *I've ever ridden*: Andrew Devonshire, *Park Top*, 149
211 *Duke of Newcastle*: *Political Quarterly*, July 1961

Index